THE ECONOMIES OF SMALL

For Natasha, 18

The Economies of Small

Appropriate technology in a changing world

RAPHAEL KAPLINSKY

IT PUBLICATIONS in association with
APPROPRIATE TECHNOLOGY INTERNATIONAL 1990

Intermediate Technology Publications,
103/105 Southampton Row, London, WC1B 4HH, UK.

Appropriate Technology International,
1331 H Street, N.W.,
Washington, D.C., USA 20005.

Appropriate Technology International (ATI) implements its mission
with public funds made available through the Agency for
International Development. ATI's programme is carried out in
cooperation with the Employment and Enterprise Division of the
Office of Rural and Institutional Development within AID's Bureau
of Science and Technology.

British Library Cataloguing in Publication Data

Kaplinsky, Raphael
 The economies of small.
 1. Appropriate technology
 I. Title
 600

 ISBN 1–85339–072–0
 ISBN 1–85339–071–2 pbk

Typesetting by J&L Composition Ltd, Filey, North Yorkshire.
Printed in Great Britain by Short Run Press, Exeter

Contents

Figures

Tables

Acknowledgements

Ton de Wilde initiated the idea of writing this book, commented on various drafts and reminded me of the various deadlines about to be missed. Ajit Bhalla, Neal Burton, Erik Hymen, Nicholas Jequier, David Kaplan, Jormo Ruotsi, Frances Stewart and Adrian Wood offered constructive comments on earlier drafts. And Annie Jamieson, Bill Watson and Irene Williams provided invaluable assistance at various stages of the manuscript's preparation. I'm very grateful for their help, but none of them is however responsible for the remaining errors and misinterpretations.

Acknowledgement is given to Appropriate Technology International for financial assistance in the preparation of this book. ATI is not of course responsible for its contents. The author and the publishers would also like to thank the following for the use of copyright material: Oxford University Press (Table 1.1, Figure 1.1 and Figure 6.1); UNCTAD (Figure 1.2); Antony Sheriff, International Vehicle Program, MIT, Working Paper 1988 (Figure 6.4); OECD (Figure 1.3); Donald Meade (Tables 7.1 and 8.1); N.L. Kent, *Technology of Cereals with special reference to Wheat*, 1964, Pergamon Press PLC (Table 3.12); the Friederich Ebert Foundation (Table 5.12).

Abbreviations

AT	Appropriate Technology
ATDA	Appropriate Technology Development Association
ATI	Appropriate Technology International
CBA	Cost Benefit Analysis
DC	Developing Country
HDTV	High Definition Colour Television
IAC	Industrially Advanced Country
IRR	Internal Rate of Return
ITDG	Intermediate Technology Development Group
LDC	Less Developed Country
NGO	Non-Governmental Organization
NIC	Newly-Industrializing Country
OPS	Open Pan Sulphitation Sugar Technology
RK	Rotary Kiln Cement Technology
SCBA	Social Cost Benefit Analysis
TNC	Transnational Corporation
VITA	Volunteers for Technical Assistance
VP	Vacuum Pan Sugar Technology
VSK	Vertical Kiln Cement Technology
UN	United Nations
UNEP	United Nations Environmental Programme
USAID	United States Agency for International Development

Currency conversion rates used in case studies

		1977	1982	1986	1989
Botswana	Pula: Sterling			0.50	0.50
	Pula: Dollar			0.45	0.39
India	Rupee: Sterling		15.52	19.42	
	Rupee: Dollar		10.63	16.05	
Kenya	Shilling: Sterling	14.43	20.53	23.16	
	Shilling: Dollar	8.23	14.06	19.14	
Tanzania	Shilling: Sterling			76.55	
	Shilling: Dollar			63.26	

CHAPTER 1
Origins and nature of the AT movement

Introduction

MUCH OF the world's population lives in a state of extreme poverty, being barely able to reproduce its subsistence needs. It is tempting to explain this poverty by referring back to nineteenth-century social commentators — of whom Malthus and Ricardo are probably best known — who predicted that the world economy would run into steady-state subsistence as the best agricultural lands were used up and population growth overwhelmed food production. However, these predictions proved inaccurate, largely because new technological innovations extended the productivity of agricultural land, enabling increasing numbers of people to be adequately fed. So successful and sustained has been this technological change, that current global problems with malnutrition have more to do with the way in which international food supplies are distributed rather than a shortfall in production.

For many years the central role played by technological change — crucial to understanding the historical development of agriculture — seemed to have little impact on economic theorists and planners, especially those concerned with industrial development. They ploughed a narrow and unchanging furrow, preoccupied with increases in the value of capital investment and in the numbers employed. The emphasis was on quantity, with little attention being given to the quality of inputs into production. Indeed it was only two or three decades ago that the issues of technological choice and technological development began to be explicitly and widely recognized in policy formulation.

There were a number of reasons why planners and academics came to be convinced that the issue of technology could not continue to be placed on the sidelines. Most importantly, a series of econometric studies had shown that most of the growth of output had resulted from qualitative changes in capital, land and labour, rather than increases in their quantity.[1] Moreover, the striking success of Japan in transforming the structure of its comparative advantage away from traditional labour-intensive industries towards those with greater value-added concentrated the minds of observers on the dynamic aspects of technology. The fact that Japanese productivity growth continued to rise during the 1960s and 1970s whilst it was falling in the older industrialized countries emphasized the need to understand the role of technological progress in economic growth. Finally, with the major contributions coming from development studies,[2] many observers came to question

1

the identification of economic growth with economic and social development. How was it that economies could continue to show 'progress' while at the same time the living conditions of significant segments of the population were becoming increasingly intolerable? Could part of the reason be that inappropriate technologies were being chosen?

Since these insights began to penetrate the world view of economists and planners in the late 1960s, there has been an explosion of interest in technology-related issues. There is little doubt that the bulk of this global concern lies with the problems of the industrially advanced countries (IACs), and with the rate of technological progress. But there is a significant, and growing, body of opinion which has also come to question the direction which this technological change is taking and to place more attention on the needs of the mass of the world's population and the environmental consequences of economic progress. How much of technological change really is 'progress', who benefits from it and what effect is it having on environmental sustainability? Moreover, the determinants of technological choice are also under increasing scrutiny in order to understand more clearly why there has been a systematic bias towards the introduction of technologies which have adverse social, economic and environmental consequences, despite the existence of more benign technological alternatives.

This book is largely concerned with the inter-relationship between patterns of human living and technological choice, that is with the appropriateness of technology. The major focus of attention lies in the role which technology plays in meeting the needs of the poorer segments of the global population living in developing countries (DCs). But as will become evident, there is also an important current of opinion which links technology, environmental degradation and adverse forms of social and economic organization in both the developing and industrially advanced countries.

The evolution of analysis of Appropriate Technology (AT) and the developing role played by AT institutions have not been without their critics, the most prominent of whom has been an American economist, Eckaus.[3] His first contribution to the literature (in 1955) had been to assert that at any one time there is only a single efficient technique, and that generally (because of the concentration of Research and Development (R&D) in the IACs) this is capital-intensive in nature. (Efficiency, here, was defined in terms of economic criteria: the merits of this restricted approach are discussed in Chapter 2.) If this were true, then labour-intensive technologies can only create more employment in the short run, and this will necessarily be at the cost of lower living standards. The response to Eckaus's assertion was an intensive body of empirical research during the 1970s.[4] This showed that there were many sectors in which there *was* a choice between economically efficient technologies.

These detailed studies were, nevertheless, often ignored and did not prevent prejudicial analysis of the issue. For example, in 1982 the French

2

Marxist Emmanuel argued that not only was Eckaus's assertion correct, but since the efficient technology was almost always owned by transnational corporations, foreign investment had a progressive role to play in DCs.[5] More recently, Eckaus has returned to the attack, arguing *inter alia* that

- AT 'is a nebulous concept with indistinct boundaries and vague criteria. With few exceptions only, the logic is dubious' (p. 63)
- there is little scholarly analysis of AT and no general insights can be obtained from these studies
- the basic assumption of the AT movement is technologically determinist, believing that merely making new technologies available will be a cure for social ills
- related to this technological determinism, the AT movement 'lacks an economic and social analysis' (p. 66); it romanticizes pre-industrial life and fiddles around by trying to solve major problems with a restricted range of new techniques.

Eckaus concludes that it is because of these failings that the achievements of the AT movement have been limited. A complementary critique of AT, also largely informed by prejudice, is that prevalent in many developing countries, especially those in Africa and Latin America which have a poor tradition of small-scale enterprise. In these countries AT is often regarded as second-best, a way in which poor countries are being kept poor by the denial of modern 'efficient' technology. But, as the severity of the economic crisis in these countries has worsened and as the success of many newly-industrializing countries (NICs) in Asia which have had a long and successful tradition of small-scale production has become more obvious, these pre-judicial views are beginning to wane. Especially in Africa there is now the recognition that alternative technologies produced by other DCs, especially those in Asia, offer significant growth and developmental opportunities.

Whilst this book on AT is aimed at a wider audience than sceptics such as Eckaus and Emmanuel, it addresses many of the points which they raise. They are wrong to assert that there is no theory of politics in the AT movement, or that it suffers from an absence of critical insights. They are wrong to assert that ATs are necessarily economically and technologically inefficient. Empirical analyses (such as those contained in later chapters here) also show that the obstacles to the widespread diffusion of AT do not lie in the preoccupation by activists with technological solutions but with the strength of vested social and political interests. Indeed, instead of running away from these political realities, the AT movement has often confronted them head-on.

The following chapters not only consider the analytical issues raised by Eckaus and Emmanuel but also provide case-studies to rebut their assertions. This first chapter reviews a number of general issues relevant to AT. It begins by addressing the historical context in which concern with the nature of technology became prominent. This makes it possible to contextualize the origins of the AT movement and to identify the similarities and dissimilarities between groups working in the developing and in the industrially advanced countries. After considering briefly the growth of the global AT movement, the chapter concludes by identifying some of the major policy issues relevant in enhancing the role of AT. Chapter 2 addresses the meaning of 'appropriate technology', identifying its relativity and distinguishing between the major characteristics of appropriateness. These include the dichotomy between private and social costs and benefits, as well as environmental, social and economic dimensions.

The bulk of the book consists of detailed case-studies, covering bread making, brick manufacture, sugar processing and cement manufacture (chapters 3–6). They are not intended to provide comprehensive analyses of all of the issues in AT. Instead each of the case-studies illuminates the specificity of the problems since, as will become clear, AT is inherently relative. The studies also illustrate the complexities of policy choice. These conclusions point the way to interventions by an AT-enabling state as well as by non-governmental organizations (NGOs) at the micro-level (that is, the operating unit), the meso-level (that is, the sector or district) and the macro-level.

These sectorial studies relate exclusively to DCs. Yet the appropriateness of technological choice and change is not an issue restricted to poorer countries, and there is increasing ferment about the content of technology in the First World. Therefore, in Chapter 6 the discussion turns to the question of whether there is a similar 'crisis' of technology in the industrialized countries. The prospects for AT in the IACs are considered in relation to the optimum economic scale of technology. Chapter 7 considers the problem of policy formulation, especially in relation to the conflict between market forces and state intervention in the diffusion of AT. The characteristics of an AT-enabling state are explored in Chapter 8 which focuses on the policy implications of earlier chapters. It also draws out the implications for the international AT agencies.

A word of caution and explanation before the empirical chapters are read. Some of the data contained in the case-studies are old, and most are specific to individual environments. Yet, since the primary purpose of this book is to illuminate the broad issues which are raised in the development and implementation of AT policy, the specific nature of this empirical data is not a major problem — the issues which come to the fore in the empirical chapters are of general significance and are relevant to AT policy formulation in other sectors, in other environments and at other times.

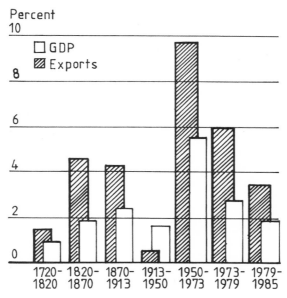

Figure 1.1. *Historical trends in the growth of real GDP and exports in selected countries, 1720–1985. Source: World Bank,* World Development Report, *1987.*

Contextualizing the origins of the AT movement

Slowdown in the global economy and the emergence of the AT movement
The IACs reached their present levels of prosperity after centuries of sustained effort. Their economic growth appears to have occurred in various phases and with important regional variations. Economic historians hotly debate the precise characteristics, timing and causalities of these various phases of economic growth,[6] but most are in general agreement that temporal and geographic unevenness has been a constant historic thread. Figure 1.1 provides a measure of the changing pace of economic growth for the world's major economies since 1720. Four major characteristics emerge from this data. First, there have been significant variations in the speed of economic growth. Second, the 1950–73 period saw growth at a rate unparalleled in any previous period — it is for this reason that it is often referred to by economic historians as 'The Golden Age'. Third, although the signs of slowdown first became evident in the late 1960s, there was a sharp reduction in growth rates

5

after the early 1970s, emphasizing the historical uniqueness of the Golden Age. And, finally, the rate of growth of international trade in the post-1950 period exceeded, in fact it almost doubled, this historically unprecedented expansion in overall output. The outward orientation of most economies thus increased significantly after 1950 although, as with variations in the rate of economic growth, there have also been cycles in the extent of international integration.

The explanation for these varying patterns of global economic growth is a contentious issue. But, as will become clear later in this chapter (and in Chapter 6), an understanding of these recent developments in the path of growth is highly relevant for a discussion of AT. Therefore it is helpful to consider, briefly, a set of historically informed analyses which provide especially helpful insights into the links between technology and society.[7] Essentially there are two major sets of analysis of the post-1970 slowdown which focus on technological factors and which have a bearing on the discussion of AT — that which explains swings in economic performance in terms of long waves and that which does so in terms of mass production.

Long-wave theorists lean on the empirical observation that global economic history over the past few centuries has been characterized by a series of approximately 50-year economic cycles of boom, recession and regeneration. Each of these cycles is said to be driven by a key, 'heartland' technology, such as the textile industry in the last quarter of the eighteenth century, the steel and railroad technologies of the mid-nineteenth century and materials-intensive technologies (such as chemicals and the internal combustion engine) in the first half of the twentieth century. Most recently in the post-1950 period, microelectronics has become the technological engine of growth.[8] For these heartland technologies to operate optimally an appropriate socio-institutional framework has to be constructed, involving the development of physical infrastructure, institutions and organizational procedures.[9] Economic slowdown (often referred to as economic crisis) — as has occurred since the late 1960s — arises when there is a mismatch between the socio-institutional framework of the old cycle and the emergence of the heartland technology of the new cycle. The political and policy struggles involve the reformation of the anachronistic institutions, rules and procedures which were relevant for the old but which are inadequate for the new.

The characteristics which define a heartland technology are that it is perceived to have a low, and descending cost; that it is in virtually unlimited supply; that it has pervasive potential applications; and that it has the capacity to reduce costs and improve product characteristics. Examination of these characteristics shows the key role currently played by electronics and identifies the flexible organizational structures required to take advantage of the opportunities which this new heartland technology offers. It also helps identify the previous wave as one being driven by materials-intensive

6

technologies, especially the perception of cheap and unlimited supplies of energy, and a resilient physical environment.

These long-wave explanations for the observed pattern of varying global economic performance are increasingly informed by related analyses of the nature of mass production. The theorization is as follows. Towards the second half of the eighteenth century, the system of mass production came to dominate. It was characterized by the production of homogeneous final products — a Model T Ford 'in any colour as long as it is black' — using special-purpose and inflexible machinery and involving a particular method of organizing production. This provided major opportunities for sustained economic growth, involving scale economies over time, and culminating in the development of 'world factories' producing 'world-products'. After the late 1960s, however, the mass production paradigm began to fracture not only under its own internal contradictions but also when the institutional structure began to show signs of increasing socio-political conflict. The conditions of certainty required to sustain ever-growing scale economies evaporated at the same time as the growth of these scale economies came to be eroded by the emergence of *dis*economies of scale. This explains the slowdown of productivity growth and the rapid rise of economies in parts of the world (such as Japan) where the socio-institutional structure was appropriate for more flexible and descaled production.

A number of insights can be drawn from this brief discussion of the causes of the post-1970 slowdown. The previous wave was one in which mass production dominated, based upon cheap materials (especially energy) and the perception of a robust environment. Towards the end of the 1960s this system of accumulation ran into difficulties. Raw material supplies — especially energy — were constrained and mass production began to suffer from various internal difficulties which led to a slowdown in productivity growth. The increasingly uncertain conditions of production made it difficult to realize scale economies and the incentive to invest in new and even larger plants was dulled. The adverse environmental impact of this path of growth led to growing costs of clean-up and pollution control.[10] These developments led to a slowdown in the rate of economic growth. At the same time, some parts of the world had begun the transition to a new post-mass production form of production, so that there was increasing unevenness in global economic performance.

Slowdown in the developing world
The issues of global slowdown and its effect on the origins and nature of the AT movement will be treated later in this chapter (and in Chapter 6). What is important at this stage is to note its effect on the Third World. For most of the 365 years reflected in Figure 1.1 the productive base in the developing countries remained relatively unchanged. There were obvious variations between regions and within regions over time, but most of their populations

remained relatively untouched by the industrial progress which was transforming living and working conditions in the industrializing economies. Some of these DCs, most notably India (after 1850) and Korea (after 1900), began the path of industrial development and agricultural transformation earlier than others, but in general the DCs really only began to experience significant structural and economic change during the Golden Age years after 1950. The most striking progress was to be found in the industrial sphere, where the share of DCs in global manufacturing value-added grew from 8.1 to 11 per cent between 1963 and 1982.[11] To some extent this was reflected in a rapid increase in manufactured exports, where the DCs share of the global total grew rapidly from 4.3 to 13.7 per cent between 1963 and 1987. But participation in this growth was limited to an increasingly restricted number of countries. The combined share of Taiwan, Hong Kong, South Korea, Singapore and Brazil rose as a proportion of total DC manufactured exports from 61.8 to 71.7 per cent between 1973 and 1987.[12]

A significant feature of this post-war Golden Age was that the DCs consistently outperformed the IACs. They also did not experience the economic slowdown suffered by the latter during the 1970s. Whereas, in aggregate, the DCs grew on average by 2.5 per cent p.a. faster than the industrialized capitalist economies between 1963 and 1973, this superiority grew to 3.4 per cent p.a. between 1973 and 1980. There were two basic reasons: first, a restricted group of newly industrializing countries — especially Taiwan, South Korea, Hong Kong and Singapore — saw very rapid and sustained economic growth and this buoyed-up the overall DC average. But, more relevant for the concerns of this book, much of the Third World borrowed itself out of the post-1973 recession. The ready availability of petro-dollars for onward lending by the commercial banks provided the possibility for escaping what were perceived to be the short-term cyclical problems of the world economy.

This strategy of external borrowing became increasingly unsustainable as the decade wore on (the debt exceeded $800bn by 1987). The high share of debt and interest payments in exports meant that DCs were sensitive to fluctuations in imports when commodity prices fell — as they did. In addition, as interest rates increased in the First World, so did the debt-repayment burden, and the commercial banks became increasingly reluctant to step-up the flow of funds to the Third World to sustain their industrial growth. Finally, the second oil-price increase of 1979 meant that for many countries there was no longer any real possibility of extending this boom in economic growth. The ratio of debt to total annual export has grown dramatically in many countries — to over 16 times in the case of Sudan in 1987 — so there is little prospect of these debts ever being repaid in full. Perhaps the greatest irony of this situation is that instead of money flowing from the rich to the poorer countries to help them with their development, the repayment of past debts, linked to a paltry inflow of new funds from the

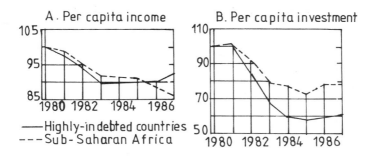

Source: UNCTAD, Trade and Development Report 1988

Figure 1.2. *Per capita income and investment in highly-indebted countries and sub-Saharan Africa (1980 = 100)*

IACs, has meant that the DCs are actually paying more to rich countries than they are receiving. In 1988 this involved a net resource transfer from poor to rich countries of around $30bn.

In this environment, two groups of countries suffered particular difficulties and have faced growing economic problems throughout the 1980s. The first is a group of fifteen highly indebted countries identified in 1985 by US Secretary of State, James Baker. Most of these are in Latin America. These are Argentina, Bolivia, Brazil, Chile, Colombia, Ecuador, Ivory Coast, Mexico, Morocco, Nigeria, Peru, the Philippines, Uruguay, Venezuela and Yugoslavia. The second group is the sub-Saharan African countries. Figure 1.2 shows how adversely these two groups of countries were affected, both in their capacity to invest for the future and in relation to their real standards of living. In sub-Saharan Africa, real standards of living fell by almost 15 per cent between 1980 and 1987; their capacity to invest fell even more significantly. For the highly indebted group, the major impact was a fall (of amost 40 per cent) in their capacity to invest, and a drop of almost 10 per cent in their real per capita incomes over the same period. Other areas in the developing world also suffered. In Central America real GDP fell between 1981 and 1986 by 20.7 per cent in Guatemala, 16.7 per cent in El Salvador, 13.8 per cent in Honduras, 14.1 per cent in Nicaragua and 11 per cent in Costa Rica.[13] When population growth is taken into account, the fall in real per capita incomes was even greater.

9

Table 1.1. Some development indicators for three groups of countries, circa 1987

	Poorest 40	India and China	22 capitalist IACs
Population (m)	957	1,866	747
GNP capita ($)	280	300	14,670
Foreign trade[a] (deficit)/ surplus ($bn)	(110)	(10.3)	(86)
Savings as % of GDP	15	31	21
Life expectancy at birth (yrs)	52	64	76
Population living in rural areas (%)	76	67	23
Population working in agriculture (%)[b]	71	72	7
Fertilizer use (hundred gms/ha)	318	997	1,163
Index of food production (1979–81)	106	119	103
Energy consumption per capita (kg oil equivalent)	116	390	6,573
Population growth 1980–87 (%)	2.8	1.6	0.6
Population per doctor (1984)	13,550	1,640	450
Population per nurse	3,130	1,700	130
Infant mortality per 1000 births	103	62	9
Daily calorie intake	2,227	2,463	3,390
Population in tertiary education (%)	2	3	39

[a] Merchandise trade only, i.e. excluding services, profits and remittances.
[b] 1980.
Source: *World Development Report*, 1988.

So far the plight of these DCs has been discussed in the aggregate, observing that between 30–40 economies have suffered acute problems over the past decade. But, were this to have been coupled with redistributive developmental policies, it would not necessarily have been associated with increasing poverty for the mass of their populations. On the other hand, if systematic attempts were not made to alleviate the adverse impact on the poor, then their plight could only have worsened. So how have the poorer groups in these poorest countries fared?

Before attempting to answer this question it is helpful to establish under what sort of conditions the poor live and how this contrasts with living conditions in the First World. Table 1.1. compares a selection of developmental statistics for three groups of countries — the 40 lowest income countries, India and China (who are amongst the poorest group but, being so large, are really special cases) and the 22 richest industrially advanced capitalist countries (grouped in the Organisations of Economic Co-operation and Development (OECD). A number of points relevant to later discussion on AT can be inferred.

- Although China and India belong in the group of poorest countries in terms of per capita incomes — being eighteenth and twenty-first respectively — they appear to perform better in terms of these indicators of development and show signs of greater industrialization (for example they have a lower share of their populations in agriculture).
- The gap between the IACs and these DCs is very large indeed, despite higher growth rates in the DCs between 1960 and 1980. In part this is reflected by lower per capita incomes, in part by lower availabilities of medical personnel and in part by lower calorie consumption.
- Almost three-quarters of a developing-country population are engaged in agriculture and an even greater proportion live in rural areas.
- All of the DCs are in deficit on their foreign trade account. Whilst the IACs are also in deficit in aggregate, once the UK (deficit exceeding $30bn) and the US (deficit exceeding $100bn) are stripped out, their trade is in surplus. Moreover, if service earnings and capital flows are included, the dominance of the IACs is further strengthened.
- The rate of savings, and hence the sums available for investment, are low for the poorest group of countries, but not in the case of India and China.
- The intensity of synthetic resource use (measured here by energy and fertilizer consumption) is far greater in the IACs.

Most DCs have experienced a significant fall in per capita incomes during the 1980s, especially those in the poorest group of countries. This has occurred amidst already low standards of living and, in almost all DCs, a very unequal distribution of income. For example, the poorest 40 per cent of the population received the following percentage of GNP — Brazil (7), Peru (7), Panama (7.2), Ivory Coast (8.6), Kenya (8.9), Mexico (9.9), Venezuela (10.3), Zambia (10.8) and Malaysia (11.2). This compares with 22.4 per cent in the Netherlands and 21.9 per cent in Japan. Interestingly, with the exception of Brazil, none of the most unequal countries has experienced relatively rapid growth, and almost all of the rapid-growth countries have relatively equal distributions of income.[14]

These problems of falling average per capita incomes and unequal distribution of income have been exacerbated further during the 1980s by the structural adjustment policies which many of these countries have been forced to follow. Their high levels of debt have compelled them into a series of agreements with the International Monetary Fund (IMF) and the World Bank which have only provided additional funds on condition certain policies were adopted.[15] The net economic consequences of such 'structural adjustment'

11

— at least by the end of the 1980s — appear to have been deleterious. A study commissioned by the United Nations Children's Fund (UNICEF) calculated the number of country-years between 1980 and 1985 in which 'IMF-assisted' countries have experienced improved growth rates. These totalled 71 and compare with 115 years in which the effect was insignificant or negative.[16] Leaving aside the impact of this conditionality on economic growth, one of the central features of these IMF/World Bank Structural Adjustment programmes has been to substitute user charges for previously free services such as health and education. In other words, the social wage which provided non-monetary services to those unable to afford to buy them on the market has been cut, thus adding to the hardship already faced by the world's poorest population.

Surveying these various developments, UNICEF assessed a decade of experience since the 1979 Year of the Child. Its conclusions are depressing:

> For almost nine hundred million people, approximately one sixth of mankind, the march of human progress has now become a retreat. In many nations, development is being thrown into reverse. And after decades of steady economic advance, large areas of the world are sliding backwards into poverty.
>
> Throughout most of Africa and much of Latin America, average incomes have fallen by 10% to 25% in the 1980s. The average weight-for-age of young children, a vital indicator of normal growth, is falling in many of the countries for which figures are available. In the 37 poorest nations, spending per head on health has been reduced by 50% and on education by 25%, over the last few years. And in almost half of the 103 developing countries from which recent information is available, the proportion of 6-to-11 year olds enrolled in primary schools is now falling.
>
> ... And in tragic summary, it can be estimated that at least half a million young children have died in the past twelve months as a result of the slowing down or the reversal of progress in the developing world.
> [UNICEF (1989), p. 1]

The development and diffusion of AT has a positive role to play in the alleviation of global poverty. Despite assertions to the contrary, there is evidence that such technology can be output- and growth-enhancing and, by making intensive use of labour and other local resources, also contribute to the alleviation of poverty and a reduction in regional and income inequalities. These points will become clearer in later chapters.

Origins of the AT movement

It is in the context of the slowdown in global economic growth and the prevalence (and rising extent) of poverty in DCs that widespread concern has grown about the nature of technology. Three major branches of the AT movement have emerged: the social/political, the consumerist/environmental and the economic/developmental (These are treated in more detail in Chapter 2.) Their origins can be traced to a common reaction to the pattern of post-war global economic growth in both the First and Third Worlds. Inevitably, there are differences in perspective and in the origins of activist groups within each of these three categories, and also important variations in analysis and approach between them. But these differences must not obscure their essential similarities and the commonality of their response to a particular paradigm of economic growth.

In order to understand these common roots and before discussing them in more detail, it is necessary to return briefly to the historical explanations of fluctuating growth rates in the world economy. To recapitulate: it has been argued by some economic historians that global economic history can be classified into approximately 50-year economic cycles. A key organizing principle of the cycle which came to an end in the late 1960s was that of material intensity — especially cheap energy and a robust environment. Another complementary set of analyses of the post-1970 slowdown is that which is based upon the degradation of the mass production paradigm in which economic and social conditions proved to be increasingly unable to satisfy the requirements of ever-growing increases in the scale of production.

These two attempts to theorize the degradation of the post-war global economic system provide insights into the development of the AT movement. The environmental/consumerist branch of the AT movement reacted to the belief in the unlimited supply of raw material imputs, doubted the carrying power of the biosphere and questioned the unfailing demand by undiscerning consumers for undifferentiated products. Concern with the economic and developmental characteristics of technology arose because of the problems experienced by mass production technologies (especially, but not exclusively, in the Third World) in attaining planned levels of efficiency, in meeting the basic needs of consumers and in utilizing local resources. Mass production technologies were also associated with unequal patterns of income distribution, alienating working conditions and social problems associated with large-scale urban agglomerations. What is interesting, as Ellis, McRobie and Darrow point out,[17] is that whilst these three branches of the AT movement represent a common response to the degradation of the materials-intensive mass production paradigm, they arose in different parts of the world.

The major impetus underlying the social/political critique of technology was to be found in Europe where there has long been an interest in the inter-relationship between patterns of social relations and types of material technology. Its roots go back to Marx and Robert Owen in the nineteenth century and surface again in the twentieth century both within activist movements and in academia. In both there has been an ongoing debate between the technological determinists (who believe that technologies determine social relations) and those who have argued that it is possible to

13

restructure technology by first remodelling the social relations under which it is produced and utilized.

For example, in the 1970s shop-stewards in Lucas Aerospace in the UK proposed that instead of manufacturing military weapons, the firm should produce a range of socially useful goods such as kidney dialysis machines and combined rail-buses. None of these ideas was picked up by the company, proving to many that without prior political change ATs would never be adopted. But some of those involved in this initiative have proceeded, with funding from the EEC, to develop further the concept of a more human technology.[18] They have attempted to design flexible manufacturing equipment and computer-aided design systems which can be easily programmed by the user and which complement rather than substitute for human skills. It is in Europe, too, that individual firms have begun to experiment with transformations in the way in which work is organized and in the technology which is utilized.[19] Moreover, as Piore and Sabel have shown, there have been large swathes of European industry in which mass production technology and organization were never really able to assert their dominance.

By contrast, the consumerist/environmental tradition has been most clearly evident in the USA. One of the key markers was the growing rejection of 'mass production life-styles' and the products which it produced. Ralph Nader's *Unsafe at any Speed* (an attack on a General Motors car in the early 1960s) focused attention on the extent to which the pursuit of profit had adverse consequences for consumers. This provided a focal point, and a lift, for various consumer lobby-groups. At about the same time Rachel Carson's *The Silent Spring* (on the environmental consequences of the indiscriminate use of DDT) provoked wider interest in the environment.[20] These and other studies ultimately led to a major international debate around the environment with the Club of Rome's Report on *The Limits of Growth* in 1972, the intent of which was

> to examine the complex of problems troubling men of all nations: poverty in the midst of plenty; degradation of the environment; loss of faith in institutions; uncontrolled urban spread; insecurity of employment; alienation of youth; rejection of traditional values; and inflation and other monetary disruptions. (p. 10)

It predicted that

> If the present growth trends in world population, industrialization, pollution, food production, and resource depletion continue unchanged, the limits to growth on this planet will be reached sometime within the next one hundred years. (p. 23)

and pleaded for a reduction in growth targets and the use of more environmentally sound technologies utilizing better waste collection, more recycling, improved product design, the harnessing of solar energy, the movement towards natural forms of pest control (instead of chemicals), the introduction of more efficient contraceptive technologies and the development of advanced medical techniques.[21]

The third major branch of AT — that concerned with its economic characteristics — had its origins in the Third World where the inappropriateness of large-scale mass production technologies was increasingly obvious. In some cases the concern was expressed by DCs' nationals, as in the case of Gandhi's emphasis on village-level technology. Colonial administrators were another pressure point for AT, frequently introducing simple pieces of equipment such as solar vegetable-driers, charcoal fridges and various water cleaners. But it was Fritz Schumacher who crystallized these views most articulately. An employee of the British National Coal Board (which has had a long obsession with large-scale technology) Schumacher was moved by his visits to Burma and India. His critique of the the post-war global economy was similar to those of both the long-wave theorists and the mass production paradigm:

> The poor of the world cannot be helped by mass production . . . [which is] based on sophisticated, highly capital-intensive, high energy-input dependent, and human labour-saving technology. The technology of mass production is inherently violent, ecologically damaging, self-defeating in terms of non-renewable resources, and stultifying for the human person. (Schumacher (1973), p. 165)

Instead, argued Schumacher, there was the need for an intermediate technology:

> a £1-technology [per workplace], while that of the developed countries could be called a £1,000 technology. Such an intermediate technology would be immensely more productive than the indigenous technology (which is often in a condition of decay), but it would also be immensely cheaper than the sophisticated, highly capital-intensive technology of modern industry. (Ibid., p. 167)

Each of these three branches of the AT movement addressed similar problems. They also had the foresight to see the limits of mass production based upon the intensive use of materials, especially energy. This does not mean that they always drew the same conclusions or that their prescriptions for all appropriate technology were identical. Some features were common to all three branches and in all three localities. For example, they generally not only called for the development and diffusion of ATs, but also preached and (to some extent) practised alternative lifestyles. All three also favoured simple, small-scale technologies making use of local resources and catering for local needs. Natural, as opposed to synthesized, raw materials were generally preferred and the call for long product-life (as opposed to rapid obsolesence) was frequently heard.

But there have also been signficant differences in approach. The environmentalists have tended to reject the need for further economic growth, whereas those calling for more economically appropriate technology in DCs have seen this as a way of increasing the pace of economic advance. An example of these differences has surfaced recently in Brazil where large areas of the Amazon jungle are being cut down to provide the charcoal used in labour-intensive metal foundries.

What emerges from this brief comparison of the different branches of the AT movement is that whilst their origins reflect a common reaction to the previous 'technological paradigm', they do not share a coincidence of views on the most desirable future. It is not yet clear whether an effective global AT coalition can be constructed and, if it can, whether it can be sustained. The real challenge of course will come if and when the AT movements assume significant power over the allocation of resources. Until then it would seem that the commonality of their reaction against the existing pattern of global development outweighs the as yet unrevealed differences in the policies which they propose.

The growth of AT institutions
The modern focus for these disparate groups was the foundation by Fritz Schumacher, George McRobie and Julia Porter of the Intermediate Technology Development Group (ITDG) in London in 1964. Much of ITDG's early work, and especially its links with other AT groups, was concerned with the problems of alternative technology in the First World. But links were soon established with a variety of similar groups in other countries focusing on the problems of DCs. These included the Appropriate Technology Development Association in India, the Technology Centre in Ghana, Volunteers for Technical Assistance (VITA), in existence since 1959, in the USA and the Brace Research Institute in Canada. An international network of AT activists began to emerge in the late 1960s and this was given much greater impetus with the formation of Appropriate Technology International in 1976 by the US Agency for International Development.

Detailed analysis at the beginning of the 1980s by the OECD Development Centre of 277 of the world's most active AT institutions shows that although there was a sprinkling of AT organizations in existence before the Second World War, it was only in the second half of the 1960s that the movement took off. The next significant step occurred towards the end of the 1970s when international institutions (such as the United Nations) began to show a more active interest. Since the completion of the OECD study in 1979, a number of developments has consolidated the AT movement. The growing interest in gender issues has led to a focus on the development and diffusion of technologies which might enhance the lot of women.

Probably more significant in terms of influencing decision-makers have been the critiques of the sustainability of a mass-production, materials-intensive industrialization. Many of these critiques were developed in the Business School, the 'brain' of contemporary industrialism. They have

16

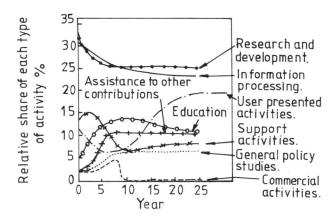

Source: Jequier and Blanc(1983), p.160.

Figure 1.3. *Typical evolution in time of an appropriate technology centre mix of activities*

schooled the new generation of managers to acknowledge the exhaustion of the old paradigm and to adjust their corporate perspective.[22] In the late 1980s concern grew, with the environmental impact of technology especially in relation to the greenhouse effect, the possibilities of further Chernobyl-like nuclear accidents, and the spread of acid rain. The political expression of the environmentalist, the Green movement, has begun to make major strides, especially in Europe.

Two other points are worth observing. First, at least by the beginning of the 1980s, there appears to have been a clearly evolving pattern of activity in almost all AT institutions as they matured (see Figure 1.3). In terms of personnel, the median size seemed to settle at around 15, and within the first decade of their founding, their pattern of activities, with two exceptions, had stabilized. The exceptions were that after initial exploration there was a strong movement away from commercial activities and a progressively growing

17

commitment to user-oriented activities such as technology diffusion and extension services. Both of these exceptions reflect the voluntary nature of the AT movement and the fact that unlike other diffusers of technology (such as private-sector capital goods firms) they have not been driven by the profit motive. They have not always had to cover their costs since, being for the most part charities, they have been able to rely on donations from the public or funding from the government.

The second point concerns the direction of the AT movement as a whole. Here it is possible to detect something of a return to the original focus of these institutions. Schumacher's seminal book, *Small is Beautiful* (1973), was partly a response to the view that unless the political structure could be got right, then there was little hope of implementing AT. For example, Dickson (writing at about the same time as Schumacher), argued that both political and social structures had to change fundamentally before ATs could be generated and widely diffused:

> technological change must be viewed as a political process, reinforcing the interests of a dominant social class. It also implies that development of a non-alienating, non-exploitative technology requires more than just a nominal change in ownership of the machines we now have. It includes a complete reshaping of our attitudes towards the function of technology in society — a simultaneous change, in other words, of both political and technological consciousness. (Dickson (1974), p. 95)

Schumacher provided some form of release from the over-deterministic politicization of the issue. He argued that by empowering the disadvantaged, AT would be a liberatory force; the first step was to make ATs more widely available. Thus attention turned, and the second phase of the modern AT movement began. This concentrated on the dissemination of knowledge about suitable ATs, beginning with ITDG's catalogue of technologies relevant for rural production and costing less than £100, *Tools for Progress: A Guide to Small-scale Equipment for Rural Development* (1967). This rapidly sold several thousand copies and had a wide impact on public consciousness, especially in the development community. Other guides were soon published, such as the Gandhian Institute's *Directory of Appropriate Technology*, VITA's *Village Technology Handbook*, the Brace Research Institute's *Handbook of Appropriate Technology* and even the Melanesian Council of Churches' *Liklik Buk*.

Not long after this, and despite the information made available in these various handbooks, economists were forced to react to the widely-accepted assertion by one of their number that ATs were economically inefficient, that is, that there was in effect no real choice of technology.[23] A series of studies was undertaken, most of which were to show by the mid-1970s that there was indeed a range of efficient technologies available in many sectors, but that these were often linked to particular product characteristics. The choice of technology was thus as much a choice of product as of process, a subject given more consideration in Chapter 2.

18

By this time the AT activists had begun to shift their focus away from merely publicizing the range of available technologies. They were becoming concerned with increasing the range of technologies and began to undertake a series of technological developments. In some cases, this even involved some technological research. By the end of the 1970s the OECD study showed that almost one quarter of global AT expenditure was on R&D, with a further one-fifth devoted to information dissemination.

This survey seems to have marked yet another turning point. After considerable experience with publicization and after devoting increasing inputs into technological development, AT organizations such as ATI and ITDG came to see the need for ensuring that these technologies were disseminated, particularly to their target groups such as women and the rural poor. Two basic approaches were applied — often, despite the fact that these were contradictory, they were implemented concurrently by the same AT institutions. The first was to focus on market failure and to use NGOs as the primary vehicles of diffusion. The second was to rely on market forces. ATs were designed to allow for profitable operation (thereby neglecting other technologies with a high social and low private rate of return). In addition, venture capital funds were made available in an effort to grease the market allocation of resources, hopefully in appropriate directions.

But as the decade of the 1980s wore on, it became clear that there were severe political obstacles to the widespread diffusion of AT. The wheel had turned full circle, for as Stewart pointed out:

> Although the need for appropriate technology is widely agreed upon, as evidenced by the enormous literature . . . and the many institutions which promote AT . . . the achievements in terms of actual use of appropriate technologies have been relatively small.
>
> [A] major reason for the relative failure of AT — in terms of actual on-the-ground investment — has been a near-exclusive focus by those promoting AT primarily (and often exclusively) on micro-interventions . . .
>
> Unavoidably such interventions can only affect a very small proportion of the total investment decisions. (Stewart (1987c), p. 271)

Thus, in the 1990s argues Stewart, logic dictates that the efforts of the AT movement should primarily be placed on changing the policy environment in which ATs are to be diffused. But appropriate action cannot be conceived without a prior understanding of the nature of political power in any economy. The relatively recent awareness by the AT movement of these political dimensions is illustrated by the OECD's 1979 survey of the 277 leading AT institutions. This showed that whereas 23 per cent of global resources were put into R&D and a further 19 per cent into information dissemination, a mere 3.6 per cent was placed in each of policy analysis and political lobbying.

In encouraging the development and diffusion of AT it is helpful to distinguish between three sets of policy interventions. Those at the

19

micro-level, influencing the behaviour of individual enterprises, have received most attention. Governments and NGOs have attempted to upgrade training, provide credit, develop new technologies and diffuse technologies to existing and new enterprises. It follows logically from micro-level interventions that action should be co-ordinated at the meso-level. Generally these policies are targetted at the sectoral level, for example aiming to upgrade all sugar or brick producers, or encourage the widespread diffusion of fuel-efficient charcoal ovens. Sometimes meso-level interventions are also aimed at specific districts, especially in DCs when poverty is geographically uneven. More recently, since the mid-1980s, there has been a growing awareness of the need to fashion macroeconomic policies to encourage the development and choice of more ATs. Whilst all these levels of intervention have a different role to play in the development and diffusion of AT, they are optimally constructed to complement each other, as will be shown in Chapter 8.

Major issues in AT

As seen in earlier discussion there has been a shift in the focus of the AT movement from the political arena, through information dissemination, the development of new technologies, the support of diffusion and back to the political stage. At the same time as these common concerns were emerging in many parts of the world, they were confronted simultaneously by the inherent relativity of AT (Chapter 2), and so caution must be exercised in generalizing the experience from one part of the world, and from one period of time, to other parts, and other times. Common experiences do exist, but each faces particular circumstances.

The political economy of technological choice and technological change
The varied criteria for judging appropriateness, which are discussed in greater detail in Chapter 2, can be grouped under five headings: the relative context of implementation, the distinction between private and social costs and benefits and the economic, social and environmental dimensions. From this it is obvious that, by definition, no technology can be universally appropriate — not merely in terms of geographical location but even within a particular site. There will, moreover, inevitably be trade-offs between different objectives, for example balancing environmental impact against the desire to maximize output. There will also be unavoidable trade-offs between different groups of people affected directly or indirectly by the introduction of the technology, however 'appropriate'.

As will become clear in Chapter 2, many characteristics of appropriateness are inherently unmeasurable. Hence attempts to quantify accurately the degree of appropriateness in terms of a single *numeraire* — money — necessarily rule out a consideration of the full spectrum of criteria. One form of unmeasurable effect is that of politics, defined here as the power to determine outcomes in situations of conflict. These conflicting interests may not always be expressed, as when the power of a particular group is so great that no challenge to its interests is launched. The poor articulation of small-scale, rural and informal sector interests in many DCs is a case in point.

Power relations are a central (albeit often implicit) feature of technological innovation. Consider, for example, the decision of a foreign investor to build a large-scale, capital-intensive plant in a DC. This may only encounter poorly articulated opposition since some powerful interest groups will gain from the inward investment as suppliers, customers and recipients of tax revenues (and perhaps also bribes). But the new investment may damage the operations of small-scale indigenous entrepreneurs operating in the informal sector and rural areas. It may also rule out future domestic investors whose operations may ultimately have a more beneficial economic, social and environmental impact.[24] Indeed, experience has shown that the identity of the entrepreneurs may have the most significant impact on the use of technology. This 'composition of units', which as will be shown in later chapters has an important bearing on the diffusion of AT, is inherently a relation of power.

This centrality of power relations is not confined to the choice of technology. It also pervades the generation of technology. A case in point here is that of seed production where the large chemical companies own most of the major seed companies.[25] This biases the nature of new seed production towards varieties which utilize chemicals intensively. The alternative technological route — designing seeds which are less dependent upon chemical inputs — is largely being neglected, reinforcing the power of the transnational chemical companies. A disturbing trend over the past decade has been that the power of the TNCs in technical change relevant to DCs seems to have increased. In the previous round of agricultural innovation — the Green Revolution — much of the basic research took place in the public domain and was thus less susceptible to biases which favour large-scale corporate interests.

A further form of power relation affecting AT generation and choice is that involved in the provision of aid. In theory there is no necessary reason why this aid should be associated with particular types of technology. But in reality there are biases in the sorts of technologies which are utilized and these reflect the power relations underlying both the giving and receiving of aid. In most cases the pressures at work (such as tying aid to purchases from non-competitive donor country firms) reinforce the tendency in DCs towards the acquisition of imported, capital-intensive and large-scale technologies. Power relations within recipient DCs will also influence the choice of technology. For example, in Kenya there is evidence that large-scale sugar technology was introduced as a direct result of corruption — a 10 per cent margin on a large investment proved to be a significant carrot in greasing the licensing procedure. But this bias of aid agencies towards large-scale and

21

capital-intensive technologies is not always the case. Some aid programmes have 'windows' which are specifically oriented towards the utilization of technologies with different characteristics.

As will become obvious in the case-studies which follow (especially in relation to the diffusion of bakeries in Kenya discussed in Chapter 3 and the development and diffusion of sugar processing technologies described in Chapter 5), it is the balance of power relations which largely determines which technologies are ultimately utilized. Unless these power relations are acknowledged, then policy prescriptions will necessarily be sub-optimal. The 'room for manoeuvre' — the extent to which technologies can be introduced which undermine rather than reinforce these power relations — is the key problem facing the AT movement. And here it is difficult to generalize since the 'political space' for actions varies between environments and over time.

The sources of AT

With the formation of the Intermediate Technology Development Group in 1964, Schumacher publicized his notion of an intermediate technology. As we have seen, he argued that the choice of technology tended to be that between the £1 per workplace traditional technologies of the DCs and the £1,000 per workplace technologies of the IACs. Schumacher believed instead that DCs should invest in intermediate, £100 per workplace technologies. In a sense, although the debate has moved beyond this concept of intermediate technology towards that of appropriate technology, Schumacher's intent remains at the heart of the discussion. Some set of techniques should be found which is both more efficient than the traditional variety and more appropriate than the technology currently being offered by capital goods suppliers, most of whom are based in the IACs.

The problem lies in identifying the source of these new appropriate technologies, and here it is possible to distinguish four major groups:

- AT drawn from the technological shelf — technologies which are available but which are unknown to potential users. It is these technologies which the various AT handbooks of the 1960s were designed to tap. As will be shown in the case of India's small-scale sugar technology, improvements in both furnace design and in cane crushing were based on previously utilized — but almost forgotten — IAC technologies.
- AT based upon the improvement of traditional technologies, sometimes referred to as 'upscaling'. In these cases old, indigenous techniques hold potential for improvement but have been left unchanged due to political economy factors driving technical change. Once again Indian sugar technology is a case in point (Chapter 5) but it is also demonstrated in the case of cement (Chapter 7). A recent variant has been the phenomenon of 'technological blending' in which advanced subsets of technologies are combined with traditional techniques.[26] A particularly striking

22

example here is that of micro-hydroelectric power which is discussed in Chapter 7.

- AT based on modified modern technologies utilized in the IACS, sometimes referred to as 'downscaling'. Most often these involve a reduction in scale and in the complexity of controls. Sometimes these changes may be possible without making expensive design-changes to the core technology itself. As has often been pointed out, most productive enterprises represent a combination of various sub-processes and many possibilities arise for combining these sub-processes in different ways. One of the most successful examples of downscaling has been in shrimp production in Indonesia, where small-scale producers account for 20 per cent of exports. Possible areas for downscaling have been identified in both shoe and sugar production,[27] and in principle can be applied to a wider set of technologies. Prospects exist in some sectors for changing the design of the central process itself, in some cases to reduce scale but also to change other features such as the organization of work, and environmental impact.
- AT based upon the design of wholly new technologies. Oral rehydration therapy (a simple and low-cost solution of salt and minerals which has significantly cut the death-rate from diarrhoea) is perhaps the most striking, cheap and effective example. Others are to be found in the field of renewable energy, where solar and wave power and even more novel forms of energy generation look likely to have a significant future impact. These renewable energy technologies relate not only to the economic criteria of appropriateness but also to the environmental and social criteria discussed in Chapter 2.

In the case-studies which follow, two of these sources of AT will be repeatedly evidenced. In bakeries, cement and sugar processing, this involves the improvement of existing technologies. And in sugar processing, off-the-shelf designs have been instrumental in improving performance. There is as yet no sign of 'blending' in any of these sectors, although a clear potential exists. The downscaling of modern state-of-the-art technology has been mooted in both the case of sugar processing and cement, but as yet there have been no tangible developments. The absence of both of these sources of AT is one of the consequences of the global distribution of technical change resources remarked on above. Were more of these to be allocated to meeting basic needs in the DCs, then there would be much more likelihood of the downscaling and blending of technologies.

Efficiency in a dynamic context
The question of 'efficiency' often arises in the discussion of AT. In many cases this involves a confusion of meanings. On the one hand there is the issue of 'economic efficiency', discussed in Chapter 2. The argument is that if a technique has lower productivities of both capital and labour (or other

inputs, if these are considered), then it is economically inefficient and there are no circumstances in which its use can be justified. On the other hand, there are also questions of 'engineering efficiency', which relate to the technical nature of the physical processes involved.

These two conceptions of technology may or may not accord with each other. This is evident in the case of sugar processing (discussed in Chapter 5) where the small-scale technology is economically efficient but achieves significantly lower yields of sugar from cane. It has been common to condemn the small-scale technique as being inherently undesirable because of its poor transformation of cane which involves the devotion of greater tracts of land to meet a given demand for sugar. Neither of these — or any other partial — types of efficiency can be utilized rationally to determine the appropriateness of technology. For, as has been pointed out, there are multiple objectives and inefficiency in some areas can be overridden by other considerations. For example, in the case of sugar processing, the greater land-using character of the small-scale technique can be offset by its savings of capital. Both factors are in scarce supply in India and neither can assume primacy. Similarly, there may be cases in which economically inefficient techniques may be highly desirable because they empower small-scale producers or provide valuable industrial experience which facilitates alternative technological trajectories in the future. Riskin argues that despite the fact that many of the small-scale techniques utilized during the Great Leap Forward in China (1958–60) were inefficient from both the economic and engineering point of view,

> [m]any of the thriving regional industries of today had their origins in a primitive workshop established in 1958 . . .
> Even where the shops established during the great leap were forced to close, however, the initial experience with industrial methods they had afforded the peasants and the lessons, both positive and negative, to which they gave rise, proved invaluable later when local industrialization was again pushed vigorously. (Riskin (1979), p. 54)

One of the issues highlighted by the Chinese experience is the long period which is often required for ATs to be developed. The present day technological capabilities of the IACs have a long history, even in the case of Japan which began its industrialization in the last quarter of the nineteenth century. It is also seldom recognized that many of the newly industrializing DCs have a long experience of industrial production so that their recent successes are less a miracle of policy changes in the 1960s than a reflection of their long history of industrial production. What is true for countries is also true for individual sectors and individual firms.

Many studies of technological capability have shown that progress, at national, sectoral and firm level, is of a cumulative nature. The fanciful idea of new entrants buying their way to the technological frontier is just that —

24

fanciful. Similarly, the conception of 'learning by doing' is also misleading in the sense that it suggests that technological capabilities arise merely as a consequence of doing something, that they come for nothing. Both of these common misconceptions — that technological progress is a costless consequence of production experience and that it is a short-run phenomenon — have been belied by a variety of detailed studies. It is true that the process can be speeded up and that costs can be reduced, but these are only qualifications of three 'rules' which have been widely observed: developing technological capability is expensive; it takes time; and the greater the scientific content in production, the greater the cost, and the longer the wait.

This experience with technological change has a number of implications for AT. It is clear that in most cases, deriving AT from any of the four sources discussed above will require the explicit commitment of resources to technological development. This is clear from the experience of cement and sugar, as will be shown in later chapters. But what also emerges from these case-studies is that in general the AT movement is ill-equipped to finance or organize such developments. Without developing close links to capital goods producers who specialize in the commercial production of ATs, there is bound to be a deficiency in their supply.

A second characteristic of appropriate technological development is that notwithstanding the point made above, relatively speaking many ATs do not require large technological inputs. Moreover, precisely because their development has been neglected in the past, the returns from investing resources into changing these technologies are often very high. This has been the experience of Indian small-scale sugar, but as will be shown, similar lessons can be drawn from bakery development and the optimization of small-scale cement technology in China and India.

Finally, given the time involved in technological development, especially in the more complex sectors, there may be problems in pursuing macroeconomic strategies which are relevant to the furtherance of AT. For example, as a consequence of their debt burdens, many DCs have been forced by the IMF and the World Bank to accept structural adjustment programmes. Such programmes are based on the premise that DCs should adopt a greater outward orientation and that they should remove trade barriers which are thought to be propping up inefficient domestic industries. In some cases this may be an appropriate trade strategy, particularly when potentially competitive small-scale producers are overwhelmed by subsidized large-scale domestic producers. But in other cases — as in the case of sugar technology discussed in Chapter 5 and in other relatively more technologically complex sectors — these trade policies being forced on DCs may be too narrow in orientation and may make it difficult to develop potentially successful ATs.

25

Engineering and bureaucratic decision-makers

One important element affecting both the processes of technological development and the choice of technology is the world-view of those making decisions about technological choice and the performance criteria under which they operate. These attitudes are defined at a number of levels, including the cultural, the institutional and the ideological. Wells developed the concept of 'engineering-man' to help him understand the choice of technology in the Philippines.[28] He recounts a large number of cases where the decisions to introduce certain types of (inappropriate) technology were driven by considerations of engineering excellence rather than economic rationality.

James found a variation of this when he investigated the choice of technology by parastatals in Kenya and Tanzania, neighbouring countries with apparently different political systems.[29] One would have expected these two differing systems to have produced varying choices of technology, but in reality few such differences emerged. To explain this James utilizes the concept of 'bureaucratic man' in which the success criteria for senior managers in both sets of parastatals is short-run output maximization. Yet in itself this concept of 'bureaucratic man' needs to be fleshed out since as will be seen in the case of bricks in Chapter 4, two sets of 'bureaucrats' working at the same point in time made very different technology-choice decisions in Tanzania.

Thus the tension between definitions of appropriateness in the abstract may be belied not only by the political economy of technical choice (considered earlier) but also by what may be called the sociology of technical choice. A similar process occurs in relation to the direction of technical change where one of the more convincing discussions of the process of R&D identifies 'technological trajectories' which represent particular orientations of technical progress drawn from a range of potential alternatives.[30] Since most global R&D occurs in the IACs the dominant technological trajectory is one which produces technologies appropriate for IAC rather than DC operating conditions. And since this process of technological change is predominantly driven by the search for profit and hence by market prices (ignoring externalities in production), environmentally harmful technologies are often produced.[31] All of these factors impinge on both the choice and the development of technology, and hence on the implementation of AT, both in the industrially advanced and the developing countries.

How small is small?

There is some ambivalence in the AT movement concerning the appropriateness of small-scale technology. Essentially this difference of views (which is seldom explicitly recognized, and is mostly implicit in the activities of different arms of the AT movement) arises because of the varying reference points concerning the criteria of appropriateness. For those who are

26

primarily driven by the economic criteria, the optimality of scale is that which is relative to the demand-profile of the particular national economy rather than the production-scale of the most advanced IAC technology. On the other hand, activists who are more concerned with the local mobilization of resources and the participation of the masses in production are more concerned with the absolute scale of the technologies in question.

At the end of the 1980s these diferences surfaced in relation to two particular technologies — sugar processing and cement. In the former case, the small-scale plant crushes between 100 and 250 tons of cane per day, compared with around 10,000 tons for the most technologically efficient plants. In cement around 50–100 tons are produced per day compared to over 2,000 tons in the large plants. In both cases the ATs are relatively small but, with capital investments exceeding $2m, they are absolutely large. Are they therefore 'appropriate'? Are these the sorts of technologies which the AT movement should be pursuing?

This is an important issue since at stake is the general involvement of the AT movement in the intermediate goods sector. In capital and consumer goods there is often a much clearer choice in the absolute scale of production, whereas in intermediate products the major area of choice lies in relative scale. The contrast between the size of investments in brick, cement and sugar processing compared with that in bread making, is one of the more striking features of the case-studies in later chapters.

Production for or by the masses?

Given the multiple objectives involved in the determination of appropriateness, it is possible that the technology considered most appropriate is not that which produces output at the lowest cost, but that which employs the greatest number of people. Alternatively, although local production may be favoured because it stimulates long-run regional growth, it might involve higher output prices. So a key question which arises is whether the technology involves production for the masses (for example producing cheap wage goods with capital-intensive technologies) or production by the masses (producing expensive wage goods with labour-intensive technologies). And, further, however cheap wage goods may be, if the mass of the population does not have the jobs which provide the incomes to purchase these goods, their availability is of little use.

Schumacher addressed these issues in *Small is Beautiful* and argued that no such conflict between objectives existed:

> The system of production by the masses mobilizes the priceless resources which are possessed by all human beings, their clever brains and skilful hands, and supports them with first-class tools ... The technology of production by the masses, making use of the best of modern knowledge and experience, is conducive to decentralization, compatible with the laws of ecology, gentle in its use of scarce resources, and designed to serve the

human person instead of making him the servant of the machine. (Schumacher (1973), p. 143)

Yet it would be fortuitous if this were always to be the case and as will be shown for the case of brick production (Chapter 4), the AT movement has often found itself to be caught between these two desirable aspects of appropriateness — production by or production for the masses. This is perhaps one of the most acute dilemmas facing the AT movement and provides a particularly sharp contrast between action at the micro-level (to ensure mass participation in production) and that at the macro-level (to provide cheap wage goods).

The interaction between technology and society
A variety of policy prescriptions arises from the analysis of AT undertaken in this book. But before policies can be identified it is necessary to understand the interaction between technology and social relations. This is a particularly complex issue, for at its heart lies the distinction between correlation and causality. The correlation is as follows. DCs, as was shown in Table 1.1, face problems of capital and foreign-exchange shortage, have predominantly rural populations and are generally characterized by the unequal distribution of resources. They also often use capital-intensive technologies, many of which are imported. More often than not these operate on a large-scale and are located in urban areas.

The question is whether the pattern of poverty and dominant form of technology utilized in the DCs are linked in any causal way. Usually such a suggested link is that it is the utilization of these particular technologies which in some way explains the prevalence and characteristics of poverty in the Third World. Essentially this is a variant of technological determinism and is a world-view ascribed to the AT movement by the critiques of Eckaus (see pp. 2–3). For example, it is argued that because capital-intensive technologies are generally imported, their utilization worsens both the savings and foreign exchange problems faced by DCs; it also necessitates location in urban areas and this leads to the concentration of social services (such as schools and health) and infrastructure (such as electricity) and the consequent neglect of rural areas. Hence, goes the argument, it is the nature of the technology which is utilized which explains the unequal distribution of resources and the slowing down of economic growth.

An entirely different pattern of causality can also be offered, arguing that the primary explanation for inequality is to be found in the social and political arenas. Unequal concentrations of income and power lead to the adoption of large-scale capital-intensive technologies since it is these which reinforce the dominance in society of the already powerful groups.

Both perspectives begin from the same observed correlation, yet the causal explanations offered are diametrically opposite; they also lead to different

perceptions of policy. If it is the technology which is seen to be the prime mover of social patterns of behaviour, then the encouragement of different types of technology will in itself lead to reduced inequalities, social betterment and enhanced rates of economic growth. On the other hand the alternative perspective suggests that the solution lies in political and social change. Crudely speaking, without prior revolution, little prospect is seen for the widespread diffusion of ATs. Merely altering the pattern of technological choice will only lead to their distorted use in the maintenance of existing political structures.

This difference in view of the relationship between technology and social structure is, as has been shown, reflected in the very history of the AT movement. At various times different elements have argued either that prior revolutionary change is a necessary precondition for the adoption of ATs or that changing the pattern of technological choice will induce more equitable patterns of social relations. But, as will become obvious in the case-studies which follow in later chapters, the real world is much more complex than either of these contrasting perspectives. It will be possible to find examples which support both. Yet seen in totality, what emerges is a dialectical interplay between technology and social relations which offers possibilities, yet simultaneously constrains the room for positive action. Policy interventions are therefore often of a complex nature, and even when successful, generalization across time, between sectors and over space may not be possible. As will be repeatedly stressed in coming chapters, appropriateness is inherently relative.

CHAPTER 2
Definitions and measurement

What is AT?

In Chapter 1 a bridge was constructed between global economic slowdown, increasing poverty, and patterns of technological choice and technological change. The correlation of these factors does not necessarily confirm a technologically determinist perspective since, as was noted, it is at least as possible that technological choice derives from the nature of social relations as the converse. But once the correlation between technology and social relations is acknowledged, attention necessarily falls on problems of optimality. Are the observed patterns of social relations desirable? Are there more appropriate types of technology? If so, will their diffusion be associated with more desirable social outcomes? In other words, are there more appropriate structures and technologies than those which currently dominate?

The definition of what is appropriate has spawned a substantial body of writing and this is reflected in a variety of approaches each of which ultimately affects the nature of the policies which are prescribed. Unfortunately, in most cases the different perspectives adopted on appropriateness are often implicit, so that many apparent conflicts in policy perspectives in reality reflect underlying differences in the meaning given to this concept. It is possible to distinguish at least three basic dimensions to appropriateness — the economic, the social and the environmental. Two other elements of appropriateness can be identified which have widespread relevance in analysis and policy — its inherent relativity and the distinction between private and social appropriateness.

AT as the utilization of local resources: an economic approach

In 1976 the US Agency for International Development (USAID) set out a programme for AT. Of the three major criteria proposed, two can be identified clearly with the utilization of local resources. (The third relates to social structure and will be considered below, pp. 37–9.) These are that

> In terms of available resources, appropriate technologies are intensive in the use of the abundant factor, labour, economical in the use of scarce factors, capital and highly trained personnel, and intensive in the use of domestically-produced inputs.
> In terms of small production units, appropriate technologies are

30

small-scale but efficient, replicable in small units, readily operated, maintained and repaired, low cost and accessible to low income persons. (USAID (1976), pp. 11–12)

The first of these two sets of specifications involves the question of factor use, the second concerns the scale of production. Often these two sets of economic criteria are considered to be too limiting and are supplemented with others. For example, in the mid-1970s the United Nations Environmental Programme (UNEP) set out a list of economic criteria for appropriateness which includes not only the utilization of local resources, but also production for local consumption and for technologies which promote dynamic interactions of a decentralized nature.[1]

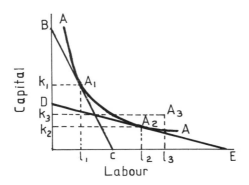

Figure 2.1. *Economic appropriateness: the production function*

Some of the factors involved in the determination of economic appropriateness are illustrated in Figure 2.1. This represents the way in which neoclassical economic theory sees the choice of technology. Curve AA, the production function, represents the range of technologies available to produce a specified good. The vertical axis represents inputs of physical capital and the horizontal axis that of labour. The price line represents the relative cost of capital and labour. In the case of BC capital is relatively cheap and labour expensive, while the price line DE represents cheap labour and more expensive capital. Obviously, BC relates to factor availability in the IACs, and DE to that in low wage economies.

Assessing AT in the context of this mode of analysis, choice A_1 is that which maximizes output at IAC factor prices; A_2 does so for DC factor prices. Thus these two points of intersection between the production

31

function and the factor price line are considered to represent the optimal choice at given factor prices, that is the appropriate technology. In this form of analysis inappropriate technologies are chosen for two major reasons. Either this is because labour intensive technologies such as A_2 are not available. Or the factor price line prevailing in DCs does not represent real factor scarcities — instead of DE, the operative factor prices in DCs is much more like that in IACs, namely BC.

One of the major strengths of this economic analysis of appropriateness is that it provides a very useful insight into what has come to be called 'economic efficiency'. This is not the same as technological efficiency and refers to the productivities of the various inputs used in production. Take, for example, point A_3 in Figure 2.1. It has a lower capital/labour ratio which is often considered to represent the most important determinant of appropriateness. Yet, reference to Figure 2.1 also shows that whilst A_2 and A_3 produce the same level of output, A_3 uses both more labour and more capital per unit of output. If the sole intent were to utilize more labour this could be done by employing technique A_2, saving capital (k_2-k_3) and setting the additional labour (l_1-l_3) to work with simple handtools. Thus, A_3 is considered to be an economically inefficient technology and should never be chosen.

The analysis contained in Figure 2.1 makes no reference to the scale of production. Yet, as can be seen from actual experience (and is evidenced in the case-studies discussed in this book), this is an important determinant of modern competitiveness. Whilst the meta-theorists writing about the problems of the mass production paradigm have considered the problem of scale from a high level of abstraction (see Chapter 1), it is important to

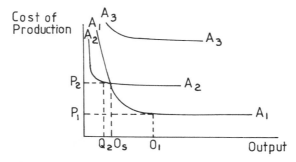

Figure 2.2. *Appropriateness in relation to scale*

understand its impact on the choice of individual technologies. Consider the example shown in Figure 2.2. This plots the average cost of production with the scale of operation. The production technique A_1 clearly has lower unit costs of production (P_1) than technique A_2 (P_2) and thus, all things being equal (that is, that factor prices reflect real resource costs), A_1 represents the appropriate choice of technology. Yet the scale of output at which A_1 achieves its lowest costs — O_1 — is considerably higher than the output at which A_2 reaches its lowest costs — O_2. In fact, at any range of output below O_S, A_2 has lower unit costs than A_1. Thus, unless A_1 operates at near its optimum scale its potential cost advantages cannot be realized and A_2 becomes the economically appropriate technique. Note that there is no scale at which technique A_3 will ever have lower costs than either A_2 or A_1. This is because it uses both more labour and more capital per unit of output than either of the alternatives.

The point here is that although there may be economies of scale to be realized in production, these can only be captured when the relevant levels of scale can be attained. In many cases this may be impossible, perhaps because the domestic market is too small or for social and environmental reasons (a phenomenon which, as will be seen in Chapter 6 is not restricted to DCs). Or, where the penetration of foreign markets is difficult, these scale economies may be illusory.

The proponents of this economic analysis of appropriate technical choice (represented in Figure 2.1) have come increasingly to recognize a series of major limitations to this simplified model. First, capital and labour are not the only inputs into production. Land, raw materials, semi-processed intermediate products as well as services all need to be taken into account. Second, these inputs are not homogeneous — labour differs in nature, and so does capital. Issues of quality are involved here, but so also is the matching of local back-up capabilities to service these inputs. Thus, one of the major concerns which arises is whether the capital equipment utilized can be locally maintained and repaired. A third and major limitation of this simplified model of appropriate technical choice relates to the assumption that each of the available techniques provides identical products. Yet in the real world, this is patently not the case.

In recent years a revision of the theory of consumer demand has led to a burgeoning interest in the appropriateness of products and the links between product and process technology.[2] Individual products are considered to be defined by their characteristics and just as process technology is assessed by its utilization of factor inputs, products are reflected by the mix of characteristics which they possess. This allows for account to be taken of trade-offs between the different attributes of alternative products. For this it is possible to specify products which possess the bundle of characteristics which best meet the needs of particular groups of consumers. Relating these properties to individual budget constraints it becomes possible to identify appropriate

33

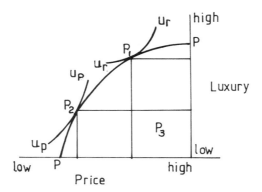

Figure 2.3. *Economic appropriateness: the consumption function*

products in the same way as appropriate products were specified in earlier analysis (see Figure 2.1).

Figure 2.3 considers what might be called the 'economic appropriateness of products'. A bundle of characteristics favoured by high income consumers is represented on the vertical axis — these might be referred to as 'luxury'. On the horizontal axis the price of commodities is plotted. Thus a production possibilities frontier (PP) can be constructed, reflecting the range of alternative product combinations which can be produced from a given set of productive resources to satisfy different requirements for price and luxury. The attribute of luxury represents the interests of rich consumers who are able to pay for non-functional attributes in products, whereas poor consumers are considered to be more interested in low price. Two sets of utility curves can thus be derived — $U_r U_r$ for high income consumers and $U_p U_p$ for low income consumers. The 'appropriate product' is thus specified as P_1 for the IACs and P_2 for the DCs since it is at these points of tangency that consumer welfare is maximized in relation to production possibilities. In the same way that P_3 represented inefficient production technology in Figure 2.1, P_3 represents an inefficient product technology in Figure 2.3. This means that for a given income a consumer could have more luxury without sacrificing any price (or lower prices without sacrificing any luxury) if they consumed product P_1 or P_2 rather than P_3.

There are a number of reasons why inappropriate products — for example, those with a preponderance of high income characteristics in a poor economy — may dominate. Technical change resources may be concentrated in products destined for richer consumers. An example of this may be the

34

current development of high definition colour televisions (HDTV) rather than lower-cost black and white receivers operating on battery power and therefore suitable for rural areas in poor countries. Another reason for the dominance of inappropriate products may be due to the power of producers to influence consumer taste patterns. Extensive evidence has been found for this in many DCs.[3] A third, and more problematic reason is that product technology may involve the same forms of economic efficiency as process technology so that a new product may be superior in the production of all characteristics, but may be relatively more efficient in respect to high-income characteristics. The comparison between detergents and soap flakes is a good example, since although detergents wash 'more whitely', their labour-saving characteristics in the washing process are more relevant to the needs of high- than low-income consumers. There may also be scale-like considerations in product technology — although a given bundle of characteristics may be produced more cheaply, there may be minimum scales of purchase (for example, for HDTV) which preclude poorer consumers from attaining these benefits.[4]

A final characteristic of product technology which is of particular importance in the diffusion of AT is its link with process technology. For many years economists undertook studies to determine whether there really was a choice of economically efficient techniques or, as Eckaus had asserted, there was usually only one efficient technique, usually capital-intensive and imported into DCs from the IACs. These empirical studies found that there was some validity to Eckhaus's view — the range of technical choice was indeed limited, often severely. But the extent of these limitations was invariably affected by the tightness with which the product was specified. For example, if a writing implement (or some form of transport) was desired, there was a very wide range of alternative technologies available. But if a Parker pen (or a Mercedes Benz) was specified, there was effectively no choice of technique. A single process technology, produced abroad and owned by a transnational corporation (TNC), was the only one available.

From here it is only a short jump to the link between the distribution of income and power and the choice of technology. If it can be shown that particular sets of consumers choose specific types of products (perhaps persuaded by particular producers), then different patterns of income distribution will be associated with varying patterns of technology utilization. Hans Singer addresses this phenomenon and also argues that technological choice not only reflects patterns of income distribution but also helps to determine it. He refers to this as the 'double appropriateness of technology':

> under a basic-needs strategy technology must bear the double burden of adapting existing or imported new technology to the general situation of the developing country and of underpinning the redistribution of incomes which goes with a basic-needs strategy. For this reason it might be called a 'doubly appropriate' technology. (Singer (1977), p. 3)

In terms of the people who use and benefit from them, appropriate technologies seek to be compatible with local cultural and social environments. (USAID (1976), pp 11–12)

This USAID concern with cultural and social compatibility is a much more restrictive specification of social appropriateness than that considered by others. Reddy, for example, basing himself on the criteria set out by UNEP, includes in social appropriateness the following characteristics:

a preference for technologies which lead to an enhancement of the quality of life, rather than merely to an increase in the consumption of goods

a preference for production technologies which require satisfying creative work, rather than boring routine labour

a preference for production technologies in which machines are subordinated to, rather than dominate, the lives of people

a preference for technologies based on communal, rather than individual, use of goods and services

a preference for technologies which blend with, rather than disrupt, traditional technologies and the fabric of social life

a preference for technologies which increase, rather than diminish, the possibility and effectiveness of social participation and control

a preference for technologies which facilitate the devolution of power to the people, rather than its concentration in the hands of elites. (Reddy (1979), p. 179)

There are clear differences between the approaches of USAID and Reddy. The first stands back from any determination of what type of social structure is appropriate and in this sense is in accordance with the inherent relativity of AT. On the other hand the specification 'compatible with local cultural and social environments' is hardly helpful. Were social and cultural environments to be homogeneous, then this level of generality might hold some water. But where they are inherently heterogeneous, with class, ethnic and gender divides, it is clear that value judgements have to be made. It is these value judgements which are clearly to the fore in the UNEP criteria.

The inclusion of social criteria in the definition of appropriateness provides an important challenge to the economistic and real resource cost approaches already outlined. But it is an approach which bristles with methodological and conceptual difficulties. How are these social criteria to be assessed and measured? Does 'blending' with the fabric of social life mean the support of patriarchal patterns of behaviour? Does providing fuel and water for women in Africa (thereby relieving them from many hours of daily effort) constitute a reinforcement (thereby freeing them to perform other tasks previously undertaken by men) or a disruption of this social fabric? Is it possible to measure the degree of 'social participation and control', and how can it be compared to improvements or further degradation in other characteristics of social appropriateness?

A second problem which arises from the attempts to specify criteria of social appropriateness is not inherent to the methodology itself but reflects the particular approach which has characteristically been adopted. Much of this derives from the school of methodological individualism in the social sciences where social compatibility tends to be seen in relation to individual actors rather than to groups such as classes, clans, tribes and trade unions. Little attention is given to political empowerment; emphasis tends to be placed instead on the welfare implications of technological innovations. Not only does this approach often fail to identify the political levers for social change, but by focusing on the welfare content, it is often static in character.

Finally, these attempts at specifying social criteria raise the question of technological determinism (which was discussed in Chapter 1 and will be considered further in Chapter 8). The implicit explanation offered in the social criteria listed above is one in which the choice of technologies leads to particular social and cultural outcomes, or reinforces or undermines these outcomes. Yet some would argue that the 'social impact' of technology is neutral — the same technology can be utilized in very different sets of cultural milieu with no discernible influence over the social outcome.[5] Therefore the idea that technologies can be assessed in relation to their interaction with social and cultural phenomena is based on a fundamentally unsound explanation of the relationship between technology and society.

It is as well to keep in mind the complexity and relativity of these issues. In some circumstances technological choice may have little impact on social relations; in other cases it may have a fundamental role to play in empowering groups and enabling them to mobilize for fundamental political change. Whilst social criteria can often be given a misplaced importance in the analysis of AT, it is also clear that they cannot be ignored.

AT and the environment

When looking to the origins of the AT movement (see Chapter 1), it can be seen that groups focusing on the environment have played an important role, especially in the IACs. They have reacted to the fact that many environmental costs are not reflected in the costs paid by the direct producer. (These are referred to as external diseconomies, and are discussed in more detail on pp. 40–43.) Nor are they always measurable. Yet, particularly in relation to DCs, little attention has been given to the nature of the environmental criteria for appropriateness.

Schumacher's early account of AT objectives paid more attention to environmental issues than many subsequent works. He argued that the origins of environmental degradation lay in the distinction between 'man-as-producer' and 'man-as-consumer':

> But since the two are the same man, the question of what man — or society — can really afford gives rise to endless confusion.
> There is no escape from this confusion as long as the land and the creatures upon it are looked upon as *nothing but* 'factors of production'. They are, of course, factors of production, that is to say, means-to-ends, but this is their secondary, not their primary nature. Before everything else, they are ends-in-themselves. (Schumacher (1973), p. 97)

The consequences of this mis-specification of priorities are that agriculture has been treated as if it were an industry, rather than a biological process, and that the earth's resources have been depleted. But, perhaps most critically, Schumacher fused ethical concerns with the necessity for action, since

> No degree of prosperity [can] justify the accumulation of large amounts of highly toxic substances which nobody knows how to make 'safe' and which remain an incalculable danger to the whole of creation for historical or even geological ages ... The idea that a civilization could sustain itself on the basis of such a transgression is an ethical, spiritual, and metaphysical monstrosity. It means conducting the economic affairs of man as if people really did not matter at all. (Ibid., p. 135)

For Schumacher, there was little conflict in achieving the goals of environmental, social and economic appropriateness simultaneously:

> Small-scale operations, no matter how numerous, are always less likely to be harmful to the natural environment than large-scale ones, simply because their individual force is small in relation to the recuperative forces of nature. (Ibid. p. 31)

Shortly after Schumacher's book was published, UNEP was formed. As part of its process of targetting the ATs, UNEP provided a set of criteria by which appropriateness could be judged. These include:

> a preference for energy-production technologies based on renewable, rather than depletable, energy resources

> a preference for technologies which produce goods that can be recycled and re-used ... and that are designed for durability, rather than quick obsolescence

> a preference for production technologies based on raw materials which are replenishable ... rather than exhaustible

> a preference for technologies of production and consumption which inherently minimize noxious or dangerous emissions and wastes, rather than those which require 'fixes' to curb their intrinsically polluting tendencies

a preference for technologies of production and consumption which incorporate waste minimization and utilization procedures as integral components

a preference for technologies which blend into natural ecosystems by causing them minimum disturbance, rather than those which threaten the biosphere with major perturbations

a preference for technologies based on the rational sustained use rather than indiscriminate rapid devastation, of the environment. (Reddy (1979), p. 178)

AT — relative or absolute specifications

Broadly speaking, there are two basic approaches to the relativity of AT. On the one hand there is the view that at a strictly logical level all technologies are simultaneously both inherently appropriate and inappropriate. They are appropriate because they were developed and innovated in order to maximize a given set of objectives; counter-insurgency weapons are a case in point. At the same time they are inappropriate since in theory (if not in practice) it is always possible to conceive of techniques which would satisfy the desired objectives even more thoroughly. Moreover if a different set of objectives were to be specified — revolution rather than repression, to carry through with the above example — then the same technology would be classified as inappropriate. The concept of appropriateness is thus seen being as inherently relative. It has meaning only when particular objectives are identified and when specific operating environments are taken into account.

On the other hand there are other observers, probably in the majority, who regard this type of analysis as a form of academic hair-splitting. They take it for granted that the function of AT is to improve the living conditions of the poor (sometimes specified as the rural poor) and rapidly move to the specification of items of technology. Only those technologies which involve rural production by or for the poor, which operate on a small-scale with labour-intensive technologies and which utilize local inputs are deemed to be appropriate.

Between these two views are those who believe that a middle path exists. Bhalla, for example, distinguishes between 'broad priority areas' and a specific 'toolkit' of techniques:

appropriate technology is a concept which implies a suitable policy framework and a broad-based pattern of development. It is *not* a toolkit of a selected number of technologies with technical and engineering specifications which could fit in with the requirements of all Third World countries ... However, although it is wrong to look for particular technologies as appropriate for all climes and times, it is possible to examine broad priority areas in which technologies should be developed and upgraded. (Bhalla (1979) p. 46)

For Bhalla, the broad priority area associated with AT is that which furthers the satisfaction of basic needs, but this may not involve any great specificity in the technologies which are identified.

The discussion which follows in later chapters broadly follows Bhalla's approach. When considering DCs, the priority areas are seen to be those with a more beneficial 'environmental footprint', technologies which relate to the needs of the poor and which are relatively labour intensive and small-scale and which use local resources. They are also technologies which, wherever possible, improve the quality of social life and which involve enriched, rather than degraded work. With regard to the IACs, technologies which operate on a small scale, have a benign (or positive) effect on the environment and which improve conditions of work are considered to be appropriate.

As will become clear, these priorities can only be mapped out in the broadest terms and the appropriateness of specific techniques will be relative to both the individual circumstances of production and to the weightings placed on these different objectives. Trade-offs between objectives are an inevitable component of AT choice.

AT — private and social, positive and normative considerations

The economic analysis so far has glossed over the issue of who pays for the costs of production and who receives its benefits. A major reason why this issue cannot be overlooked is that in reality factor prices seldom reflect the real opportunity cost of resources.[6] The optimality of choice from the private perspective may be very different from that which is appropriate from the economy-wide point of view.

Consider, for example, the cost of capital. For one reason or another, the market price of capital may be at variance with its real availability or, as is more often the case, large-scale producers alone may be offered capital at 'artificially' low prices. This may then lead them to invest in capital-intensive technologies, which are often imported. The result will be a lower availability of capital for other users (such as small-scale producers) who may potentially utilize this capital far more productively. It will also lead to a worsening balance of payments (since labour-intensive technologies not only use less capital but also often have a higher local content as well) and a reduction in overall employment.

A second reason why there may be a divergence between private and social optimality is when there are spillovers from production to the external environment. These may be of a positive nature, most notably in the case of training. A particular plant may offer formal or on-the-job training to its employees which is transferable to other firms. In this case the training firm is unable to capture all of the benefits which it is providing. But these external effects may also be negative, most clearly in the case of pollution. The real social and environmental costs involved in displacing effluent into the physical environment may not be felt by the producers themselves, and may,

40

after being borne by rivers or atmospheric changes, be experienced many miles or decades away. An associated concern is the issue of resource use over time. The market valuation of inputs generally reflects the current costs of production rather than the future depletion of resources. The further in the future is the depletion of resources and the greater the cost of capital,[7] the more likely this is to be the case.

Finally, private and social returns may be affected by normative concerns of what is socially desirable. For example, placing a premium on social equity may bias choice towards technologies which can be utilized in under-developed regions. Technological development and choice may also involve gender considerations, perhaps by placing a premium on technologies which involve the employment of women or which may affect their lifestyle. Normative concerns may even incorporate values which are widely considered to be 'regressive', actively favouring the already advantaged at the expense of the relatively disadvantaged. In all cases these social objectives might undermine private profitability. Thus the distribution of income and power may be an important component to be considered in the determination of appropriateness.

The consequence of these divergences between private and social costs and benefits, as well as the consequence of considering normative distributional considerations, is that market prices may lead to a socially undesirable pattern of technological choice. What may be appropriate for particular private parties — usually private entrepreneurs attempting to maximize their profits over time — may not be appropriate from a social perspective. This may either involve limited concerns with maximizing the utilization of local resources (and hence the rate of growth and output) or wider objectives relating to equity, welfare and the environment.

Measuring AT

It is thus possible to determine a number of criteria in terms of which AT can be judged. Interest then turns to the problem of measurement in any particular case. Is it possible to estimate the extent of appropriateness and thereby to compare the desirability of alternative choices? There are basically two approaches to this problem: the first believes that a clear basis for measurement both exists and is meaningful, and that this can be translated into a monetary equivalent; the second is more sceptical of the power of financial analysis, even when corrected to take account of social and environmental costs.

It is not surprising that it is the economists who are most firmly wedded to the measurement of AT. The basic technique utilized, often referred to as the social welfare approach, it to begin with market prices and to correct these for the distortions which represent real resource costs. This leads to the generation of a series of 'shadow prices', most typically in the case of DCs correcting for 'imperfections' in the markets for capital and foreign exchange (generally thought to be undervalued) and labour (generally thought to be overvalued). In his well-known summary of the extent of technical choice conducted in the mid-1970s, Morawetz described this evaluative procedure in the following way:

> Appropriate technology may be defined as the set of techniques which make optimum use of available resources in a given environment. For each process or project, it is the technology which maximizes social welfare if factor prices are shadow priced. (Morawetz (1977), p. 517)

In some cases it is not only the distortion of factor prices which is considered in the measurement of AT but also normative ideas of social welfare. Income distribution weights are applied to the different groups involved in production and consumption. The stream of these various (corrected) costs and benefits is discounted over the lifetime of the project at what is considered to be the appropriate social rate of discount, and this leads to the calculation of total net social benefit. The project with the highest net social benefit (or sometimes that which has the highest net-social-benefit-to-cost-ratio) is deemed to be the appropriate technology.

The alternative 'specific characteristics', approach to evaluation involves multiple criteria — economic, social and environmental.[8] It is proposed that technologies be assessed in relation to these criteria, and assumes the relativity of appropriateness. Measurement does enter the evaluative procedure in the sense of illuminating and comparing particular characteristics of different technologies, for example with respect to capital cost or labour utilization. But this measurement plays a qualified role since it is not used in a summing-up of the diverse characteristics of the alternative technologies under consideration.

The social welfare approach has two clear advantages over the specific characteristics procedure.

- It allows for an explicit trade-off of conflicting objectives, facilitating the process of choosing between alternatives. For example, if extra employment is to be created, it is possible to weigh up these costs against a group of other costs and benefits, such as capital usage and the level of final output which results. The rate of trade-off can thus be easily assessed, and if used in a non-mechanistic way, various forms of sensitivity-analysis can also be employed to show how sensitive these conclusions are to variations in the values ascribed to individual parameters.
- As long as positive factor prices are utilized (that is, productive units should not be paid to employ labour or use capital) it avoids the blindness which comes from ignoring considerations of economic efficiency. As mentioned above, ignorance of the principles of economic efficiency can readily lead through an 'employment at any cost' objective to a situation in which techniques are adopted which make more use of all inputs per unit

of output. In these circumstances, although there may be greater employment in a particular plant, this will be not only at the cost of lower employment in other plants and in the economy at large but also to the disadvantage of consumers, who have to pay higher prices.

These advantages of the social welfare approach should not be discounted, but they have to be weighed against its disadvantages, of which the following are most important.

- In terms of its own logic, there is considerable discussion concerning the estimation of shadow prices (particularly in large projects) and the determination of the appropriate distributional weights.[9]
- It lends itself only to a consideration of the measurable aspects of appropriateness, thereby largely confining analysis to the economic components and effectively excluding most of the social and environmental criteria discussed above.
- Not all measurable criteria can be reduced to the financial *numeraire* utilized in the discounted computation of net benefit. For example, it is possible to measure environmental effects in physical terms but it is very difficult to place monetary values on these phenomena.
- Even if environmental criteria can be measured and monetized, they are only poorly reflected in the discounting procedures utilized by the social welfare approach. Take the problem of carbon monoxide emissions and the greenhouse effect. The consequences are to be felt so far into the twenty-first century that even if they could be monetized and even if a low discount weight were to be utilized, the discounted value of these environmental costs would be negligible.
- The approach has an ideological component — it 'hides' social weightings and subsumes them and factor prices in a single figure of net social welfare. By contrast, the specific characteristics approach forces a consideration of the detailed implications of choice in terms of a range of criteria, and thus (as Stewart (1987) points out) provides various 'signposts for action'. These make it more likely that policy interventions will be implemented to ameliorate the negative aspects of alternative technologies.

For these various reasons AT practitioners are generally drawn to an eclectic methodology. Most make primary use of the specific characteristics approach, although some give greater weight to the incorporation of social welfare techniques to inform their analysis. In adopting this eclectic attitude, the AT practitioners often run up against the opposition of the economics profession as well as administrators of aid programmes, many of whom are schooled in economics and accountancy skills. The reaction of economists such as Eckaus (discussed in Chapter 1) is a good example of this professional opposition.

CHAPTER 3

The political economy of diffusion: the bread industry in Kenya

In the previous chapter it was argued that AT is an inherently relative concept, varying with physical location, over time and (especially) in relation to whose interests are being considered in the evaluative process. Despite this inherent relativity, there is widespread agreement on the identification of social appropriateness with meeting the basic needs of the world's poor but there is less accord on whether this necessarily implies a direct role for the poor in production.

In this chapter examining the bread industry in Kenya, the appropriate technology under consideration is one which produces consumption goods for the poor and which involves production with labour-intensive technologies. It is also a technology which utilizes local resources and builds up local capability. Moreover, there is a congruence between the social appropriateness of the technology and the way in which private appropriateness is defined by economists. And yet, despite this, it is the inappropriate technology which dominates the bread industry in Kenya. The central concern of this chapter is to explain how and why this happens, and in so doing the focus of analysis is cast on the political economy of diffusion.

The research on which this chapter is based was undertaken in the late 1970s, yet the analytical issue which is identified — the political economy of the choice of technology — is of enduring importance and the insights which are obtained are relevant to the diffusion of technology in other sectors,[1] in other countries and in different periods of time.

Bread in the Kenyan economy

Most of the gains in average per capita incomes in Kenya were made during the first decade after Independence (1963–73). Towards the mid-1970s this relatively high growth rate began to tail off and the Kenyan economy increasingly felt the pressure of severe balance of payments deficits, relieved occasionally by commodity price booms (especially coffee and tea). But behind these stagnating aggregates has lain a continual change in the structure of production, especially in the growing monetization of production and consumption in agriculture. Processed foods, of which bread is an example, have become an important component of survival for much of the country's population.

As in most other African countries, bread was introduced into Kenya by immigrants. For most of the twentieth century it remained a consumption good for settlers (especially those from Europe) and it was only after Independence in 1963 that the consumption of bread by the indigenous population became widespread.[2] This change in consumption patterns reflected growing urbanization (for bread is an important convenience food), rising per capita incomes and a new marketing strategy by the largest producer, Elliots, which launched a 10 cent mini-loaf in 1973. It also reflected a fall in the relative price of bread: between 1966 and 1977 its price rose by only 87 per cent, compared with well over 200 per cent for all other processed foodstuffs.

Thus after 1965 bread consumption rose substantially faster than other processed foods, reaching an index of 210 in 1974 (1969=100) compared to 143 for all processed foodstuffs. Much of this consumption growth occurred in lower income households. For example, in Mombasa (the second largest city), the income elasticity of demand for bread in 1969 was above 1 for average monthly household incomes below KSh 750. As incomes rose, this elasticity fell from 1.24 for monthly household incomes of KSh 160–300 to 0.63 for incomes between KSh 1,000–1,400.[3] In the same year the average monthly earnings for all salary earners in Mombasa was KSh 540. In other words, for many lower income consumers, especially those dependent upon the cash economy and living in urban areas, bread had become a staple consumption good by the early 1970s. Yet at the same time, for those living in the rural areas or only marginally dependent upon the cash economy, it was a luxury good, something to be purchased on special occasions. Of course there were also regional taste preferences, with bread consumption being better established at the coast where there had been a longer history of foreign settlement. Temporal variations in consumption were also important, rising at the end of the month (when salaries were paid) and peaking during harvests and at Christmas. These variations in consumption were also more marked in rural areas.

The alternative technologies

Bread baking is an age-old skill, stretching back over five millenia. For most of this time processing equipment remained relatively simple, with the more substantive changes in product appearance and quality resulting from the types of cereal flours used. Despite the substantial changes which have occurred in recent decades, many items of current equipment are similar to those used in the early twentieth century.

The only pieces of equipment which are essential for bread production are storage and mixing receptacles, moulding tables and ovens. Yet in most countries only a small proportion of commercial production results from such very labour-intensive bakeries and the following major sub-processes have been subject to various stages of mechanization:

45

- *Storage and feeding* Various forms of bulk storage and automatic feeding have become increasingly prevalent in the industrially advanced countries, but it is possible to use simple containers and to feed ingredients by ladle.
- *Mixing* This is an arduous task and was consequently the first sub-process to be mechanized. A combination of mixing techniques is available, ranging from hand-powered ladles (or feet, in some cases!) to rotary mixing in bowls (basically larger versions of the hand-held food-processors) to continuous and high-speed mixing. Continuous and high-speed mixing have become important, especially in the UK and the US where mass-produced bread finds a ready market. Their major advantages are that they save on time by effectively eliminating fermentation; bread production is reduced from eight to two hours. This reduces work-in-progress and storage space, and it also results in a very even-textured dough, making it possible to reduce variability in the weight of bread loaves. Most importantly, it increases the yield of flour since more water can be absorbed — about 4 per cent more loaves can be obtained from the same input of flour. On the debit side this equipment is scale-intensive (most commonly processing two tons of flour per hour), requires significant electrical power and is very expensive. Because it produces a homogeneous rather than a differentiated product in high volumes, bread produced with high-speed mixers generally requires extensive transporting, reducing the possibility of fresh-bread sales. It is also very sensitive to temperature and to operating procedures.
- *Dividing and moulding* Dough can be divided and moulded into separate loaves manually, or with various degrees of mechanization. A major characteristic of the automated technologies is that they produce fewer variations in bread weight, especially when they are combined with mechanical mixers which produce a more evenly textured dough than that which results from manual mixing.
- *Proving* Moulded loaves can be left to 'prove' (that is, allowing the yeast to rise) either by standing in a warm space, or through being placed in heated chambers.
- *Ovens* This sub-process provides the most significant choice of technology and is the technological category utilized in subsequent analysis. Basically three variants of oven are utilized in Kenya (see Figure 3.1). The first is those constructed from brick. The ovens are heated by wood burnt inside the chamber with the ashes moved aside to allow room for the baking tins. In general they are small in scale, seldom baking more than 240 half-kilo loaves at a time. (This number of loaves is generally obtained from a single 90kg bag of flour). The second are the peel ovens, generally involving two or three chambers (each baking between 40–150 loaves) and heated by an external source.[4] Most often this power source is electricity, but sometimes diesel is utilized and occasionally these peel ovens are also heated by wood fires. Finally there are the travelling tunnel ovens, in

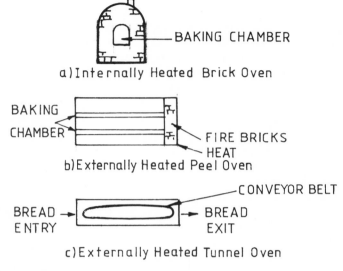

a) Internally Heated Brick Oven

b) Externally Heated Peel Oven

c) Externally Heated Tunnel Oven

Figure 3.1. *Three basic oven technologies*

which the loaves are passed through the chamber on conveyor belts. These ovens are heated externally by electricity or diesel, and are very large in scale, with the smallest of the Kenyan tunnel ovens baking around twelve bags of flour (that is almost 3,000 loaves) per hour.

- *Wrapping and slicing* Wrapping can be undertaken either manually or by mechanized means, although the technology for this automation is relatively complex.[5] Slicing however can only be practically undertaken by machine and although this equipment is relatively inexpensive, it does require electrical power.

In the mid-1970s there were around 90 bakeries in existence in Kenya. Of these, 60 were being actively operated, and the percentage of these which utilized mechanized equipment was as follows: 79 per cent machine-mixing (with no high-speed or continuous mixers in operation), 44 per cent moulders, 71 per cent dividers, 26 per cent provers, 26 per cent brick ovens, 69 per cent peel ovens, 5 per cent tunnel ovens, 52 per cent slicers, and only 9 per cent possessing mechanized wrappers.

There is of course a great variety of combinations of available technology.

47

But broadly speaking it is possible to describe three modal types of bakeries, each defined in relation to the core oven-technology utilized. The first was those working with brick ovens. Generally such bakeries make little use of mechanized technology, with the exception of mixing. This is both an arduous task and one which has an important influence over product quality. At 1977 prices the average mixer would have an installed cost of around $7,500. Thus the total fixed capital cost (excluding buildings) of this type of bakery was in the region of $10,000. The second major type of bakery was that using a peel oven. Almost always this involved mechanized mixing, and was often associated with a slicer, a divider and a moulder. A small single-oven bakery would have involved an investment of $20,000. Finally in the three tunnel-oven bakeries, mechanization was virtually complete, albeit of a low technological level by comparison with IAC plant-bakeries (that is, no continuous or high-speed mixers were involved). They also required significant investment and a new tunnel oven alone cost about $150,000 in 1977. Total plant investment would have exceeded $250,000.

Of the 60 active bakeries, just over one half (55 per cent) were located in the urban areas. Considering the groupings of these bakeries in different output-sizes — measuring output here, as is common in the industry, by consumption of 90kg bags of flour per year — 31 per cent consumed less than 2,500 bags, 40 per cent 2,500–10,000 bags, 19 per cent 10,000–20,000 bags, and 14 per cent 20,000–50,000. One bakery using a tunnel oven processed 50,000–100,000 bags of flour and the remaining two tunnel-oven bakeries each consumed in excess of 100,000 bags of flour per annum. The average size of rural bakeries was 6,277 bags a year; for urban bakeries 11,510 bags a year (excluding the three tunnel-oven bakeries). Considering size by technology, average annual flour consumption was 3,000 bags a year for brick-oven bakeries, 10,407 bags for peel-oven bakeries and 234,267 bags for bakeries using tunnel ovens.

From the point of view of the consumer, there is considerable debate about what constitutes quality in bread and, as will be shown later, this is generally a socially defined characteristic. From the perspective of the producer, two product characteristics stand out in importance: the first involves the keeping-characteristics of the final product and this is in part affected by the cleanliness of the plant, in part by the type of flour utilized,[6] and in part by whether various stabilizers are included in the dough; the second concerns the weight of the final loaf. This is especially important when (as in Kenya) the legal definition of weight is based on minimum rather than average loaf-weight. This is because the greater the degree of variation of weight (which, as has been explained, correlates with the labour intensity of mixing, dividing and moulding), the greater must be the average weight of the final product. This, as will emerge in later discussion, is one of the most important factors affecting profitability.

Specifying the appropriate technology

It is possible here to distinguish between the private and social appropriateness of these various baking technologies. The analysis begins at the private level by focusing on the relative profitability of the various technologies. It then examines broader social considerations.

Private profitability[7]

Private profitability reflects a combination of the real operating performance of alternative technologies and the prices of their inputs and outputs. It is helpful to compute real factor productivities before considering prices. Labour inputs are fairly easy to measure; although it is difficult to take skill differences into account, baking is a relatively unskilled operation, mostly involving on-the-job training. Measuring output is not quite as easy as it seems since the various bakeries produced different mixes of breads, as well as confectionary. Based on the observed differences in time and other inputs, the output of all these bakeries is thus converted to ordinary-bread equivalents, that is to standard quality, price-controlled half-kilo loaves. Finally, capital is frequently measured in relation to acquisition costs but this is unsatisfactory because it makes no allowance for varying machinery lives or for inflation since the equipment was purchased. Therefore an annual capital charge is computed, based upon the replacement costs of the varying items in 1977 and estimates of their respective economic lives.[8]

All this enables the computation of the coefficients of production, namely the productivity of capital and labour and the capital/labour ratio (Table 3.1). Considering the capital cost per workplace, there is a marked difference between the three different types of technologies. Jobs in modal brick-oven bakeries cost almost half those in peel-oven bakeries and less than one-seventh the cost in bakeries using tunnel ovens. Considering the issue of economic efficiency (see Figure 2.1. in Chapter 2), the peel-oven bakeries are inferior since they have the capital productivity of the tunnel-oven bakeries but a much lower productivity of labour. However, the relatively large scale

Table 3.1. Coefficients of production of alternative technologies

Type of Bakery	Capital/[a] Labour (KSh)	Output/ Labour (bags pa/ worker)	Output/ Capital[a] (bags/ KSh)	Size of Sample
Brick	555	203.1	1.92	15
Peel	1,043	272.2	0.46	40
Tunnel	4,095	1,049.0	0.46	3

[a] Annualized capital cost based on estimated economic life of all items of equipment.

of these tunnel ovens means that their capacity utilization in many parts of the country would be low and this diminishes both their effective capital and labour productivities. Competition from brick ovens is also constrained due to environmental controls on wood-burning in the major cities. These factors (amongst others) consequently provide the 'space' for these economically inefficient peel-oven bakeries. These coefficients of production make it possible to plot the industry's production function (Figure 3.2). From this it is clear that a substantial number of bakeries, particularly those using peel ovens, is some distance from the production possibilities frontier.

These factor productivities limit the physical parameters in which profitable operation can be defined. However to calculate private profitability they have to be mated to prices of inputs and outputs, and these vary significantly, especially between urban and rural areas (and thus largely between brick-oven and peel/tunnel-oven bakeries). Moreover, for various reasons discussed below (p. 51), the bread yield from a given input of flour varies considerably and this obviously has an important bearing on profitability. Although the calculations which follow are based upon detailed observations of costs and selling prices in the 60 most active

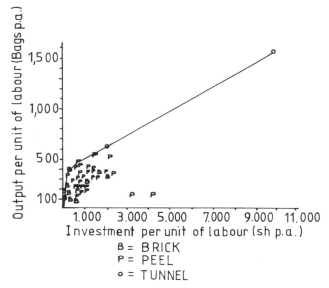

Figure 3.2. *Production function for bakeries*

50

bakeries, some costs proved to be difficult to measure accurately. The most important of these non-measured costs are: transport; selling costs; rent (because in some cases premises are owner-occupied and in other cases they are rented); management and other overheads; repair and maintenance; and working capital costs. The analysis thus begins with the calculation of measured costs and returns, and proceeds to discuss the impact of non-measured costs on profitability.

As a backdrop to the subsequent analysis it is helpful to begin with a summary of the shares of the major measured items in total unit costs — fixed capital (2.4 per cent), labour (5.3 per cent), energy (5 per cent), flour (77 per cent), other material inputs (5 per cent) and wrapping (6 per cent). It is clear from this that the efficiency with which flour is utilized is the most significant determinant of profitability. Here the small-scale, predominantly rural brick-oven bakeries might be seen to be at a double disadvantage. First, as was shown earlier (p. 46), there are technical reasons why mechanized equipment makes it more feasible to achieve predictable bread-weight. The definition of bread-weight in terms of price control as a minimum (rather than average) weight ensures that the bakeries with a more variable weight of output have to produce a higher average weight of final product, utilizing more flour. And, second, many of these small-scale bakeries are insufficiently schooled in business management to realize the significance of keeping bread-weight to a minimum.

In reality, though, the most significant factor affecting bread-weight is not the type of technology used, but the fear of prosecution.[9] Comparing bakeries in district/provincial headquarters towns where price control staff were more active (some of which were in rural areas) with those operating in other areas, the respective average bread-weights were 506.6gms versus 484.9gms, whereas the difference between bakeries using mechanical and manual dividing was only 496.1gms versus 498.9gms.

Total costs of production were also influenced by the price of flour. The officially regulated price of a 90kilo bag was KSh 206.55, but this was at the mill factory-gate. As will be shown, the largest two tunnel-oven bakeries were owned by the monopoly supplier of flour, and this has had an effect on the actual prices paid for flour. But more significantly, the rural bakeries (including most of those using brick-ovens) were forced to pay a high cost to transport the flour from the mills. Thus the three tunnel-oven bakeries paid an average of KSh 206.66, compared to KSh 207.85 for the peel-oven bakeries and KSh 216.74 for those using brick ovens.

In contrast to the higher costs paid for flour inputs, the brick-oven bakeries benefited from lower costs in two major respects. Because they seldom sliced and wrapped their bread, this yielded a considerable saving over the tunnel-oven bakeries (of an average of KSh 13.16 per 240 loaves). They also faced much lower wage costs, and rural bakeries paid an average wage of KSh 259.60 per month compared to KSh 369.50 in Nairobi. This helped to reduce the extra unit labour costs arising from the labour intensity of their technologies.

Another significant factor affecting relative profitability was the selling price of bread. Although the maximum retail price of ordinary bread was price controlled at KSh 1.40 per half-kilo loaf in most of the country and KSh 1.45 in areas more than 15 kilometers from a tarred road, there was a significant variation in the ex-factory prices realized. Bakeries selling direct to the urban public generally obtained KSh 1.40 per loaf. In very small bakeries there were few resource costs involved in this selling, since this occurred after the bread had been baked and was considered part of the working day. In some rural areas, however, consumer incomes were low and some small brick-oven bakeries sold to the public at a discount of 5 cents. Larger bakeries, including those in higher income urban areas, were forced to employ distributors and in most areas this resulted in an ex-factory wholesale price of KSh 1.30–1.34. Finally, for the very largest tunnel-oven bakeries, bread had first to be delivered to these wholesalers, so that for them the ex-factory price was around KSh 1.28 per loaf. Thus the average revenue realized per 240 loaves was KSh 322.31 for the brick-oven bakeries, KSh 319.41 for those using peel ovens and KSh 313.28 for the tunnel-oven bakeries.

Table 3.2.   Unit costs, revenue and margins and an estimation of private profitability

Type of bakery	Costs (KSh/bag)	Revenue (KSh/bag)	Margins (KSh/bag)	Proxy internal rate of return
Brick	278.55	322.31	42.82	317.3
Peel	268.64	319.41	52.51	131.1
Tunnel	267.30	313.28	45.98	103.5

Table 3.2 draws together the various data to calculate the costs of production, revenue and margin per bag of flour utilized. In itself these estimations of gross profit margins are a poor indicator of profitability since they take no account of production volume or of the scale of initial investment. Therefore Table 3.2 also calculates a proxy internal rate of return (IRR), based upon a discounted stream of net revenues. These proxy IRRs are unrealistically high since they exclude a variety of non-measured costs. However for almost all of these non-measured costs — the transport of final output; the cost of selling; overheads, rents; and repair and maintenance — there were clear reasons why the small-scale bakeries utilizing brick ovens were more favourably placed. They sold directly to final customers and

therefore had no need to deliver their bread; by contrast, the higher transport costs they paid in obtaining their inputs were included in the measurement of production costs. Managerial costs and selling were part of the working day of production workers (and have thus been included in the cost-calculations) in small- but not large-scale bakeries. The lack of mechanization meant few repair costs, and premises were generally very modest. Only in the case of working capital was there a hint that the small-scale rural bakeries are adversely affected because of the higher interest rates which they tend to pay.[10] Thus the proxy IRRs in Table 3.2 tend to underestimate the relative profitability of small-scale bakeries utilizing brick ovens.

The results of these financial calculations are fairly clear. The large-scale capital-intensive tunnel-oven bakeries had the lowest measured production costs and the labour-intensive brick-oven bakeries the highest. However, these higher measured costs were more than offset by the need of the large-scale bakeries to sell via wholesalers, rather than direct to final customers. In terms of unit margins the peel-oven bakeries did best since they had relatively low production costs and relatively high margins. Yet because both these peel-oven and tunnel-oven bakeries had much higher investment costs than their brick-oven competitors, the rate of profit of the small-scale, predominantly rural brick-oven bakeries was substantially higher than their predominantly urban-based and larger-scale mechanized counterparts. The degree of this superior profitability is sufficiently high to offset any reasonable measurement errors. Moreover the inclusion of non-measured costs further accentuates the relative profitability of these rural small-scale brick-oven bakeries.

Yet all these figures represent averages and there was of course a considerable degree of variation in profitability, especially amongst the larger samples of peel-oven and brick-oven bakeries. Detailed analysis shows that one particular type of bakery — in the smallest size category, operating in rural areas and using brick ovens and a simple mechanized mixer — is clearly the most profitable type of bakery in Kenya.

Social optimality
As was argued in Chapter 1, the determination of social optimality, that is identifying the AT, requires a different, broader set of criteria than the rate of profit to the private investor. Without a clear specification of whose interests are to be considered, no clear determination of appropriateness is possible. It is useful, perhaps, to begin with the expressed views of the Kenyan Government during the time period relevant to this analysis of the bakery industry. In relation to employment generation:

> The Government adopts as its long term policy that all householders will have access to either wage employment or to land in order to assure that all possess the means of earning an acceptable level of living. (Sessional Paper No. 10, 1973, on Employment, p. 24)

The government also committed itself to the dispersion of economic activity outside of the main urban centres in order to spread the fruits of economic growth and reduce the costs of infrastructure. The Second Development Plan of 1970–74 stated that 'It is the Government's intention now to locate industries to a great extent . . . outside Nairobi and Mombasa' (p. 324). This was emphasized in the well known Sessional Paper on Employment of 1973, which emphasized that

Where the Development Plan 1964–70 focused upon rapid growth, the second Plan for the period 1970–1974, attempts to shift the locale of growth towards the rural areas. In fact, rural development, the improvement in the quality of rural life, is the first priority of the Government. (Ibid., p. 15)

Finally, with regard to the utilization of local resources, and in the context of a growing balance of payments deficit, attempts were made to reduce import intensity and to promote the development of local technological capability. Two of Kenya's most distinguished social scientists observed of the various development plans that

The [Development] Plans have called for increasing mobilization and utilization of local resources which are complementary to available human skill to reduce unemployment for example through labour-intensive rural works. The aim was also to reduce dependence on capital and technology acquired from outside. (Mbithi and Mighot Adholla, untitled mimeo, 1977)

With this perspective on official policy it is possible to consider the specification of AT in terms of the three sets of criteria — the economic, the social and the environmental.

Economic appropriateness It is relatively easy to consider the economic criteria of appropriateness through various forms of measurement. Shadow prices can be attached to market prices and the effects can be shown on total costs, revenue and profitability. Nevertheless spurious levels of precision can be misleading, and for this reason a form of sensitivity analysis embodying a range of shadow prices is utilized, illustrating their effects on relative costs of production. The impact on final 'social profitability' can be read off from these various cost calculations.

Given the emphasis on labour utilization, and the existence of large numbers of under- and unemployed people, shadow-pricing labour inputs is a useful first step in the analysis. This is done in Table 3.3 in which all labour inputs are discounted by 25 and 50 per cent respectively. This reduces the costs of all three types of technology, but least for the most capital-intensive tunnel-ovens.

A second input which can be shadow-priced is that of capital. In Table 3.4

Table 3.3. Shadow-pricing labour: effects on costs of production (KSh per bag)

	Market prices	0.75 weight	0.50 weight
Brick	278.55	274.09	269.62
Peel	268.64	264.78	260.92
Tunnel	267.30	265.52	263.74

all capital costs are weighted by an extra 25 and 50 per cent, in an attempt to capture the scarcity of this input into production. Because of the small share of capital in total unit costs, this form of shadow-pricing has little effect on the relative ranking of these three technologies.

Table 3.4. Shadow-pricing capital: effects on costs of production (KSh per bag)

	Market prices	1.25 weight	1.50 weight
Brick	278.55	280.81	281.47
Peel	268.64	270.05	271.47
Tunnel	267.30	268.66	270.01

Foreign exchange is another — and perhaps even more important — input whose supply is constrained. Hence in Table 3.5 its use is weighted by 25 and 50 per cent and the effects are computed on relative costs of production. Since almost all of the capital inputs into the small-scale brick ovens were produced locally and only a few baking ingredients were imported, these bakeries were relatively beneficially affected by shadow-pricing the import content. Yet because capital costs are only a small proportion of total unit costs, the absolute advantage derived from this exercise is limited.

Table 3.5. Shadow-pricing foreign exchange: effects on costs of production (KSh per bag)

	Market prices	1.25 weight	1.50 weight
Brick	278.55	279.20	279.86
Peel	268.64	270.96	273.28
Tunnel	267.30	269.00	270.69

The cumulative effect of these three shadow prices is shown in Table 3.6. This shows that, relatively speaking, the brick-oven bakeries are favourably affected by the utilization of these shadow prices which reduce their costs of

55

production from KSh 278.55 per bag to KSh 274.42. Since, by contrast, the costs of production of both the peel-oven and tunnel-oven bakeries increase, from the perspective of economic appropriateness the brick-oven bakeries clearly score much higher than those using other types of technology.

Table 3.6. Shadow-pricing labour, capital and foreign exchange: effects on costs of production (KSh per bag)

	$L_w = 1$ $I_w = 1$ $FE_w = 1$	$L_w = 0.75$ $I_w = 1.25$ $FE_w = 1.25$	$L_w = 0.50$ $I_w = 1.50$ $FE_w = 1.50$
Brick	278.55	276.34	274.42
Peel	268.64	268.82	269.60
Tunnel	267.30	268.91	271.19

A final element of economic appropriateness which can be considered, but which is very difficult to measure, is the link with indigenous technological capability. The tunnel-oven bakeries score very poorly in this regard since virtually all of their equipment has to be imported. By contrast the core technology in the brick-oven bakeries, that is the oven, is built locally, from indigenous materials. This is not to suggest that this small-scale sector has become a focus for technological development, since there has been little optimization of design (see pp. 69–70). Earlier designs were based on Indian technology and involved the utilization of fire-bricks, constructed into a self-supporting domed oven, yet new materials such as cement and scrap-iron (which can allow for the less costly and more energy-efficient construction of rectangular-shaped ovens) have not been incorporated. Indeed, the capital goods industry as well as science and technology institutions seem entirely divorced from this sector's needs. An attempt has been made to manufacture peel ovens locally, but this was based upon a poor understanding of engineering principles. The metal used for the steam-tubes which heat the baking chambers proved to be inadequate to cope with the corrosion inherent in the process and whilst the designs worked and were utilized profitably, no links were made with the capital goods sector or the science and technology system, so that the growth of sustainable domestic capabilities was limited.

Social appropriateness Estimating social appropriateness is considerably more complex, since whilst the economic criteria can be considered in relation to their real resource cost, social criteria are inherently normative; they are also difficult to measure. Nevertheless, in terms of the sort of criteria considered of relevance to social appropriateness — see Chapter 2 — there can be little doubt that the bakeries using brick ovens are more appropriate. They are smaller in scale and lend themselves more readily to local construction. Hence the barriers to entry of rural entrepreneurs and poorer people in these rural areas are much lower than in the case of the peel-oven and tunnel-oven bakeries.

One negative feature of these small-scale bakeries is that they are difficult to control, and the government might find it hard to impose minimum standards. For example, it has already been shown that the further the bakeries are from district/provincial headquarters, the greater the possibility that the bread will be underweight, sanitary conditions poor — since health inspectors are unlikely to inspect these small establishments as often as the larger ones in urban and peri-urban areas — and working conditions inferior with lower wages and longer hours. A particular characteristic of this is that since most of these small bakeries are family run, social inequity is likely to be intra-familial, rather than class-based.

A possible measure of social appropriateness is its effect on income distribution. One way in which this might occur is through the multiplier-effect from consumption by the owners of these bakeries. It might be argued that the consumption basket of large-scale capitalists was much more import-intensive than those of small-scale entrepreneurs, but the effects of this are likely to have been limited. More important, probably, is the distributional impact of wage-incomes. In Table 3.7 the consequences for regional income distribution are computed through the shadow-pricing of rural labour. Although this is an imperfect measure of distributional concerns it can be seen that its consideration has the effect of significantly reducing the cost disadvantage of production by the brick-oven bakeries, most of whom are in rural areas. Since some of the peel-oven bakeries are also in rural areas, they, too, gain from this exercise.

Table 3.7. Income distribution weights: discounting rural labour costs only (KSh per bag)

| | Costs of Production (KSh/bag) | | |
	Market prices	0.75 weight	0.50 weight
Brick	278.55	274.68	270.81
Peel	268.64	267.71	266.77
Tunnel	267.30	267.30	267.30

Environmental appropriateness The major environmental issue in bakeries is the utilization of energy. Here the balance between the three forms of technology is probably more even. The brick ovens use firewood, which is in short supply in Kenya. They thus contribute to the destruction of soil cover and a consequent rise in soil-erosion and to a possible reduction in rainfall (due to lower plant-perspiration). In addition, carbon dioxide and particulates are released in burning wood, possibly contributing to an acceleration of the greenhouse effect. On the other hand, these small-scale bakeries utilize little machinery, and their need for electricity is insignificant. This not only affects their foreign exchange intensity but also has energy implications.[11] Thus, in the bakery industry, the brick ovens themselves involve much lower energy inputs in their production than do peel and tunnel ovens. In addition, bakeries using brick ovens tend to have much less ancillary automation than do the peel-oven and tunnel-oven bakeries.

To the extent that the peel and tunnel ovens utilize electricity generated by hydroelectric power, their environmental impact is less deleterious. Yet most of these bakeries utilize oil and the proportion of Kenya's electricity supply which is generated through renewable energy sources is small. Moreover the burning of oil also releases large volumes of carbon dioxide into the atmosphere with negative environmental consequences.[12] Finally, the larger the bakery, the greater the need to deliver their products. In its baked form bread is 50 per cent greater by volume and 20 per cent greater by weight than the purchased inputs. This is because in the process of baking, much water is absorbed and air is entrapped by the gluten in the flour. Hence delivering bread, rather than its ingredients, is wasteful of energy and places an additional burden on the transport infrastructure.

The diffusion of bread-making technologies

The full history of the Kenyan bakery industry is obscure. The first comprehensive records on formal sector production go back only to the early 1950s. They record a constant number of about 50 bakeries employing more than five people until the early 1960s. Whilst this number is not very different from those operating in the mid-1970s, the overall scale of output was much lower since almost all of these bakeries were of a very small-scale nature.

There have been four major periods in the development of this industry (Table 3.8). Before the Second World War most bakeries were in the urban areas, using brick or peel ovens. Then, between 1945 and Independence in 1963, there was an expansion in the number of urban peel-oven bakeries and the first rural brick-oven bakeries were established. The bulk of bread production was however concentrated in Nairobi and Mombasa (where the major markets lay), with a limited number of peel-oven bakeries rising to dominance, and it was in this period that Elliots Bakery was established. In the period between 1963 and 1970, when the consumption of bread grew most rapidly, all three tunnel ovens were introduced — two as new investments and the third as a substitute for a peel oven in the largest established Nairobi bakery. The fourth period, 1971–6, saw the wider diffusion of brick-oven bakeries in rural areas.

The introduction of these three large-scale tunnel ovens in the 1960s further accentuated the market concentration which was emerging in the

Table 3.8. Vintage of bakeries[a]

	Brick		Peel		Tunnel	
	No.	%	No.	%	No.	%
Pre-1945	4	28.6	3	9.7	1[a]	33.3
1946–63	0	0	14	45.2	0	0
1964–70	5	35.7	7	22.6	2[a]	66.7
1971–6	5	35.7	7	22.6	0	0

[a] By number of plants. Elliots Bakery has two tunnel ovens, both introduced between 1964 and 1970, which are the largest in the country. The Nairobi oven was substituted for a peel oven in the 1960s.

post-war period. The proportion of output accounted for by the largest four firms (not plants, because since the late 1960s Elliots has produced on two sites) rose from around 55 per cent in the mid-1950s to about 74 per cent in 1976. There are a number of dimensions of inequality in this market structure: by location, by size and by type of technology (Table 3.9). The major cause for these types of inequality was the existence of a single large firm, Elliots Bakery, accounting for 62.9 per cent of total national production in two tunnel-oven urban plants.[13] While 25.9 per cent of bakeries used brick ovens, their share of production was a tiny 2.2 per cent. Rural bakeries made

Table 3.9. Market structure, location, size of bakery and type of technology

	No.	Output (bags pa)	Share of number (%)	Share of output (%)
Location				
Urban[a]	32	223,776	56.1	28.8
Rural	25	90,425	43.9	71.2
By Size (bags pa)				
0–2,499	18	11,630	31.5	1.4
2,500–9,999	23	70,684	40.4	8.4
10,000–19,999	11	87,573	19.3	10.4
20,000–49,999	4	80,600	7.0	9.5
50,000–100,000	1	63,700	1.8	7.5
Over 100,000	2[b]	531,750	3.6	62.9
By Technology				
Brick	15	18,272	25.9	2.2
Peel	40	232,175	69.0	27.5
Tunnel	3[b]	595,452	5.2	70.4

[a] The urban category excludes the three tunnel-oven bakeries which, given the spread of their deliveries, are better considered as national bakeries.
[b] In fact these are two plants owned by a single firm.

up 43.9 per cent of the total, and produced only 28.8 per cent of total output. The smallest size category, consuming less than 2,500 bags of flour a year, comprised 31.5 per cent of all bakeries, yet produced only 1.4 per cent of total output.

How is this pattern of diffusion to be explained? The contrast between market concentration and the appropriateness of the various technologies is striking. The small-scale brick-oven bakeries operating in rural areas make greater use of local resources, have a closer 'fit' with the smaller scale of social organization amongst the indigenous population and are in harmony with official development policy. Much more puzzling is the disjuncture between these market shares and private profitability. The small-scale brick-oven bakeries also have a far higher rate of profit than their large-scale capital-intensive counterparts. If this is the case, how is it that 'market forces' do not lead to their supremacy, as would be predicted by economic theory (and as exemplified in Figure 2.1)? To understand this it is necessary to delve into the political economy of technical choice.

The political economy of the choice of baking technology

There are of course a large number of factors which have in one way or another determined the choice of technology in the Kenyan bakery industry. Four explanations stand out in importance and all can be considered to be in the realm of political economy:

- the particular characteristics of monopoly power in the Kenyan food processing industry
- the nature of entrepreneurship in the bakery sector (Stewart's 'composition of units')[14]
- the role of state policies
- the determination of consumer tastes

Before considering these major political economic explanations, it is useful to consider one potential explanation for the disjuncture between market shares and profitability which lies within the realm of economic analysis. If the relative cost of capital has risen significantly, then past investments in capital-intensive technologies may appear economically irrational in the present but will have been rational at the time investment decisions were taken. Whether these now sub-optimal techniques are scrapped in face of the changes in factor prices depends on whether their marginal costs of operation are greater than the total *ex ante* costs of the most profitable technique available. In other words, if it is assumed that their capital costs are sunken, are the running costs in these sub-optimal bakeries lower than the total costs (including the repayment of capital) which any prospective new investor would expect to recuperate before undertaking a new investment?

This increase in the relative cost of capital is an unlikely explanation for the dominance of these highly inappropriate bakeries. First, there is no evidence of any significant change in relative factor prices in the period under consideration. The only possibility of such a change would be during the Second World War when the inability to import from Europe may have effectively ruled out the prospect of any peel or tunnel ovens being introduced, effectively putting a very high price on the cost of capital. But as can be seen from earlier analysis on the vintage of bakeries, this explanation is not relevant. A second reason why this economic explanation for the choice of inappropriate technology is convincing is that in the case of bakeries, capital costs are only a small component of total costs and variable costs are dominant. A writing-off of these fixed costs is unlikely to explain the continued dominance of relatively unprofitable past investments.

Monopoly power in the Kenyan food processing industry[15]

The dominance of the bread industry by a single producer, Elliots, must be seen in historical perspective. Its roots lie in the arrival of the earliest white settlers at the turn of the century. For many years the dominant political settler leader was Lord Delamere who initially reared sheep on a 100,000-acre farm which he acquired in 1904. He then turned to wheat farming with a view to supplanting wheat imports, then worth K£10,000 a year. In 1908, with five other farmers, Delamere established the first wheat mill with the expressed aim to keep milling charges low in order to provide a market for local wheat. It was called '*Unga*', Swahili for flour.

In return for a protective duty on imported flour (imposed in 1922) and a complementary railway-tariff structure (which was higher for imports than exports), Delamere undertook to hand Unga over to the Kenya Farmers Association (KFA) in 1926. This was on the agreement that milling would not be run as a profit centre but as a means of ensuring a market for wheat. By 1939 Unga accounted for 95 per cent of Kenya's wheat-milling capacity. The same principle of reducing milling costs to a minimum was involved when the KFA came to dominate the maize-milling industry, and after a brief bout of competition in the late 1940s, the largest maize-milling competitor (Maida) was taken over by the KFA, and closely integrated with the operations of Unga.

After the war the horizons of Kenya's settlers moved to the regional level and similar control was established in the grain-milling industries in Tanganyika and Uganda. In the 1950s two major steps towards diversification were taken, one planned and the other enforced. The planned investment was the establishment of an animal-feed company (Proctor and Allan), using byproducts in grain-milling. The enforced diversification led to the acquisition of Elliots Bakery. This had been established by a number of European settlers in 1948 and soon became the largest bakery in Nairobi. But in the early 1950s the premises were destroyed by fire, and being a time of commodity-price boom, the owners preferred to redirect their insurance-repayments into coffee-farming. The KFA (through Unga) was thus forced to take over Elliots in order to maintain a market for its wheat flour and, having done so, proceeded to increase baking capacity in line with market demand and the availability of wheat. In addition, in the early 1970s a second tunnel-oven bakery was established in Nakuru, a large town in the Rift Valley.

But what explains the policy of minimizing milling-charges and concentrating profits from the overall food-chain in the agricultural sector? The key to this lies in the political basis of settler economic power which was always concentrated in agricultural rather than industrial capital. Their political power over the colonial state enabled these settlers to exclude competition from Asian and African capital in farming,[16] but not in industrial production. This racial basis of power was made quite explicit in the grain and food processing industries. Whilst Highland wheat farmers were, by law, exclusively of European origin, European domination in milling was entrenched through two non-legal mechanisms: processing margins were kept low to reduce the incentive to competition; and non-European owners were excluded from KFA associated processing industries by the statutes of these enterprises. Indeed it was only just before Independence in 1963 that Unga removed from its Articles of Association a clause which specified that

> No transfer [of shares] shall be made to any person who is not of pure European descent or to any Company or Corporation any shareholder of member thereof is not of similar descent.

As Independence drew near it became clear that such racist policies were untenable. In both Tanganyika and Uganda, 50 per cent of the shares were sold to parastatal bodies in an attempt to forestall outright nationalization, a stratagem which in fact failed. In Kenya the shares of the holding company Unga were sold off, some to KFA members and the rest to the public. A complex restructuring was undertaken, with overall control being vested in a publicly quoted company (Mercat) in which no single interest was dominant. It was a management-controlled enterprise. One of the primary functions of this restructuring was to disguise the extensive interests of Mercat via indirect holding companies such as Kenya National Mills. The management remained as before and even in 1976 the three most important members of the Boards of Mercat and its affiliates, the Group Director, the Group Technical Director and the Group Finance Director, were long-term employees of the firm.

The overall structure of the Mercat Group is shown in Figure 3.3. Its dominance of the Kenyan food processing industry in the late 1970s was almost overwhelming. It accounted for over 60 per cent of all bread production through Elliots. Unga and Maida between them produced over 90

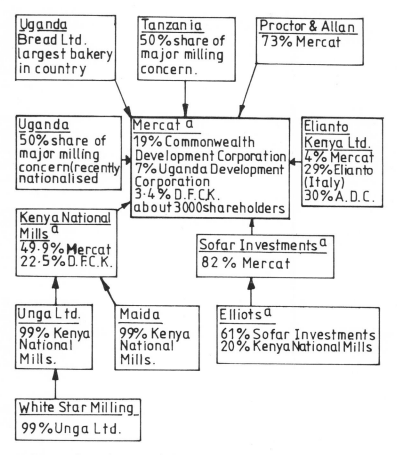

Uganda Bread Ltd. largest bakery in country

Tanzania 50% share of major milling concern.

Proctor & Allan 73% Mercat

Uganda 50% share of major milling concern(recently nationalised

Mercat a
19% Commonwealth Development Corporation
7% Uganda Development Corporation
3·4% D.F.C.K.
about 3000 shareholders

Elianto Kenya Ltd.
4% Mercat
29% Elianto (Italy)
30% A.D.C.

Kenya National Mills a
49·9% Mercat
22·5% D.F.C.K.

Sofar Investments a
82% Mercat

Unga Ltd.
99% Kenya National Mills.

Maida
99% Kenya National Mills.

Elliots a
61% Sofar Investments
20% Kenya National Mills

White Star Milling
99% Unga Ltd.

D.F.C.K.– Development Finance Corporation of Kenya.

A.D.C. – Agricultural Development Corporation

a – Public Company quoted on the Nairobi Stock Exchange

Source: Company Records, Registrar General

Figure 3.3. *Structure of the Mercat Group (1978)*

63

per cent of wheat flour and over 40 per cent of all large-scale maize milling. Proctor and Allan produced over 50 per cent of grain-based animal feeds (the major source of feed), and much of the breakfast-cereal market. In the mid-1970s Mercat went into a joint venture to produce vegetable oil with an Italian firm in which Mercat had the largest share (41 per cent) of the equity. Finally, until the mid 1970s Mercat also possessed a 50 per cent share of the monopoly grain-milling firms in Tanzania and Uganda, and held the major share in the largest bakery in Uganda.

How does this history of Mercat account for the rise to dominance of Elliots bakeries and the use of less profitable and socially inappropriate technologies? There are four major explanations. First, as mentioned earlier, the exclusion of African and Asian farmers from cash-farming meant that if profits from the food-chain could be concentrated in agriculture, not only would they be safe from appropriation by other racial groups, but there would be less competition in downstream milling and baking since profits in those sectors would be low. Thus, in a dissenting note to the 1929 Tariff Committee, the Asian representative (who was Chairman of the Indian Merchants Chamber in Mombasa) complained that

> in the wheat industry mills have paid the highest prices possible to growers, limiting mill profits to sound business dividends of six per cent. Wheat is a highland crop in the hands of the Europeans.

Thus the low profits in downstream processing made it an unattractive proposition for potential competitors using similar technologies.

A second reason why Elliots was able to maintain its dominance over bread production related to the distribution of flour during periods of flour shortage. These shortages were endemic in the bakery industry until a change in policy in the late 1960s allowing for the freer import of flour. Many medium-sized bakeries in the urban areas had bitter memories of differential treatment in the colonial period in which Elliots was able to run at near-full capacity, while they were provided with reduced quotas and had to lower production significantly. One recounted a story whereby he had tried to supplement his ration of flour from Unga by buying from the seemingly independent Maida, only to be informed that he had already obtained his quota from Unga.

These two explanations for Elliots market-dominance reflect the monopoly market-power of the KFA combine. But there was also a series of intra-firm internal economies which benefited Elliots, although these were not of overwhelming significance. In some cases intra-corporate loans were made available or payments for flour deferred during times of financial stringency. For example in 1975 when bank credit was limited, Elliots borrowed K£62,000 from associated companies. In better years it leant money to them — K£93,000 in 1974 and K£55,000 in 1972. But there were also non-financial internal economies. In Nakuru the bakery was built adjacent to the flour mill and flour was provided through a conveyor belt, effectively removing delivery costs. Also, bread yields are optimized in relation to the specific characteristics of the flour input, and Elliots were in constant touch with Unga and Maida in fine-tuning this.

But these three factors only explain the market-dominance of Elliots. They do not account for the choice of an apparently less profitable technology. To unravel this it is necessary to understand the nature of managerial preferences and the ability to appropriate profit at the corporate level from production at the plant level. In the colonial period the Mercat complex was controlled by the Kenya Farmers Association; after 'dismemberment' in the mid-1960s, it was controlled by the same management, with the diversified 'owners' never attempting to influence policy or even the composition of the managerial board.[17] This settler management had no interest in small-scale, informal-sector type enterprises. They were housed in smart offices in the centre of Nairobi, and were chauffeur-driven to large-scale modern enterprises. Their world-view was far from Kenya's rural informal enterprises — indeed the name Mercat, which was only assumed in the post-colonial period, was in fact drawn from the name of a town in Scotland where one of the senior managers was born. Their technological links were also stronger with equipment suppliers in the UK than any potential local suppliers and these foreign machinery suppliers were familiar with large-scale mechanized technologies and knew little of brick-ovens or hand-dividing.

As important as this world-view in determining the choice of technology was the problem of appropriating profits from individual plants. There is little doubt, as can be seen from the previous analysis, that both the total profit and the rate of profit would have been much higher from 750 small-scale brick-oven bakeries producing at two bags of flour a day than from two large tunnel-oven bakeries. But how could these 750 small bakeries have been controlled? How could their real level of profitability be computed and how could this profit be appropriated? (Moreover, some of this profit was derived from low wages or associated with unsanitary conditions, factors which a large bakery chain such as Elliots would be unable to sustain.)

There is a clear link between the pattern of market dominance of the Mercat Group and the type of technologies which were utilized. Contrary to restricted economic theory, merely understanding the relative profitability of the various technologies available explains little of the overall picture of diffusion. The identity of entrepreneurship is of considerable importance.

The nature of entrepreneurship in the bakery industry
Given this identity between settler-owned and -managed enterprises and the utilization of large-scale capital-intensive technologies, it is clear that particular patterns of technological choice are associated with types of entrepreneurship. Table 3.10 provides data of some relevant features of different racial groupings. The major differences arise between the indigenous African/Arab and the Asian groups of entrepreneurs, since the sample for the European

bakeries (2) and the publicly owned bakeries (1, with 2 plants — Elliots) is too small. From this is it clear that African/Arab owned enterprises are more likely to have started their enterprises and to have been recent entrants to the industry. Because of this they were less likely to have expanded production and their relatively precarious market position forced them to provide more credit to customers; yet at the same time they found it more difficult to obtain credit from their suppliers (notably Mercat who provided them with flour). They also had more loans outstanding and appear to have had a greater number of other enterprises in operation. If the Asian bakery owners can be said to be members of the petit-bourgeoisie, the African/Arab bakeries make up a proto petit-bourgeoisie.

Table 3.10. Entrepreneurship by racial group

Racial group	Original owners (%)	If take- over, how long (yrs)	Providing credit (%)	Receiving credit (%)	Loans out- standing (%)	Other busi- nesses (%)	Technology B P T (%)		
Africans/ Arabs	77	1.9	48	38	62	32	45	55	0
Asian	39	8.0	43	53	30	26	9	87	4
European	50	17.0	50	50	50	0	0	100	1
Public	na	—	100	100	na	100	0	100	0

na not available B = Brick oven P = Peel oven T = Tunnel oven

These various characteristics are reflected in technology choice, with the indigenous-citizen owned enterprises utilizing the more profitable and socially appropriate brick-oven bakeries. They predominantly also operated on a very small scale, with 55 per cent producing less than 2,500 bags a year. By contrast the Asian owned enterprises generally operated on a larger scale with only eight per cent operating at less than 2,500 bags and 60 per cent at between 2,500 and 10,000 a year. The difference in the choice of technology is almost certainly explained by the fact that whereas the small-scale brick-oven bakeries provide a greater rate of profit, the overall quantum of profit is too small to satisfy the socially-defined consumption needs of Asian business people. Their alternative of producing on a large scale with a number of small-scale brick oven bakeries is only a theoretical possibility since they would face the same problem of appropriating profits from numerous bakeries as did Elliots. In consequence, therefore, the nature of entre-preneurship has a pervasive implication for the choice of technology. And these determinants of profitability are not technical — they are social and political.

The role of state power

There are three major areas in which government policies affected the market shares of different types of bakeries.

- *The distribution of wheat* Since the early twentieth century most of Kenya's flour needs have been met from local production, except for the import of some quantities of hard wheats which cannot be grown locally.[18] For most of this period, wheat could only be marketed through the Wheat Board, made up of representatives from government, the wheat-growing farmers and the milling industry. Traditionally the Board struck a balance between supply and demand by limiting milling-capacity through licences. Until the early 1960s, this licensing system hindered non-European participation in milling and contributed to the growth of monopoly power in the food processing industry. For example, in 1937 an Asian-owned mill (Sun Mills) was forced to sell out to Unga because it was denied adequate inputs during a period of wheat shortage, and a similar event occurred shortly after the Second World War when Tanga Mills was denied the opportunity to expand.

- *The growth of lending facilities targetted at small-scale African entrepreneurs* There have been a number of such 'windows', especially the Industrial and Commercial Development Corporation (ICDC). Between 1961 and 1976, the ICDC gave loans to 16 bakeries, and of the 60 bakeries involved in this sample, 12 had received ICDC loans. Eight of these were for new bakeries while the remainder were to enable the takeover of European/Asian enterprises. A signficant biasing factor of these loans is that they were always provided against security. This either meant that the entrepreneurs involved had extensive farms or other businesses, or were forced into the use of inappropriate peel-ovens, because these peel-ovens could be easily repossessed and sold to businesses in other areas. This was obviously not possible for brick ovens. Nevertheless, to the extent that the industry had been dominated by European and Asian entrepreneurs who had a vested interest in utilizing the most inappropriate technologies, this lending programme by the post-Independence state played a role in reducing industry-concentration and in widening the spectrum of technology choice.

- *Pricing policies* As bread became a major wage-good during the 1960s and 1970s, so its political sensitivity became more apparent, and since 1966 the prices of both flour and bread have been controlled through the Price Control Act. In the late 1970s the official price of KSh 1.40 per half-kilo loaf of ordinary bread was under heated discussion since various types of 'premium bread' were not price-controlled. Basically there were three protagonists in this debate over prices. On the one hand the members of the Bakery Association were pressing for an increased price. The Association was predominantly made up of medium-sized bakeries, using peel ovens and selling various types of bread to upper income markets in Nairobi. These markets were relatively price inelastic and the Association reasoned that any fall in consumption as a consequence of higher bread prices would be more than made up by an increase in price.

On the other hand Elliots were caught in a vice. They had to balance the costs of capacity utilization with bread margins. Since they were predominantly selling to a very price sensitive African population, any increase in prices would have the effect of reducing overall consumption, thereby reducing their rate of capacity utilization; since their operations had a relatively high proportion of fixed costs (machinery plus overheads), this would be undesirable. At the same time a reduction in bread prices would also be problematic since they were only just breaking even at KSh 1.40 per loaf retail price, which gave them an ex-factory price of around KSh 1.28 (see p. 52).

Finally, the small-scale rural bakeries using brick ovens often sold at a discount to the KSh 1.40 price ceiling because their consumers were poor and their markets were thus price sensitive. Moreover, their higher profitability made this selling price possible. They would have therefore been indifferent to a fall in the official price, rather than an increase.

Faced with these divergent views, the Price Control Board could have moved in either direction: higher prices would have favoured the medium-scale bakeries using peel ovens; lower prices would have favoured the small-scale rural bakeries because the urban bakeries would not have been able to afford to deliver bread across the country. A fall in price would also have favoured the consumer, perhaps after an initial fall in the availability of bread. Leaving the bread price stable, which is what actually happened, most favoured Elliots.

This decision reflected a long history of close links between large-scale industry and the state in Kenya which has been associated with similar patterns of inappropriate technological choice in other sectors.

The determination of consumer tastes
The analysis of relative profitability earlier in this chapter coped with the problem of product diversity by reducing all production to 'standard bread equivalents'. The conversion factors used were based upon the actual performance of operating bakeries and are a reasonably accurate reflection of real operating conditions. As was pointed out, in terms of volume, the production of cakes and special breads was only a small component (less than 5 per cent) for almost all bakeries. But because there was no price control on these products, their contribution to total revenue and to profits was disproportionately high. So one of the major reasons why the seemingly less profitable peel-oven bakeries continued to thrive in the urban areas was because of their diversification into non-price controlled premium bread and

cakes.[19] This option was of course not open to rural bakeries since their customers had much lower incomes than those in urban areas.

In addition to this diversification of output, another factor explaining the continued existence of the very largest producers is the power of brand names. Others have documented this phenomenon in Kenya and have found that Kenyan consumers are heavily influenced by the demonstration effect provided by those with higher incomes.[20] The fact that so many foreigners live in Kenya — Nairobi has the third biggest UN employed population of any city in the world — has certainly contributed to this phenomenon.

The result of this has been that in the bakery industry a great premium has been placed on Elliots' market power, the Elliots' brand names and its wax wrappers (which require expensive machinery to be used). One peri-urban baker in Eastern Province (about 50 miles from Nairobi) complained about this with particular bitterness, and offered the following story. Faced with the reluctance of locals to eat his bread he went into a cafe to enquire the reason. They responded by saying that his bread was not up to Elliots' standards, so he left the cafe, bought an Elliots' loaf, and transferred its wax wrapper to his own product. He re-entered the cafe with this 'Elliots' loaf', the customers opened it and told him that this was the proper way for bread to be cooked. This form of producer power, backed in Kenya by a social system which often seems to favour the foreign more than the local,[21] is a powerful determinant of consumer preferences and helps to explain the continued presence of socially inappropriate and less profitable technologies.

The political economy of technological development

The extent to which a technology can be improved in large part reflects the degree of effort specifically devoted to this activity and the extent to which optimization has already occurred in the past. As is to be expected, almost all the formally trained workers are employed in the largest, urban bakeries. Of the three master bakers not working for Elliots, two worked in bakeries in the 20,000–50,000 category. Elliots employed over 20 trained staff, of whom 15 had been trained abroad. But most of these skilled personnel reflect the higher skill content involved in operating these bakeries rather than the attempt to systematically improve bakery design.

As to past efforts put into improving technology, it stands to reason that the greater these have been, the lower the marginal returns to further investments of resources. Both the imported peel- and tunnel-ovens have been subject to intensive technical-change inputs over the years, whereas almost all of the local brick ovens have been built by non-specialized users. The consequence of this lack of specialization is particularly apparent in fuel costs. Four factors affect fuel-efficiency:

- The amount of heat lost by an oven reflects the proportion of surface area to baking area. Consequently, as a general rule multi-tiered ovens are much more fuel efficient than single-chamber ovens.
- Since most designs of brick oven burn fuel internally, they require enough oxygen for combustion (although this can be affected by the design of the draught). The peel ovens, by contrast, are heated externally, so that the size of the chambers can be reduced to the size of the baking tins.
- External heating allows for a multiplicity of fuel courses (including rubbish) whereas internally-heated ovens are confined to firewood.
- Heat loss is also affected by the degree of insulation. In order to minimize loss, some brick ovens have been lined with a glaze made of molten lime, glass and salt, but many others have not. Even in those which are glazed, the proportions needed to make this glaze vary, so there is little evidence of optimization.

The consequence has been that many of these rural brick ovens, whilst being relatively profitable, remain sub-optimal. During the course of this research engineers were induced to leave their laboratories and were appalled at the degree of heat loss. Designs were produced which were estimated — and this was corroborated by other engineers — to save 30–60 per cent of unit fuel costs. And since unit fuel costs (around KSh 10 per bag) were about double unit capital costs, this would have significantly accentuated the relative profitability of these brick-oven bakeries. In addition these savings in energy could have been achieved with lower capital costs since, with the availability of scrap-metal, rectangular ovens could have been constructed rather than ovens with self-supporting arches.

This distribution of inventive resources is of course a political–economic phenomenon since up to now only the interests of a narrow group of powerful producers utilizing imported capital-intensive equipment have been considered. The skilled workers are confined to these large-scale capital-intensive bakeries and the engineers from the university and the Industrial Research Organization are locked away in their classrooms and laboratories, far from the needs of small-scale producers in the rural areas. At the same time the returns to their efforts would have been far greater in these rural enterprises than in the already relatively well-endowed urban bakeries. Finally it is notable that with the exception of Lamu Island, an Arab community some distance from any major concentration of population and industry, there was no specialized capital goods firm concentrating on the design and manufacture of brick ovens.

Evidence from other sectors: breakfast cereals

The diffusion of bakery technologies in Kenya has been explained by a combination of four political–economic factors — monopoly power, the nature of entrepreneurship, the role of the state and the determination of consumption patterns. These help to explain the dominance of baking technologies which are not the most profitable, and which are also least socially appropriate. But how specific is this to the bakery industry?

Events in the Kenyan breakfast cereals industry in the late 1970s suggest a similar pattern. In this sector, however, it is not only process technologies which are affected, but also those of products. The contrast here arises between the traditional breakfast porridge made from maize flour (*ugali*), and Weetabix and other Western-type convenience cereals. *Ugali* has been, and remains, the staple food of most of Kenya's (and indeed Southern and Central Africa's) population. It is made by grinding whole maize into flour and cooking it. Urban residents and rural populations whose grain stores are empty buy sifted maize flour produced by the large mills (such as those owned by Unga and Maida — see pp. 62–4). This generally comprises about 60 per cent of the whole maize; it is easier to cook, but the germ which is not included in the flour is much the healthiest component of the cereal.[22]

Towards the mid 1970s, Western-style breakfast cereals became increasingly popular. A number of locally produced alternatives became available, including corn flakes made under licence from General Foods of the USA and Weetabix and Weetaflakes made under licence from a British company. The value of domestic production of these foodstuffs was about K£300,000 in 1977, and growing rapidly. Table 3.11 shows the unit costs of these various forms of breakfast foodstuffs. In general the traditional category was much

Table 3.11   Unit cost of different breakfast foods (1977)

	KSh/100gms
Staples	
Traditional	
Maize flour — 100% extraction	0.10
Maize flour — 85% extraction	0.17
Modern	
Wheat flour — 85% extraction	0.25
Bread	0.30
High Income Foods	
Locally Made	
Post Toasties	2.70
Weetabix	1.99
Weetaflakes	2.49
Imported	
Special K	9.00
All Bran	3.68
Puffed Wheat	8.01
Shredded Wheat	4.77
Rice Krispies	7.25

cheaper than the modern category of staples, and both were much cheaper than the Western-style breakfast cereals.

Since these various foodstuffs are made from different cereals and involve a variety of processes, they have different nutritional components, whose unit costs bear little relationship to the relative costs shown in Table 3.11. This is for two reasons. First, in general the traditional foods are less intensively processed and have far higher levels of nutrient per unit of weight than do the Western-style foodstuffs. But, for 'perverse' reasons, the Western-style foodstuffs also have added nutrients, and in some respects this reduces the unit costs of their nutrients. (The 'perverse' reasons are that in the case of breakfast cereals affected by UK-based laws, nutrients were added in response to the exemption of foodstuffs from value added tax in the early 1970s. However there was so little nutritional content in these cereals that they could only qualify as 'foodstuffs' if synthetic vitamins were added during processing!) It can be seen from Table 3.12 that in terms of nutrient cost these Western-style products were clearly inappropriate to the needs of the mass of consumers. The relative attractiveness of bread as a convenience staple is also evident from this data.

Table 3.12. Differential between unit nutrient costs for 100 per cent extraction maize flour and locally manufactured breakfast cereals

	Carbo-hydrates	Protein	Fat	Ash	Fibre	Calories	Thia-mine	Ribo-flavine	Niacin
								Vitamins	
Weetabix/ maize flour	18	19	45	55	22	21	9	3	4
Weetaflakes/ maize flour	22	30	64	68	29	24	12	3	5
Bread/ maize flour	4	4	4	17	na	4	2	1	1

Source: Nutrients of cereals from N L Kent, *Technology of Cereals with Special Reference to Wheat*, Oxford, Pergamon Press. Nutrients of bread from Y Pomeranz (ed.) (1964), *Wheat Chemistry and Technology*, Minnesota, American Association of Cereal Chemists. Maize and wheat flour nutrients from FAO/UN and US Department of Health, Education and Welfare, *Food Composition Tables for use in Africa (1968)*. Nutrients for Weetabix and Weetaflakes from manufacturers.

This inappropriateness in product finds its parallels in the inappropriateness of process technology. The Weetabix plant had annual sales of around K£160,000. But since 5 per cent of sales was remitted in terms of the technical services agreement, and most of the machinery and some inputs were imported, annual value aded tax was lower. The plan cost around K£600,000 and employed 15 people. By contrast, each hammer-mill cost K£2,000 and produced domestic value added of around K£5,000 per year.[23]

So the same capital sum invested in the two types of technologies produced K£130,000 value added and employed 15 people in a single Weetabix plant located in Nairobi, whereas it would have involved 300 dispersed hammer-mills, employing over 600 people with domestic value added of K£1,440,000.

A number of factors explain the existence and expansion of this inappropriate technology. In part it reflects the residence of an expatriate community; in part the convenience of instant cereals.[24] But the market for Weetabix and other Western-style products is not confined to high income expatriates. Weetabix was engaged in a conscious attempt to expand its market to lower income consumers. Advertising expenditure on Weetabix and Weetaflakes alone was double the total advertising expenditure on all maize and wheat flour products.

This advertising was pitched at 'European' consumers, but with the conscious strategy adopted by the dominant transnational affiliate in the food industry (East African Industries, a subsidiary of Unilever) of 'sticking it in at the top of the market and letting it sink down'. The advertising agency responsible for the Weetabix promotion modelled itself on this approach, believing that 'it is easier for products to go down [market] than up [market]'. This marketing approach was affected by an earlier experience of launching a locally made beer (Jambo Beer) in the early 1970s which was pitched at working-class consumers. 'If you want to kill a product,' observed the head of one of the largest advertising agencies in Nairobi, 'give it a Swahili name.'

This pattern of social determination of consumption preferences, modelled on foreign lifestyles and high incomes, is peculiarly strong in Kenya.[25] What is especially interesting about these two case-studies, bread and breakfast cereals, is that the primary actors were not, as Langdon documents for other sectors, transnational corporations. They were local firms, but firms whose behaviour was heavily conditioned by the presence of TNCs and by the consumption patterns which this foreign-owned sector and its attendant expatriate population tended to foster. This phenomenon is not unique to Kenya, nor is it confined to capitalist economies. In the 1960s the revolutionary Cuban government tried to reorient consumption patterns in order to change the choice of process technology. But being so close to Miami it proved virtually impossible to blot out US radio stations and there was significant consumer dissatisfaction with the inability to obtain Coca Cola, Ford cars and other branded consumer products.

The institutional framework of AT development and diffusion: brick manufacture in three African countries

Introduction

The state as a direct agent of innovation and diffusion, and the relationship between this and market forces, has become an increasingly prominent debate in the development literature and development practice,[1] and will be considered in subsequent chapters. In this chapter attention is focused on the role played by states and markets in the development and diffusion of a particular AT (for manufacturing bricks)[2] in three sub-Saharan African economies, Botswana, Kenya and Tanzania. But it is not only the state and private capitalists who are active in this process, since non-governmental organizations, some of whom are based in the industrially advanced countries, have also played a prominent role. What can be learnt from this experience of these different development agents in promoting alternative technologies? And, insofar as ATs have diffused, do the activities of these development agents favour particular types of technology and particular sets of producers?

Setting the Schumpeterian motor to work

In attempting to explain technological progress and diffusion, economists have drawn a distinction between a number of important subprocesses and social roles. The first of these is that of invention, the basic idea behind a new product or way of doing something. This may involve degrees of originality by the inventor from the way in which inputs are combined to fundamental or applied research. On their own, these basic ideas can seldom be translated into production without prior development. In the case of complex technologies the stage of development may require extensive resources and take a considerable time. After the completion of technological development, the new technology can be considered eligible for commercial production and this involves the process of innovation. One of the most distinguished theorists of technological change, Schumpeter, identified the role of the entrepreneur (and of entrepreneurship in general) as being the translation of inventions into commercial production.[3] By providing a technological rent (since no other producers have access to the technology) innovations enable the entrepreneurs to escape from the competitive pressures which gradually erode profitability. These monopoly profits simultaneously act as a spur to emulation, and thus a process of technological diffusion sets in.

The 'Schumpeterian motor' describes a process whereby technological change is endogenized in economic growth, one in which new technologies are continuously innovated, and replicated, in the search for protection from competitive pressures. This process seems to be well established in most of the capitalist industrially advanced countries, as well as in the newly-industrializing Asian countries. But in the socialist countries and the developing countries there is often an acute problem of integrating the subprocesses of invention and technological development with those of innovation and diffusion. In these economies, science and technology are often marginalized from production. As will be seen later in this chapter, and especially in Chapters 5 and 6 on cement and sugar, this marginalization is particularly acute for alternative technologies and there seems to be only limited effective demand for the application of science and technology to meet the problems of low-income consumers and producers.

This brief description of the literature on invention and technological development, innovation and diffusion is suggestive of important institutional issues. Schumpeter's characterization of the innovation process assumes the existence of a class of profit-hungry capitalists. But they are not always in evidence, especially in DCs, and even in the IACs the inventive process may be too complex for the private sector alone. So the state has come to play a prominent role. Other actors, too, have been important in different countries, including communes and co-operatives (in China), feudal and military rulers (in nineteenth-century Japan) and, most recently in many developing countries, non-governmental organizations. No generalizations can be made about the most suitable type of institution since its role is so clearly affected by the particular circumstances of any country, region or point in time. But the centrality of institutions to the process of AT development and diffusion cannot be ignored.

Brick technologies

Alternative forms of building materials

Most of the housing needs of the world's populations are met through the use of various types of plastered soil, mixed with water and often reinforced with wooden laths. Given the availability of excess labour (often a seasonal phenomenon) and the widespread variety of suitable soils, such forms of construction are virtually costless and it is this which explains their widespread use. These traditional building materials are not, however, without their blemishes. Their durability is low, adversely affected by heavy rains, termites and general weathering. As a consequence they require frequent maintenance and rebuilding. They are structurally weak and unable to support heavy roofs or multistories and are therefore largely confined to meeting the needs of low-income housing in economies with excess labour. Consequently, a number of alternative materials have come to dominate construction in DCs. These include cement, cement blocks, soil-cement blocks, stone blocks and bricks.

Brick is an extremely durable material, with excellent structural properties (when well made) and attractive to the eye. Given their regular shape, bricks are readily transportable and, perhaps most importantly, they are a cost-competitive type of building material under a wide variety of factor price regimes since unlike other materials (such as stone blocks) a range of efficient brick-making techniques is readily available.

The major substitutes for bricks in the IACs are materials based upon cement. This is an easily transportable input which can be made from generally available deposits of raw materials. In its most widely-accepted form, portland cement, it possesses both durability and structural soundness, although it is not nearly as pleasing to the eye as brick (which may, however, often be used to face the exposed surfaces of cement walls). Whilst the production of cement is generally large-scale and capital intensive in nature, its use can be associated with a range of contruction methods including blocks and bricks, and bulk cement.[4]

Because of the different operating environments existing in different countries (and indeed between districts within countries), it is not possible to develop easy rules of thumb about the relative costs of these alternative forms of building materials. In at least two of the three countries under consideration, detailed costings suggest that well-produced bricks are more durable than traditional materials and are an inherently cheaper form of construction than cement blocks, though this relative price advantage varies in different environments (Table 4.1).[5] In Arusha (Tanzania), for example, where for environmental reasons both bricks and cement blocks need to be plastered

Table 4.1. Comparison of constructing equivalent sized walls in Botswana (Gaborone) and Tanzania (Arusha) from concrete blocks/bricks or bricks (1986)

| | Tanzania (TSh) | | Botswana (Pula) | |
	cement blocks	clay bricks	cement blocks	clay bricks
Materials	630	160	5.50	5.50
Cement for laying	7	18	0.50	0.50
Labour for laying	42	80	2.10	2.10
Plastering materials + labour	90	90	2.50	0
Painting materials + labour	120	120	2.50	0
Total	889	468	13.10	8.10
Ratio of cement blocks/bricks to bricks	1.90		1.62	

Source: Interviews with Wade Adams in Botswana and Coviconstruct in Tanzania.

and painted, the cost of constructing one square metre of plastered and painted wall is 90 per cent higher with cement blocks/bricks than with bricks. By contrast, in the drier climate of Botswana, where bricks can be used without plastering, the costs per unit of construction of using cement blocks/bricks are only 60 per cent greater than bricks.[6]

In the face of these significant cost differentials, the major reason why bricks are not more widely used is that they are simply not available in the required quality and quantity. In Botswana, for example, most good quality bricks have to be imported from South Africa at P325 per 1,000 (produced locally at less than half the price), and this transforms the cost advantage in favour of cement products. In Arusha, good quality bricks are difficult to obtain at any price. What the analysis suggests is that should bricks be available at the calculated prices, in sufficient quantity and of adequate quality, then they will be used widely, with a strong potential for profitable production. Substituting for cement also makes more productive use of foreign exchange — in Botswana cement has to be imported and in Tanzania and Kenya its production has a relatively high import content.

Brick-making technologies

Brick manufacture involves the mixture of water and suitable types of clay soils to form a malleable, plastic substance which can be shaped into brick form. The amount of water involved in this mixture will largely be determined by the type of forming technology used. Once formed, the 'green bricks' have to be left to stand in order for some of the moisture to dry out. The speed of drying must be controlled, in relation both to the types of clay utilized and their moisture content, otherwise external surfaces would dry more rapidly than the core. With soils prone to shrinkage, this would lead to cracking, lower structural integrity and wastage. Most often this means that the formed bricks have to be dried in an environment with some form of protection from the wind and the sun. Thereafter the green bricks are fired at between 800–1,000 degrees C over a number of days, after which they have to be removed from the kiln and delivered to customers.

It is possible to distinguish five major stages in the process of manufacture:[7] the winning and transporting of clay to site; the mixing of clay; the forming of bricks; their transfer and drying; and their firing.

Clay winning and transporting   Clay soils of the appropriate variety have to be dug from the ground. These clays (whose suitability is in part determined by the pressing and firing technologies used) are generally geologically old soils, and are more likely to be found in flat terrain or near the bottoms of valleys. In the process of winning, the ground level is reduced and becomes subject to flooding. Since the soil is often harder at lower depths it is common for winning to be extensive, rather than to involve deep excavations.

There exists a wide range of winning and transporting technologies. Insofar as winning is concerned, this may be done either by labourers using simple tools such as spades or with heavy earthmoving motorized equipment. The extent of transporting required depends mostly upon the locale of the brickworks and the suitability of the local clays for, generally, a mix of soil varieties will be required. A well-chosen site will require virtually no transporting of clay, but in some cases a proportion of the inputs may have to be obtained from some distance. Transporting may occur through the use of wheelbarrows, ox-carts or motorized vehicles of various capacities, all depending upon the distance and extent of materials required.

Mixing The type of technology required to mix the ingredients largely depends upon the hardness of the clay and the scale of output. In general, damp surface clay-soils with a good amount of natural silts and sand require no crushing equipment and in small-scale plants it is a relatively easy task for labourers to mix the clay and water with simple tools. However, the mechanized forming technologies require a homogeneous clay input, since they operate with significantly drier mixtures. In these circumstances it is essential that the mixing process utilizes crushing equipment (for which there exist varying degrees of mechanization).

Brick forming There are essentially three different technologies for forming bricks. The first is that of slop-moulding. The mixture is ladelled into wooden moulds, the excess clay is removed and the moulds are then upended on a smooth floor. In this method of forming, the clay mixture has to have a high water content (which can be up to 35% but is more typically around 25%) in order to minimize the clay sticking to the wooden moulds. The bricks are left to dry, but since it is necessary to ensure that this does not proceed too rapidly (otherwise cracking is likely to occur) it may have to take place in a covered area. Typically this will involve a period of around 10 days and sometimes even up to one month. With slop-moulding, wasting is high because the soft moist moulded bricks are susceptible to cracking during drying and to deformation and damage during the transporting and drying phases.

The second major type of brick-forming technology is that of pressing. In this process the clay-mixture is placed in a mould on a horizontal work surface, and then through a leveraged action the mixture is pressed into the required shape. These presses may be manually operated, moulding two bricks per pressing and upwards of 200–300 bricks an hour. However, they may also be semi-automatic and power-driven, pressing around 2,000 bricks an hour. Because this process involves a high pressure which both bonds the homogeneous mixture and eases ejection from the mould, the water content in the mixtures is substantially lower than slop-moulding, at around 10 per cent. This offers several advantages, including lowering the rate of cracking, minimizing the need to use special sands as fillers to reduce shrinkage (and thus cracking) during drying, and reducing the energy required in firing since there is less moisture to be driven off.

Pressing offers two additional advantages over slop-moulding: first, its output is more regular in shape, which not only improves the final appearance but perhaps more importantly means that less cement has to be used in the construction of the wall in which the bricks are to be included; second, the bricks are drier and more rigid, so they dry more rapidly (around 2–3 days), and can be handled after forming without much danger of deformation and wastage. However, its relative disadvantage over the traditional slop-moulding method is that it requires an investment of fixed capital, not just in the press itself but in many cases also to homogenize the clay before mixing.

The third major type of forming technology is that of extrusion. This process developed in the nineteenth century in Europe and involves the mixing of a homogeneous clay which is then forced into a continuous process through a die which dictates the final shape of the brick. The extruded clay is cut by a sharp wire and the bricks are then treated analogously to the procedure involved in pressing. Because extrusion is a continuous process it is inherently capital intensive and modern plants of this sort will produce around 8,000 bricks per hour. Because of its capital-intensity, extrusion technology may be the preferred choice where labour costs are high. That being said, recent developments in mechanizing pressing technologies have meant that many modern brick factories in the IACs use presses instead of extruders.

Transfer and drying Of all sub-processes in manufacturing, it is generally transfer which offers the most scope for capital/labour substitution. In most manufacturing industries work in progress can be moved around by hand or by a mechanized transfer line which, in the most modern plants, is flexible. In the case of brick production, since moving lines are generally ruled out by the fragility of the unfired brick, the choice is between manually moving individual bricks or pallets of bricks.

In the case of drying it is common to leave bricks to stand in the shade in the small-scale plants, since exposure to sunlight (especially when slop-moulding is involved) may lead to excessive cracking. In large-scale plants bricks may either be left to stand (although this might create problems in that the large volumes require such large drying areas that the extent of transfer required is not only costly, but is likely to be associated with greater wastage), or dried slowly in purpose-built areas partially using waste heat from the kilns.

Firing The function of firing is primarily to strengthen the brick, although it serves the subsidiary purpose of producing the red colour which makes the product attractive to consumers. There are at least three major variations in kiln technology which, coincidentally, accord with those used in brick plants

79

in Botswana, Kenya and Tanzania. The first of these is that which is most widely used in the production of low-cost bricks, especially in the less developed countries. It involves the construction of what is called a clamp. This is a simple procedure in which bricks are stacked in the open into a largish cube-shape, approximately 2 metres high, of between 5,000–40,000 bricks. (In some cases, as in SE England, clamps contain up to 2m bricks.) The clamp is plastered on the outside with either clay or spoilt bricks from earlier firings, in order to maintain high temperature and to minimize fuel usage. Tunnels are left in these clamps in which the wood (or coal) is inserted for firing, more being added during the firing which can take 2–5 days. Thereafter the clamp is left to cool, which can take up to 2 weeks. The clamps are obviously temporary, being rebuilt with new bricks (except for the insulating external layer) for every firing.

Clamp-firing can in principle produce bricks of a regular shape and acceptable structural quality, but each batch is inherently uneven in nature with the bricks in the centre tending to be relatively over-fired and those at the rim under-fired. The production of acceptable quality bricks requires a considerable degree of skill and it is much more common for clamp-fired bricks to be of variable shape and of a lower quality than bricks produced with other firing techniques. In general they therefore tend to sell at a discount.[8]

The second major type of kiln is the purpose-built stationary kiln. This may take a number of forms but is generally of three types: the simplest is of a rectangular shape, generally with at least two parallel chambers, so that whilst one is firing, the other can be unloaded and reloaded; an alternative is the Hoffman kiln, which is built in an ellipse or circle and is fired continuously, the fire moving slowly around the kiln, with loading taking place in front of the fire and unloading in its wake; a third type is the Scotch kiln, involving the construction of a containing wall on at least three sides, with arches for the fuel to be inserted. Any of these stationary kilns produces bricks of high quality, although with poor management (such as underfiring) they are naturally capable of producing a poor quality product. A wide variety of fuels can be used, including oil, coal, wood and coffee husks.

The third and final type of kiln is the tunnel kiln, in which the bricks move through the kiln on purpose-built trolleys. This requires a most carefully controlled firing system, and generally requires gas, oil or coal. Being continuous, it tends to operate on a large-scale but by comparison with other types of kiln the final product tends to be of a high and homogeneous quality. Both continuous and purpose-built stationary kilns are widely used in the industrially advanced countries, whereas few developing countries use tunnel kilns.

Linked technical choices

In theory, while it is possible to combine any single technique in any of these five subprocesses with all of the alternatives in other subprocesses,[9] a limited number of technological and managerial paradigms have tended to emerge, involving clusters of choice. Small-scale plants (up to 2,000 bricks per day) tend to involve manual winning, mixing and intra-plant transfer and link these with slop-moulding and clamp-firing. Medium-scale plants (from 2,000–10,000 bricks per day) might involve some form of mechanization in winning (depending upon the scale of output), mechanized crushing, hand-operated or mechanized presses, palletized intra-plant transfer and specialized stationary kilns (generally Hoffman kilns in the larger plants). The largest scale plants (up to 75,000 bricks per day) almost always have mechanized winning and transport of materials to site, mechanized crushing, extruders (or sometimes a series of mechanized presses), palletized transfer lines and Hoffman or tunnel kilns.

AT in brick manufacture

The specification of AT in the brick industry hinges around the appropriateness of product. It is clear that under some factor price combinations, with available markets and suitably placed raw materials, bricks are a viable building material, especially when structural strength is required. But within the product-category of 'bricks', there are a number of alternatives. A homogeneous product, often favoured in DCs (but not IACs) as the image of modernity, requires mechanized mixing, pressing and relatively capital-intensive firing. A structurally-sound brick can be manufactured with the most labour-intensive technologies, but this requires particular skills and sound management. The final product will also vary in colour.

Given these product constraints, three modal technological combinations can be identified, based upon what exists in the three countries:

- labour-intensive mixing, slop-moulding and clamp-firing;
- mechanized mixing, manually-powered presses and simple kilns; and
- mechanized winning, mixing, extrusion-forming, intra-plant transfer and tunnel-kilns.

As specified in Chapter 2, the assessment of appropriateness should consider the relativity of the operating environment and identify whose needs are to be considered. Economic, social and environmental criteria must be taken into account, as well as the distinction between private and social costs.

In assessing the appropriateness of these technologies in the environment of East and Southern Africa, there is a greater degree of similarity than difference between the operating conditions in the three countries under consideration — they have broadly similar climates, per capita incomes and raw material availabilities. The calculation of factor productivity and cost estimates — which is undertaken only in outline form, since the primary concern lies with the institutional character of diffusion — is based upon operating conditions in Botswana and Tanzania. Environmental appropriateness is also not considered in detail, since with minor differences in the types of fuel utilized and the degree of transport involved in the transport of raw material to, and final product from, large-scale factories, there is also no great difference between the various technologies. Insofar as social appropriateness is concerned, the primary aspect raised in the case of bricks concerns the social character of innovation, and this issue is treated in greater detail, especially in relation to the institutional characteristics of technological choice.

Before considering these institutional issues, it is first helpful to undertake a brief economic valuation of appropriateness in Botswana and Tanzania. In Botswana the comparison of technological choice is between the three modal types specified above (p. 81). In Tanzania, the contrast is drawn between a medium-sized press-moulder and a fully mechanized large-scale extrusion/tunnel kiln plant. Because of the general similarity of factor prices and operating conditions, the conclusions emerging from these relative costings can be extended to Kenya. (Due to the datedness of the Kenyan plant it was not possible to identify suitable pricing parameters as the capital cost cannot be realistically calculated. So discussion only relates to its output and employment and to the institutional character of AT dissemination.)

The choice of technology in Botswana

Table 4.2 sets out the factor productivities of the two major types of mechanized technologies, a brick-pressing plant with a purpose-built stationary kiln (operating at two different scales) and a large-scale automated extrusion/tunnel plant. (Information is not provided for the labour-intensive slop-moulding plants. As they operate in the open on extensive deposits of

Table 4.2. Coefficients of production of alternative brick technologies[a]

	Capital (Pula)	*Labour*	*Output (000s/pa)*	*K/L (Pula)*	*O/L (bricks)*	*O/K (bricks)*
Small-scale pressing plant with purpose-built kiln	142,609	29	973	4,918	33,559	6.8
Medium-scale pressing plant with purpose-built kiln	268,284	53	2,306	5,062	43,515	8.6
Large-scale plant with extrusion and tunnel kiln	5,334,000	131	24,440	40,718	186,260	4.6

[a] Data for the medium-scale plant is based on scaling of small-scale plant in operation; for large-scale plant, data obtained from feasility study.

land, requiring only spades to dig the soil, the estimation of their capital productivity and capital/labour ratios is virtually meaningless.) All costs and factor productivities are based upon 1986 replacement prices. Data for the pressing technologies are based upon observation of existing technology, whereas the appraisal of the large-scale plant is based upon project documents for a proposed investment by a foreign firm.

It is clear from this data that if all output can be readily sold and with no differential in transport costs, then the small-scale pressing plant would not be utilized. It has a lower productivity of both capital and labour than the medium-scale press and is therefore economically inefficient. However, if the medium-scale plant were not available, then both the very large-scale automated plant and the small-scale pressing plant would be economically efficient. The most striking information in this table is the comparison between the large- and the medium-scale plants. The difference in initial capital cost is a factor of 20, with an almost eightfold variation in capital costs per job. The output variation is around tenfold. This means that Botswana's annual consumption of bricks (some 20m–25m bricks in 1986) could either be met by a single plant costing P5.33m, employing 131 people and operating at about 40 per cent of single-shift capacity; or five medium-scale plants costing P1.34m and using 265 workers at full single-shift capacity; or with 11 small-scale pressing plants employing 319 workers and costing P1.57m.

The figures on factor productivities, when mated to factor prices and to the gestation periods involved in constructing the plants,[10] can be used to calculate the relative costs of production. Table 4.3 shows the break-even selling price over 20 years life to achieve an internal rate of return of 12.5 per cent, the commercial cost of capital in Botswana in 1986. What is striking about this is that despite its 'economic inefficiency' the small-scale pressing plant is the least-cost producer. This is because its transport costs are lower and it faces different factor prices. If the absurdity of full-capacity utilization for the large-scale plant is removed (since its rated capacity is twice that of the whole Botswana market), then the higher costs of the automated plant would be even more marked.[11] The most significant aspect of this data is, however, the low selling price of the slop-moulded bricks and the very high selling

Table 4.3. Selling price required to break-even over 20 years at internal rate of return of 12.5 per cent

	Pula/000 bricks
Very small-scale slop-moulding with clamp-firing	50
Small-scale brick press with purpose-built kiln	68
Medium-scale brick press with purpose-built kiln	92
Large-scale extrusion/tunnel kiln	156
Imported bricks	325

price of imported bricks. The determination of product quality and market demand are probably the two most important factors determining real-world profitability. If the large-scale plant can impose its product standards on the market and produce bricks of equivalent quality to imports, then even it can run at a profitable rate. If in addition it can succeed in defining quality in terms of homogeneity rather than structural integrity, then it would have a marked advantage over smaller-scale producers not using tunnel kilns.

Assuming that product quality is similar between the three plants (a subject considered in more detail above, (p. 81), then the case for the smaller-scale variants of technology is very strong: they produce a much cheaper product, in plants of a scale more amenable to local participation; their real resource costs are lower, since they use more of the abundant factor (labour) and less of the scarce factors (capital and also, because of the poorly developed capital goods industry in Botswana, foreign exchange); plant size is lower, providing more scope for ownership by poorer local citizens; and, finally, there is no basis for suggesting that their environmental impact is more adverse than that of the larger plants.

The choice of technology in Tanzania

The analysis of technical choice in the Tanzanian brick industry is more complex since whilst two plants were being built in the interior, near Arusha, neither was as yet in operation in 1986. The histories of these two technologies are considered in greater detail below (pp. 91–4), but it is relevant here to sketch out the basic characteristics and operating conditions of the two plants. One was a small-scale enterprise with manually-powered presses and a purpose-built kiln; the other was a large-scale automated plant, incorporating mechanized winning, mixing and intra-plant transfer, an extruder and a tunnel kiln. Construction of both plants was nearing completion in late 1986.

Table 4.4 provides data on the basic operating characteristics of the two plants. It is clear from this that they are both economically efficient, but

Table 4.4. Coefficients of production of two alternative technology brick plants under construction in Tanzania

	Capital (TShm)	Labour	Output (000s/pa)	K/L (TSh)	O/L (bricks)	O/K (bricks)
Small-scale brick press with purpose-built kiln	1.6	40	1,500	40,000	37,500	0.94
Large-scale, with extrusion and tunnel kiln	86.0	110	7,500	781,818	68,182	0.09

whereas the automated plant cost over 50 times as much as the small-scale technology, it produced only five times the output. The costs per workplace in the large plant were around 20 times of those in the smaller plant.

Since both plants were under construction it is not possible to provide any clear data on private profitability. However in view of the factor productivities and capital costs of the two plants as well as the cost of inputs, it would be extremely surprising indeed if the large-scale plant were to be competitive. Moreover, whereas the smaller plant uses coffee husks and wood (both of which are in relatively abundant supply in Arusha), the large-scale plant uses oil. There is a permanent shortage of oil in the Tanzanian interior and it is therefore doubtful whether the automated plant could ever operate near its designed capacity.[12] This would increase the plant's unit cost of capital. Moreover, the frequent firing of furnaces will substantially increase energy costs — there are many other reasons why large-scale plants operate at sub-optimal capacities in Tanzania and these, too, suggest that the automated plant's production costs will be very high.

The institutional framework for the development and diffusion of AT in brick manufacturing

In all three countries under consideration, bricks are a potentially important building material. In Botswana a small-scale brick pressing plant is in operation and plans are underfoot for both a medium-scale pressing plant and a large-scale automated technology using extrusion and tunnel-kilns. In Tanzania, both a medium-scale pressing plant and a large-scale automated plant are under construction, whilst in Kenya a large-scale extrusion plant (using a Hoffman, rather than a tunnel, kiln) has operated for some years and plans are underway for a number of smaller-scale pressing plants.

Three different types of institutions are playing a role in the development, innovation and diffusion of brick manufacturing technologies in Botswana, Kenya and Tanzania:[13] the private firm, which may either be locally owned, or a subsidiary of a transnational corporation; the state, whose activities may influence production in a number of ways — it can be a facilitator to other investors, in a variety of forms,[14] but it can also be a direct investor; and the non-governmental organizations (NGOs), which may be either local or foreign. Each of these three types of institutions can operate in isolation or in collaboration with one or both of the others.

Botswana
The historical experience of Botswana cannot be seen outside of the extension of white domination in the adjacent South African economy. The Batswana, a relatively cohesive cultural group, were able to resist the advance of white control over a long period of time by keeping the British to their 1885 commitment to protect Tswana sovereignty. The price paid for this was that

over the years British administration was almost entirely funded by levies exacted on the Tswana population. Given the apparently poor resource endowment of the economy this effectively meant that a significant proportion of the male population was forced to work as migrant labour in South Africa. As Independence approached in 1966, Botswana emerged as one of the world's poorest economies, almost entirely dependent on cattle production (in which the distribution of herds was markedly unequal) and migrant labour. The country was subject to frequent droughts with over one-fifth of the population dependent on famine relief in 1966, rising to over one-half in the severe drought of the mid-1980s. But despite this seemingly desperate economic scenario, Botswana had maintained its political sovereignty and was characterized by a regionally distinct social cohesiveness.

Few could have anticipated the next two decades of post-Independence development. The Botswana economy seemed suddenly to emerge from its struggle with subsistence, achieving one of the highest compound-growth rates of any economy in a period of declining global economic performance. The source of this was the discovery and exploitation of two significant sets of primary commodities: the first, in the early 1970s, was copper, which played an especially significant role in releasing the foreign exchange constraint, followed a few years later by the diamond-boom. The consequence was a growth in per capita consumption and a boom in the construction and service sectors, although all of this was interrupted by the severe drought of the early 1980s. At the margin, there were additional increments of growth with the expansion of the manufacturing sector, benefiting to some extent from the desire of white Rhodesians to shift their assets out of independent Zimbabwe, and the onset of beef-exports to the EEC.[15]

Thus in the mid-1980s Botswana found itself on the crest of a developmental wave, although there is naturally some concern about what might continue to fuel growth. Skilled, but not unskilled labour is in short supply. There is little experience by the Batswana in the trade sector, and only the embryonic signs of an indigenous industrial class. The revenue provided to the state from the mineral sector has allowed for a series of initiatives to encourage small-scale production with appropriate technologies. The major cloud on the horizon, however, is the political situation in neighbouring South Africa.

It is against this background that the development of brick manufacturing must be seen. Botswana has a long history of brick production, probably predating colonial rule. By the mid-1980s there were two primary producers in active production, the first being a group of small-scale traditional manufacturers located in Lobatse in the south of the country. Relatively speaking (since Botswana is four times the size of France with just over 1m inhabitants), this is a densely-populated area and lies on the main arterial road running through the east of Botswana. These very small-scale producers are literally digging up the land they are living on (which is suitable for brick production), slop-moulding the bricks in their forecourts and firing them in clamps at the side of their housing complex. Their output is of only marginal quality, since the bricks are left to dry in the sun (and hence crack easily), the clay-mixes are not optimized and the clamp-firing is poorly managed. The bricks are sold for consumption by low-income households since they are considerably more durable than traditional mud and laths, and cheaper than cement blocks. Their variable quality, however, limits their load-bearing capacities. While there is some sharing of tasks between producers (as is common in Botswana culture), these producers are essentially in the private sector, depending on the market for technology and market-information. Although they also depend on the market for access to capital, their needs are slight since most labour is provided by the family and most inputs can be obtained easily through the simple application of family-labour.

The second existing producer is an NGO, the Southern Rural Development Association (SRDA). This was formed in 1978 in an attempt to create productive employment in the rural areas. Initial funders included USAID, German, Canadian and Dutch aid agencies. It was decided to concentrate early projects in a number of areas, one of which was building materials. In 1984 these building-material activities benefited from government money disbursed through the Financial Assistance Policy scheme which promoted small-scale labour-intensive plants. The various building materials and mining ventures came to be grouped together in 1982 in the Minerals Holding Trust (MHT).

Amongst the various activities of the SRDA was construction, and widespread use was made of traditional slop-moulded and clamp-fired bricks produced by the small-scale producers in Lobatse, around 60 miles distance from the centre of SRDA's activities in Kanye. Three of the elder workers, all of whom had had experience in small-scale brick manufacture in Lobatse, suggested to the MHT that it produce its own bricks; they were confident that the local clays in Moshaneng (just outside Kanye) would be suitable. Thus the MHT became involved in brick manufacture, initially using slop-moulding and clamp-firing techniques. Despite its obvious promise the brick plant ran at a loss, partly because it proved unable to compete with the low-cost Lobatse enterprises, partly because the local clays at Moshaneng were not entirely suitable and some had to be brought in from other areas, and partly because the technology was suboptimal. A series of decisions was then made to upgrade the plant, introducing manually-operated brick-presses and constructing a stationary kiln of two chambers, each with a capacity of around 60,000 bricks. Because this represented a significant change from previous operations, assistance was sought from international alternative technology NGOs.

The general funding of the SRDA (as well as the funding of its building materials division, MHT) has been supported for many years by government

87

and international non-governmental organizations (which had a commitment to self-help co-operative schemes designed to increase employment). This financial support has tended to remove market discipline from the various operations, with the consequence that heavy financial losses have built up and have frequently had to be relieved by injections of external assistance. This is reflected clearly in the operation of the brick-pressing plant.

In Table 4.3 (see p. 83) it was shown that the cost of production for a small-scale brick-pressing plant (with a capacity of 1,080,000 bricks a year) was P68 per 1,000 bricks. This compared with P92 per 1,000 for a medium-scale brick-pressing plant and P156 per 1,000 for a large automated extruder plant using a tunnel-kiln. By contrast the MHT brick-pressing plant, with a capacity of 729,000 bricks a year produced bricks at a cost of P106 per 1,000. But management of this MHT plant were not aware of their production costs and sold their output at P75 per 1,000, leading to considerable financial losses and necessitating frequent injections of topping-up finance. Since the output of this plant was of a relatively high quality by comparison with the Lobatse slop-moulders, since imported bricks cost over P325 per 1,000 and since bricks are a competitive form of building material at prices lower than P150 per 1,000, the MHT plant had absolutely no problems in selling its output. Most of this went to government departments or to upper-income local residents for house building.

Because the MHT plant ran at a consistent loss, there had been discussion within management about reducing costs, but not about increasing selling-prices. One innovation which had been tried was to provide output incentives to the workers and this had indeed had the desired effect, reducing costs from P106 to P92 per 1,000. Not only did it have lower production costs, it also led to an increase in wages. This experiment ran into difficulties, however, because of the policies of one of the key international NGOs backing the various MHT projects. They deemed these wage incentives to be 'ideologically unsound' and the experiment was discontinued.

Two other factories have also manufactured bricks in the past. One was established by a non-citizen resident of Botswana and was located near Gaborone, the capital city. Like the Lobatse producers it had used a combination of slop-moulding and clamp-firing but, being more carefully managed, produced a higher quality product. It had run into difficulties due to the unsuitability of the clay being used and is no longer in operation. In addition, in the late 1970s a Motswana who had worked in a Zimbabwean brick factory for some years developed a small and profitable slop-moulding and clamp-firing plant employing five people in Francistown, the second biggest town in Botswana close to the Zimbabwe border. In 1982 he decided to expand, but lacking access to detailed knowledge of the alternatives he went to Zimbabwe to search for equipment. There he found second-hand technology, involving a combination of extrusion with clamp-firing. It was a large-scale plant and had a capacity to produce 12m bricks a year, half of

Botswana's annual brick consumption. Mixing and extruding equipment was purchased for P45,000 but, once installed, turned out to be troublesome. It had not been used for some years (due largely, as the new owner found to his cost, to the unreliability of the equipment). This brick-venture soon ran into difficulties, partly because the machinery needed considerable attention and partly because the owner's belief that the local soil was adequate proved to be misfounded. The nearest suitable clay was 62 miles distance and, when the rains came, the heavy cotton-soil made it virtually impossible to transport it to site. Moreover, this small-scale entrepreneur, with limited schooling and no technical training, was poorly equipped to handle the complexities of a relatively large-scale and technologically-complex enterprise. So, having invested over P200,000 in the venture (not an inconsiderable sum in Botswana, and financed partly through government grants and largely through profits generated in retailing) the brick factory was sold in 1986 to an Asian family owning the largest supermarket in Francistown. Having invested P700,000 in buying and upgrading the plant, the new owners had produced a total of 500,000 bricks in two years (compared to a potential capacity of 24m) and there were considerable misgivings in the family about the attempted diversification.

To complete the Botswana picture, the Ministry of Commerce and Industry began to negotiate with a French firm for the construction of a plant to produce 24m bricks a year. This was either to be built on a turn-key basis or operated as a joint venture with a local partner. As early analysis showed, the costs of production in this plant were much higher than the smaller-scale alternatives but not nearly as high as the cost of imports. By early 1989, and after some years of discussion, no final decision had yet been made on the establishment of this plant. But it is significant that other than a proposal for a slightly smaller plant by the French supplier (which was not favoured on grounds of cost) no detailed appraisal of a smaller-scale technological alternative was undertaken by the Ministry.

Putting all this together, a number of conclusions can be drawn. First, no invention is involved in this sector in Botswana. Some limited technological development has been required, mainly to optimize input-mixes to the particular characteristics of local clays. The manual brick-presses, recently developed in Belgium, also required some small adjustments and a British brick-press had been tried and shown to be inadequate for the task. All this developmental work on the presses had been undertaken by an American non-governmental organization, Appropriate Technology International (ATI). It is significant that comprehensive clay-testing had been undertaken by the Botswana state, but the details of this had not filtered through to the existing producers. In some fortunate cases they had learnt through experience which clays were least unsuitable; in other less fortunate cases, they had paid the price of ignorance. Because of the absence of formal knowledge and testing facilities, neither the Lobatse clamp-firers nor the

MHT brick-pressing plant had really optimized their mix of clays and sand, and this lowered product quality. Some improvements had been made on the MHT mix through advice received from an ATI adviser during his visit to Botswana.

Botswana's formal sector consumption of bricks is about 25m a year based upon the prices of imports of over P300 per 1,000. Were bricks available at lower prices, the demand would be much higher, with bricks substituting for cement bricks/blocks whose basic input is imported. Yet, despite these major opportunities, local production was less than 1m bricks a year. Some innovation had occurred through the introduction of brick-presses in the MHT plant, which had previously used slop-moulders. This had been undertaken by a local NGO, with extensive support for similar international bodies. The introduction of a mechanized mixer and extruder plant in Francistown was also an innovative step and had been undertaken by a private entrepreneur. Yet his poor training and limited knowledge had led to an unviable form of innovation. His choice of technology, which was both inappropriate to local operating conditions and of poor quality, represents a case of market failure (since perfectly functioning markets imply perfect knowledge and foresight). The state, too, through the Ministry of Commerce and Industry, had been trying to stimulate innovation in large-scale technology, but the French technology supplier was reluctant to invest alone, and no suitable local partner could be found. While reliance on the market for innnovation and diffusion had led to unsatisfactory results, state involvement had not stimulated socially optimal patterns of innovation. What innovation had occurred had mainly taken place through the activities of NGOs.

The picture of diffusion is also limited. There has been extensive diffusion of small-scale slop-moulding and clamp-firing technologies, especially in the Lobatse area. In one sense this fits the classic Schumpeterian case since, through a process of intensive competition, prices have been whittled down, with the returns from this form of brick production lower than those in paid employment. These small-scale slop-moulders only produced bricks because of their failure to obtain employment in the formal sector. Yet in another sense the Schumpeterian model is not validated since there has been no innovative response arising out of these highly competitive market conditions.

By contrast, the brick-presses used in MHT had not diffused elsewhere in Botswana despite the existence of market opportunities and their demonstrated ability to produce adequate-quality products at prices which would allow for profitable production. One possible explanation for this was the pricing policy actually adopted by MHT (that is, selling at below cost) which might have suggested to potential entrepreneurs that the technology was unprofitable. This unrealistic pricing policy was a direct (but not necessary) reflection of the non-governmental status of MHT and its international backers.

Tanzania

Tanzania (then consisting only of Tanganyika) began its Independence with a fundamentally different colonial inheritance from that of its regionally dominant neighbour, Kenya. Lacking the settled white population of Kenya, the struggle for Independence had been less intense. Moreover, most of the factors which made Kenya such a 'success-story' were absent: commercial agriculture was less well developed and the industrial sector was almost primitive by comparison; the TNCs which had tended to use Kenya as a regional base in the past seemed to show little inclination to establish viable enterprises in Tanganyika, so that the Arusha Declaration of 1967 was not so much an attempt to expropriate a large foreign sector but more a response to a deficient historic rate of investment in industry and commercial agriculture.

The subsequent experience of Tanzania is well-known, albeit controversial. In terms of output growth, the performance has been significantly worse than Kenya. But the extent to which responsibility for this can be placed on the policies which were adopted is uncertain since, as has been noted, Tanzania began from a very different starting point to its neighbours. By the mid-1980s, the economy appeared to be in a state of crisis. It was not a matter of maintaining historic levels of employment, investment and output growth, but more acutely one of minimizing the rate at which incomes and output were falling. In many respects the 'modern economy' had broken down, with transport and other infrastructural investments often crippled by a lack of foreign exchange. To the extent that innovation in the non-agricultural sector had become the preserve of the state, the budgetary crisis and the very severe foreign-exchange constraint almost put an end to new investment. Much of the parastatal-led investment which had occurred, as was shown in Chapter 1, had often resulted in the introduction of inappropriate technologies.

With a clear need for labour-intensive technologies, utilizing little foreign exchange and producing at the local level, the Tanzanian state began in the mid-1970s to consider the production of bricks. It provided the prospect of meeting basic needs as well as those of urban development through the processing of local inputs. A number of feasibility studies were undertaken and the results published. These identified clear market opportunities in brick manufacture, but as no private investors emerged, the offer of technical assistance from the North Korean Government in the late 1970s was welcomed. Initially the plant was to be located in Zanzibar (an island off the Tanzanian coast), but when it was realized that no suitable clay was available there, the decision was made to establish the plant instead at Arusha, 500 miles inland. The fact that Arusha is a considerable distance from the existing cement plant at the coast, and so would help in future to reduce economy-wide transport costs, was probably an important element in this locational decision.

It was agreed that North Korea would provide the equipment and Tanzania would be responsible for the civil works and operating expenses.

91

Soil-testing began in 1979, ground-clearing in 1982 and construction in 1984. Planned output was 5m Korean-sized bricks a year, equivalent to 7.6m bricks produced by the plants considered in the earlier economic analysis (see pp. 84–5). The equipment involved is of the most modern type, with extruders and a tunnel kiln as in the automated Botswana plant. This is an especially important decision since such kilns use coal, gas or oil — the plant in question will use oil. All of these fuel inputs have to be imported and this must be seen in the context of a severe foreign exchange constraint in Tanzania, such that for significant periods of the year, Arusha region as a whole is without any fuel oil. In circumstances where the process of brick-production requires continuous firing, the consequences could be extreme. Indeed it is expected by the Tanzanian managers that the plant will only run at 70 per cent capacity, but in the light of the experience of other large firms in Tanzania, even this might be considered too optimistic.

Implementation of this project has been extensively delayed. For some period the non-availability of finance and reinforcing rods held up construction. More recently, when it became clear that fuel oil would be required (since coal supplies were so erratic), construction ground to a halt whilst the parastatal searched for the foreign exchange required for its importation.[16] By 1986 the plant was at least one year away from producing its first brick. If this schedule is kept, it will have taken almost ten years to bring to fruition after the agreement was signed, and six years after ground-clearing began.

Although appropriateness is an inherently relative concept, the inappropriateness of this North Korean plant is striking. The initial capital cost estimate was TSh12m (provided on soft-aid terms), equivalent to $1m at official exchange rates. By 1986 it had consumed TSh56m, equivalent to $3.1m at official exchange rates. It was estimated in 1986 that if the project came on stream as early as 1988, it would have cost TSh86m ($4.8m). All these estimates are in current prices, and since inflation rates in Tanzania have been substantial, the real cost of this plant will of course have been much larger. These capital costs compare with the projected price of the Botswana plant (in 1986 prices) of $3.34m for a plant of roughly three times the capacity, and of TSh8m if the same capacity of bricks were to be provided by medium-scale brick-pressing plants. When operating at full capacity, this automated Arusha plant will employ only 110 people. More significantly, if the experience of the Dar es Salaam brick factory is anything to go by, there are good reasons to doubt the level at which it will actually produce. In 1985 a Bulgarian-supplied large-scale brick factory with extrusion technology was opened in Dar es Salaam at a project cost of TSh169m (that is twice as much as the Arusha plant). Although this operates with a much better infrastructure (including oil for the furnaces), it produced only 3m bricks in its first operational year against its projected output of 20m. This does not augur well for the future of mass production in distant Arusha.

If this plant seems surprisingly inappropriate for Tanzania in general and

Arusha in particular, it is perhaps even more startling that a decision has already been made to set up a new Bulgarian-aided extruder production line on the same Arusha site, designed to produce 3.5m roof-tiles (or an equivalent amount of bricks) a year. Construction of this new line was begun in 1987, before the Korean-plant had even started production!

However, the Tanzanian state operates at a number of levels and at the same time as this long drawn-out process of innovation has been occurring, another parastatal has simultaneously been experimenting and developing a medium-scale alternative, also to be installed near Arusha. This medium-scale technology will be implemented through the initial aegis of a new parastatal, forged out of two previous ones (devoted respectively to the manufacture of agricultural implements, especially ox-carts, and the dissemination of AT). It has also been facilitated by ATI.

There are two phases to this smaller-scale project. The first phase, completed in early 1986, involved the testing of three alternative types of brick-press and two of crusher. Tests were undertaken simultaneously on local soils to determine their suitability for brick manufacture. Most of the equipment costs and some of the variable costs involved were borne by the international NGO. In the second phase the project moves to the level of innovation. It will comprise of a small-scale plant, using three presses and a purpose-built stationary kiln to produce approximately 1.6m bricks per year. The capital costs of this plant are less than TSh2m and the foreign-exchange and some of the other fixed costs of this will be covered by a five-year loan from an international NGO. It will be a privately owned venture, the shareholders drawn from the local area.

It is clear that as in the Botswana case no invention is involved. By contrast, though, technological development has been more extensive, adapting the large-scale plant to fuel availability, testing soils and various types of mixing and pressing technologies in the medium-scale plant. But the innovative process seems to have taken an inordinate amount of time — more than ten years for the large-scale and two years for the medium-scale plant.[17] Diffusion is also non-existent, except in the case of small-scale slop moulders. They produce on a very limited basis on the periphery of the largest towns, including Arusha.

Considering the institutional nexus of these events it is once again clear that despite obvious opportunities, the market mechanism, insofar as it functions in Tanzania, has not led to socially adequate levels of investment. The state has been involved in technological development, as well as in innovation. But what is especially interesting about this is the diversity of state actions. Two very different types of technological choice have been made by the 'same' state, one of an almost unbelievably inappropriate nature, the other much more relevant. An especially interesting characteristic of this activity in smaller-scale production is its links with personal accumulation by state-employees with assistance from an international body, Appropriate

Technology International. When this medium-scale technology moves to the implementation stage, the investment will not be undertaken by the parastatal itself, but rather by 8–10 individuals in their private capacity, assisted by a loan provided by ATI. Included amongst these individuals are the current director of the parastatal testing and developing the technology, the regional manager of the state-agency responsible for small-scale industry development, a local member of parliament and a prominent local lawyer. All of them owe their prominent role to their positions in the state apparatus, and will clearly be using the experience and contacts so gained to the maximum effect.

The development and innovation of the more appropriate brick-pressing technology rest crucially on the efforts of an international non-governmental organization. It has identified the technology, financed items of equipment to be tested, assisted in the testing and subsequent development process, and will provide the loans to facilitate innovation. It has substituted not only for the market but also for some of the classical functions of the developmental state.

Kenya

Of the three British East African economies (Kenya, Tanganyika and Uganda), Kenya achieved independence in the most turbulent fashion. Following a long military struggle in which the independence movement had obtained sufficient popular support, the settler-dominated government had no alternative but to grant the wishes of the mass of the population. Seemingly anticipating the inevitable at the onset of the armed struggle, the colonial government had taken steps in the early 1950s to create a class of indigenous capital, especially in the agricultural sector. The implementation of the Swynnerton Plan in 1952 was specifically designed to strengthen the tendency towards the individual ownership of land. At the same time a number of other factors contributed to the emergence of a class-stratified population. There had been an evolving tendency for the African population to participate in the trading sector, whilst coterminously the relatively advanced industrial sector had begun to spawn an African working class. Together with a growing shortage of arable land, the ingredients were there to provide for a dynamic and expansive class of industrial capital; all that was needed were the initial resources to fund industrial ventures, and these were variously provided during the 1960s, 1970s and 1980s through successive booms in commodity prices, access to the state machinery which provided monopoly rents of various sorts and occasionally also through the intervention of foreign-aid donors. (All of these various factors will emerge in our discussion below.)

In the mid-1970s it was common for Kenya to be viewed as a success story, at least in relation to growth if not with respect to development. And then the bubble seemed to burst, as a combination of high population growth and diminishing economic performance began to reduce average per capita incomes. After a brief resurgence during the coffee-boom of 1976–8, real per capita incomes continued their decline, falling by 4.8 per cent between 1980 and 1984. The prognosis for future growth does not look good, but even this pales into significance in relation to the existing and potential problem of unemployment.[18] Employment-creation, especially that in non-farm rural activities, as well as output maximization[19] will be major problems facing the Kenyan economy in the future. These are of course precisely the objectives which underlie the attempt to diffuse appropriate technologies in such economies.

Small-scale slop-moulded and clamp-fired bricks have been produced for many years and are still to be found in many rural areas of Kenya, especially in Western and Eastern Provinces. These brick enterprises are similar to those in Botswana (see pp. 86–7). 'Modern-sector' brick production is of more recent origin, beginning in the late 1940s when a plant was established near Nairobi. It has slowly expanded over the years and currently manufactures both roof tiles and bricks. In terms of brick-equivalents, production is about 17m bricks a year produced with mechanized mixers, extruders and a Hoffman kiln. Much of this equipment is old[20] and difficult to value, so detailed costings are impossible. By comparison with the two large-scale Tanzanian plants and the proposed large-scale plant in Botswana, the technology in place is relatively labour-intensive, especially for the Hoffman kiln which, unlike travelling-kilns, has to be loaded and unloaded manually. Whereas the proposed Botswana plant will employ 131 people to produce 24m bricks a year, this Kenyan factory employs 332 workers for the smaller annual production of only 17m bricks.

But since, as in Botswana and Tanzania, there is a ready market for good quality bricks and there is clearly unmet demand, there are two major proposals for extending small-scale brick production in the country. Whilst they have not yet come to fruition, their origins are of relevance to questions of innovation, particularly in comparison with what is occurring in Botswana and Tanzania. Although two separate sets of activities are involved, the respective entrepreneurs are close friends, went to the same school and, as will become apparent, are also engaged in a joint venture designed to push brick-making technology in the west of the country.

Venture A   This is funded by surplus generated in the trading sector. The entrepreneur involved is one of the country's leading commodity traders, exporting $7.5m of tea and coffee in 1986. One of his first attempts at diversification, in partnership with a local geologist, was to mine gold, but with the fall in gold prices in the mid-1980s this became unviable. His attention then turned to brick production, spurred by his recognition of the market opportunity and by his political contacts. Brick production will be underwritten by a contract for building materials on a site which he was

95

jointly developing with an Assistant Minister in Athi River, 30 miles east of Nairobi, involving the construction of 100 houses. Athi River contains soils suitable for brick production and this initial contract will be used to nurture a brick-factory into maturity. At projected costs the factory will be highly profitable, in relation both to cement blocks and the current market price for bricks. It is intended to start production with manually operated presses and, if sufficient demand exists, to upgrade these to mechanized presses, subsequently transferring the hand-operated presses to another planned site.

Subsidiary intentions exist to expand the brick interests of this entrepreneur should this housing venture lead to the successful establishment of a brick-factory. One possibility is to establish a smaller-scale brick-pressing plant at Kiambu, a densely populated site west of Nairobi, where the entrepreneur owns a number of plots which will be used as demonstrator sites for small-scale brick production. The fact that the brick-presses can be loaded onto a small pickup and have wheels for on-site transfer not only makes this type of decentralized production possible, but raises the possibility of substituting mechanized presses for the manual ones whenever adequate markets are generated. The final element in the brick-making plans of this businessman is the joint venture being considered with the second entrepreneur for diffusing the technology into the rural areas of the Western part of the country.

Venture B Whereas Venture A appears to be effectively unconstrained by a shortage of capital and to involve the employment of professionalized management, this second project is being generated by an entrepreneur who combines the four functions of invention, development, innovation and diffusion. He began as an academic and then moved into the fashionable area of energy studies. This had a dual function in so far as his brick interests are concerned: the consultancies which it spawned helped finance the development phase of his brick programme; and one of these energy-related projects took him to Thailand and resulted in his involvement in the manufacture of clay jiko-liners.[21] These liners are made from burnt clay and have provided the entrepreneur with extensive experience in clay-identification, mixing, firing and marketing.

Like Venture A, Venture B has two stages. The first involves extensive testing of soils, but with the specific intent of manufacturing soil-cement bricks. These possess three main advantages over bricks and cement bricks: they are said to use less cement (between 2–4 per cent versus 14 per cent) than cement blocks, do not require the costly firing of bricks, and can utilize a variety of soils. The major disadvantages of soil-cement are that it is as yet untested, it is unclear whether its cement content could be as low as 4 per cent and it does not yet meet the urban building standards, without which it cannot be used in formal-sector construction.[22] Phase 1 of this project therefore involves the systematic testing of these soil-cement bricks, made with soils drawn from around the country. If they fulfil promise, the brick-presses will be introduced as mobile units, going around the countryside on the back of a pickup, making soil-cement bricks on site ready for use a day later. Since the financial barriers to entry are so low in this operation (the presses cost only $2,500 each) and the presses require little skill to operate, the speed of innovation and a systematic knowledge of the varying soil characteristics are the key factors underlying success. Both these factors are recognized by the entrepreneur in question.

The second stage of Venture B involves collaboration with the Venture A trader in an operation which combines both skills in production and in trading. The central idea is that a vast potential market for either bricks or soil-cement bricks exists in the Western part of the country which is both densely populated and a long distance from the country's two cement plants. Therefore, after an initial stage in which the pressing technology's viability will be demonstrated through the mobile operations already described, the intent is to offer a package of technology and training to potential manufacturers in the Western region. The returns to this joint venture will come more from the sale of equipment than from surplus generated directly in production, although the two partners hold open their options of themselves producing if that turns out to be the most profitable alternative. As in the Tanzanian case, the initial testing phase is partly financed by an international NGO which imported the first brick-presses. It will also finance some of the costs of the Western Kenyan diffusion programme.

It is clear that unlike Botswana and Tanzania, there is some inventive activity in Kenya. Soil-cement blocks have obvious potential — they require less cement than cement blocks and, unlike clay bricks, require no firing. But despite this obvious potential, soil-cement technology is only in an embryonic state globally.[23] The private-sector entrepreneur in Venture B and the international NGO are thus both clearly involved in the process of invention, albeit of a technologically modest nature. There is also a process of technological development, merging with the 'invention' of the soil-cement formulae. Innovation and diffusion are as yet poorly developed — both ventures are still in the planning stage. But should these plans come to fruition, the 'Schumpeterian motor' has been clearly built into the stage of diffusion. Since the gains to the joint venture arise from the sale of packages of embodied technology and know-how, they clearly have a structural interest in maximizing diffusion.

Considering the institutional determinants of technological invention and development, and innovation/diffusion, the relative vibrancy of the private sector is evident in Kenya. There is already large-scale private-sector production of bricks, although the origins of this enterprise are to be found amongst the European settler population rather than indigenous entrepreneurs. The private sector is also actively involved in promoting further investments. Nevertheless the market has not operated in text-book fashion — demand is unmet and economically inappropriate large-scale technologies dominate. Moreover, without inputs from an international NGO, neither of the two proposed ventures would have been generated. Nor could they be implemented without active technological support from this NGO and, in at least one case, also with subsidized financial support.[24] Except through the role played by links with an Assistant Minister of Housing (which will allow entrepreneur A to underwrite the acquisition of basic brick-manufacturing skills), the Kenyan state seems to have played little role in technological invention/development, and innovation/diffusion.

Conclusions

From the point of view of brick production, Botswana shows signs of the least 'movement', with an unchanged pattern of small-scale informal sector production and with the one 'modern' small-scale plant being owned by an NGO. There is also little evidence of further diffusion. In Tanzania there has been some technological development in small-scale technology, but the one large-scale innovation which has occurred has been particularly inappropriate to local conditions. Only Kenya has experienced any invention and has also seen extensive technological development. But both innovation and diffusion remain undeveloped. In none of these countries has the demand for bricks been met, despite demonstrably profitable opportunities.

It is tempting to explain this varying pattern of invention, development, innovation and diffusion as a direct consequence of the particular policies adopted in each of these three countries. But this is partly to mistake cause for effect. It is, for example, at least as plausible to argue that the Tanzanian state was forced to take over the process of innovation in the 1970s because of the failure of private capital to innovate, as vice versa. Similarly, the method of project implementation utilized by the international NGO in Kenya may have been determined by the pre-existence of a class of indigenous industrial capital, rather than actually being instrumental in the formation of this group of industrialists.

However, the limitations on policy are not absolute. There is scope for sensitive initiatives, and this raises the question of institutional delivery. What is the best form for translating policy objectives into practice? In the environment of these three countries three institutions can be seen to have a role: private entrepreneurs, the state and NGOs. What generalizable conclusions can be drawn from their role in the brick industry in Botswana, Kenya and Tanzania? Are any of these three types of actors really able to meet the needs of poor consumers and poor producers?

Market failure and the role of the state
The respective roles played by states and markets in contemporary sub-Saharan Africa are an impassioned point of discussion. Following the World

Bank's influential account of the crisis in these economies it became common to ascribe poor economic performance to an overweening position being played by the state. (This is discussed further in Chapter 7.) Said to be insulated from market forces, to be prone to selecting inappropriate technologies and to be dulling of private-sector innovative efforts, much policy-focus has been given to culling the activities of parastatals and other forms of state backing for industry. Additional fuel for this approach has been provided by recent accounts of the success of the East Asian NICs in terms of their reliance on market forces[25] (even though more measured accounts of the experience of these countries have made it clear that there never was much evidence that these economies adopted the market-oriented policies which have been suggested).[26]

A casual view of the brick sector in these three countries may seem to lend support to this perspective. Kenya, in which the state has hitherto played no role, seems easily to be the most dynamic potential innovator. Moreover it is here that systematic attempts are being made to invent and develop the highly promising technology of soil-cement. It is Tanzania in which the prime example of inappropriate technology is to be found, most graphically in the case of socialist-state to socialist-state technology transfer. And in Botswana, the absence of a Schumpeterian-type profit incentive in an NGO-controlled enterprise is quite possibly the major factor limiting further diffusion of brick-pressing technologies.

Yet this characterization of 'state failure' is unjustified. Most importantly, the neglect of clear market opportunities and the utilization of inappropriate technologies in all three countries clearly represents a situation of simultaneous market failure, in which the market mechanism has proved to be a highly imperfect allocator of resources. Hence in both Tanzania and Botswana the state (or the NGOs acting as a quasi-state) initially came to be involved precisely because private capital was reluctant to innovate in the first place. Indeed, even now in Botswana the major impetus behind the construction of new brick-factories arises from the Ministry of Commerce and Industry rather than from private capital. Moreover it was in a Botswana NGO that the most appropriate (and potentially profitable) technology was first tested and implemented and much of the impetus to this was provided by the quasi-state role played by an international NGO. In Kenya, without the quasi-state role played by an international NGO, market opportunities will remain unmet for some time.

This situation of pervasive market failure cannot be explained by distortions in the price mechanism. (If this were the case, the appropriate policy response would be to reinforce the market mechanism rather than develop substitutes or complements to market allocation.) In Botswana and Tanzania (where more detailed costings are available), and almost certainly also in Kenya, relative prices are such that brick production is highly profitable. And, yet, demand remains unmet.

99

Thus instead of the situation being characterized as state versus markets, it is more accurately described as state and markets. The issue is thus one of what type of state intervention in what market context is most conducive to all four elements of the story: invention, technological development, innovation and diffusion. Instead of Tanzania being seen as an example of the negative role being played by the state, it can more correctly be seen as an example of the dual roles being played by different elements in a heterogeneous state. Moreover, amongst the aspirant owners of the small-scale brick-pressing technology are the current director of the parastatal developing the technology and the regional manager of the state agency responsible for small-industry development. Both owe their prominent role to their positions in the state apparatus, and will clearly be using the experience and contacts so gained to maximum effect. Similarly, in Kenya the nurturing of a new medium-scale brick factory is being undertaken in the protected environment of a new housing estate being built with an assistant minister and it is commonly accepted in that country that the business interests of MPs and ministers largely result from their official status and contacts.

In recognizing these complexities of market performance and state intervention, it is important to draw attention to the generalizability of individual country experiences. Kenya is a country in which class formation is most extensive and where private industrialists are actively seeking out profitable opportunities with large sums of investable funds arising in part from commodity booms, or rents provided by state-allocated quasi-monopolies.[27] Their wealth makes them less risk-averse than the smaller-scale capitalists investing in Botswana and Tanzania. For clearly understood historical reasons this is not an appropriate point of reference for Tanzania. The abolition of the role of the state in innovation there will not in itself necessarily lead to widespread innovation by the private sector. This is similarly the case in Botswana, especially in so far as indigenous small-scale entrepreneurship is concerned.

Thus, in determining the appropriate balance between states and markets, or the 'best' method of combining the two, it will not make much sense to generalize the conclusions across sub-Saharan economies, and possibly not even across different industries in the same economy. This is not to argue, of course, that the actual policies which were adopted in individual countries were necessarily most conducive to the innovation and diffusion of AT. There can be little doubt, for example, that in so far as AT is associated with the development of small-scale capitalism, the effective negation of much private-sector manufacturing investment in Tanzania for many years had the effect of slowing the development and diffusion of ATs. Similarly, Kenya's bias towards large-scale capitalist development has led to the neglect of opportunities for the utilization of ATs. Much of the parastatal investment which was substituted has been large scale and inappropriate in nature.[28]

The role of aid agencies and NGOs

Aid agencies have played an important role in the brick industries in these three countries. They have provided finance and have stimulated inventive, developmental and innovative activity. They have also been important, if not crucial, in a number of other areas, especially in the identification of ATs and (with the possible exception of soil-cement) the provision of ongoing technical assistance. Nevertheless the neglect of market opportunities suggests that it is not just the local state and private capital, but also the aid agencies which have not responded adequately to obvious market failures. And where they have responded, this has frequently been of an inappropriate nature. The North Korean extravaganza in Arusha is the clearest such example, but in a smaller way it also applies to the NGOs' preoccupation with modern-sector pressing technologies in all three countries.[29] The long-term neglect of slop-moulding and clamp-firing technologies, which is quite clearly the technological package which lends itself most readily to 'production by the masses', as well as producing output 'for the masses', is a case in point here. So, too, is the long delay involved in developing the potential of soil-cement technology.

But the NGOs cannot be placed in the same category as government-to-government aid. Unlike the latter, there are fewer powerful producer lobbies pressurizing NGOs to provide particular types of (generally inappropriate) technologies. Furthermore, the small size of technologies involved in NGO-directed aid is probably too trivial for the larger aid agencies. Similarly, the provision of ongoing technical assistance to relatively small enterprises is also beyond the experience, and probably also the capability, of the official government aid agencies.

Thus it is largely the NGOs who have come to play an important role in the development and extension of relatively small-scale technology in the brick industry in Botswana, Kenya and Tanzania. They have played a quasi-state role in the sense that in other environments where market failures are apparent these roles of stimulating investment, facilitating technological development and promoting innovation have traditionally been undertaken by state agencies. The particular strength of these NGOs has been their ability to promote relatively small-scale technologies although, as will be argued below there are reasons to believe that they could have gone further down this path than they did. By contrast, the relative weakness of the NGOs is the possibility that they are undermining the process of diffusion. The failure to exercise market discipline in NGO-funded enterprises — most graphically displayed in the case of Botswana — may well prove to be a structural weakness of this mode of institutional support.

Production for or by the masses

Although the concept of AT is inherently relative, it is widely accepted that the primary role of the AT institutions is to make available technologies which assist the mass of the population, especially that residing in rural areas. However, assistance rendered to the private sector in an attempt to quicken the pace of technological development, innovation and diffusion ('getting the Schumpeterian motor to work') may have the opposite effect of, in fact, helping the rich. Consider, for example, the dilemma posed to AT funders by the social position of the individuals involved in the diffusion of brick technology in Tanzania and Kenya. In Kenya one of the country's largest commodity exporters, operating in alliance with an Assistant Minister, stands to be a primary beneficiary; in Tanzania, the beneficiaries include a local Member of Parliament and the directors of the two parastatal agencies directly charged with the development and diffusion of AT. Thus, in so far as the Schumpeterian motor determines the rate of diffusion, this will most likely occur when the direct interests of private-sector innovators are consolidated. But these are almost always drawn from the richer, literate segments of the population who have access to the AT network. In terms of factor-incomes, spin-offs to the poor are likely to be confined to wage incomes.

On the other hand these dynamic business people are likely to ensure the relatively widespread availability of a high quality brick with uses not just in homes for the rich, but also in infrastructural investments such as schooling and hospitals. To some extent the interests of the mass of the population are served by the widespread availability of low-cost, durable and attractive building materials such as well-fired bricks. The policy dilemma for governments and aid donors is that maximizing AT diffusion (and the availability of cheap wage-goods) in the short run may well reinforce income inequalities in the long run.

This attempt to use the Schumpeterian motor to increase the rate of diffusion of ATs is, of course, undoubtedly an important question whose relevance and importance extends well beyond brick manufacture. But it is not the only distributional issue emerging from the activities of these NGOs. Although providing a relatively small-scale and appropriate technology by comparison with the large-scale extrusion and tunnel-kiln technologies, they seem to have been systematically driven towards a relatively high scale of technology provision and the neglect of the slop-moulding and clamp-firing informal sector enterprises. Their output is generally at least half as expensive as the modern-sector brick plants and their quality problems are not inherent to their technology, but reflect poor technological management. Improved management would also cut wastage and reduce fuel costs.

The direction of NGO technical assistance towards the higher income product and higher level technology appears to arise from the same sort of institutional fix experienced by government agencies, albeit at a somewhat lower level. The international AT agencies seem to feel more comfortable when collaborating with a counterpart agency than with isolated, generally illiterate entrepreneurs, many of whom do not speak English, and most of whom do not always operate 'regular hours' or maintain organized records. Such collaboration is easier to regulate and implement; it is also easier to defend when annual reviews of operations are carried out by external auditors, many of whom have no experience of informal-sector operations.

Broadly-based technical assistance to these small-scale entrepreneurs does not lead to a problematic choice of production for or by the masses, but rather it is production for and by the masses. This involves a change in orientation by international AT agencies. But these NGOs may not be able to provide the type of technical assistance which is required, necessitating sporadic contacts with apparently unreliable counterparts who are not prone to keeping books and only speak the vernacular. It is much more in the terrain of the resident volunteer (not those provided by the UN family who tend to go for the larger, intermediate upgrading of technology) than in the existing operating procedures of the itinerant international AT agency staff.

If it is true that such technical assistance inputs are not the comparative advantage of the international AT agencies, perhaps these agencies are better left to devote their attention to intermediate-level enterprises such as those using brick-presses and permanent kilns rather than slop-moulding and clamps. They will be helped in this by being able to collaborate with NGOs, and perhaps also larger-scale entrepreneurs and the state, who are already working in these areas but who (in Africa at least) are likely to push the choice of technology to a higher and probably more inappropriate plane, albeit less inappropriate than those technologies resulting from market-allocation or state investments. But if this is the case, then as has been argued already, these AT agencies may well necessarily find themselves in the constant dilemma of producing for or with the masses. Knowledge of the various projects in the portfolios of these international agencies suggests that the brick story is not an isolated case.

In this case, some of the primary tenets of the AT movement may have to be abandoned or qualified. Indeed, it was a particular concern of both Mahatma Gandhi and Fritz Schumacher, two of the pioneering spirits of the AT movement, that unless production was carried out by the masses, then they would never realize its benefits. Moreover, if the AT movement fails to ensure production by the masses, then *reductio ad absurdum* the role of the AT movement will be confined to maximizing the rate of economic growth by using descaled technologies and local inputs. Technologies will be supported because they make cheap commodities available for the mass of the population rather than because they are produced by the masses. The social content of their programmes will consequently be diminished.

CHAPTER 5

Developing an appropriate policy environment: small-scale sugar production

The AT movement has historically been preoccupied with interventions at the micro-level. Inputs have been provided to individual families, firms and plants in an attempt to upgrade their technological, entrepreneurial and managerial capabilities. Yet, as Stewart points out,[1] focusing these interventions at this disaggregated level only meets part of the problem. If the overall policy environment is unfavourable, any amount of microinterventions will have little overall effect in changing the prospects for AT. Often, the discussion of these macropolicies is confined to policy interventions aimed at 'getting the prices right', that is getting market signals to reflect the real cost of using inputs. Yet this is too restricted a focus for policy interventions, since there are a number of other macrofactors which have a significant impact on the development, innovation and diffusion of AT. Some of these macrofactors are relevant at the sectoral level, whilst others have relevance at the regional or national level.

The importance of both microinterventions and many of these wider macrofactors (including relative prices) emerges in the case of small-scale sugar technology.[2] A small-scale variant became the subject of research and development in the mid-1970s. Technological improvements were made so that in many developing-country environments it represents the economically optimal choice of technology. Yet this attractiveness is not reflected in the real world, and outside of India and Colombia, small-scale sugar plays a very minor role in sugar production.

How and why has this occurred?

Developments in the world sugar industry

Annual global sugar production (including both cane and beet sugar) is currently just short of 110m tonnes, and generally exceeds global consumption by a few million tonnes. Of this about 27m tonnes is traded between countries. However this trade occurs in a series of complicated arrangements: Cuba supplies sugar to the Eastern bloc under a special agreement; the ACP (Africa, Caribbean and Pacific) countries have preferential access to the EEC; and the US also purchases sugar from designated developing-country suppliers. These various preferential agreements account for around 7m tonnes and all involve the purchase of sugar at negotiated prices. The remainder of world trade — around 19m tonnes, less than 18 per cent of global production — is transacted at a residual price, generally much lower than the prices obtained through these quota sales. In times of shortage this residual price soars, whilst at periods of glut it plummets. Historically the high prices on the world market last for about one to two years, whilst the low prices last for around seven or eight years.[3]

Whilst the production of sugar continues to grow, demand-growth has begun to falter in recent years as alternative, particularly non-calorific sweeteners have become increasingly available. These include artificial sweeteners (such as aspartame and saccharin), high-fructose corn syrups and new intensely-sweet tree crops which are soon to come under commercial cultivation. The consequence of these long-term cyclical factors, the slow-down in demand-growth and the inherently residual nature of the global market is that the price for the 19m tonnes traded on the 'free market' is invariably lower than the costs of producing sugar. Figure 5.1 shows that in the nine years between 1978 and 85 the average daily price of sugar was less than the lowest estimated recurrent costs of sugar production.[4] At first glance, therefore, it would seem that it makes little sense for any country to produce sugar, and that it is therefore an inappropriate product. Why production continues and why this initial judgement of the inappropriateness of sugar production may not be accurate will be considered later in this chapter.

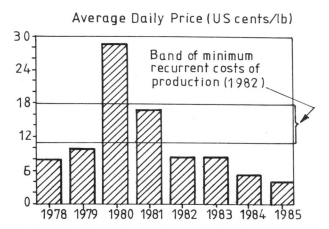

Figure 5.1. *World price and cost of sugar production*

105

The technological dimensions of choice

The production of sugar from cane involves the following major processes. First, the cane has to be crushed. The liquid which is obtained not only contains sucrose, but also a range of suspended solids, colloidal matter and other impurities. It therefore has to be clarified, during which the juice is purified prior to further processing. At this stage a liquid of water and sucrose is available, and consequently the water has to be removed by boiling the solution. This leaves a sticky residue of sugar, from which grains have to be obtained through a process of crystallization. Since not all sugar is available in crystal form (see below), the grains have to be separated by centrifuging the molasses, after which the sugar can be dried and packed.

One of the major problems in sugar processing is that there are two basic forms of sucrose: the first, which forms the bulk of consumption, is in crystal form, known in the industry as 'non-invert sugars'; the second is that of 'invert sugar', available only in liquid form and known to consumers as molasses. Since the bulk of sugar is consumed in crystal form and since this commands a higher price than liquid molasses, the major cane-processing task is to maximize the yield of non-invert granular sugar. Here there are basically three factors which affect the product mix: the purity of the juice emerging from the clarifying process; the temperature at which the water is boiled off; and the duration of the boiling process. The first of these is a relatively simple problem and has few scaling consequences. The other two are interconnected and have major implications for the choice of technology.

The nature of the boiling process accounts for the primary source of scale economies in the industry. This is because the production of undesirable invert-sugars is adversely affected by the temperature at which the water is boiled off from the juice — the higher this temperature, and the longer the process of boiling, the smaller the yield of granular sugar. It was in the mid-nineteenth century that the technological solution was found to these problems. Because the boiling point of water is lower under vacuum conditions, it was realized that granular sugar yields could be increased if the boiling process could take place in a semi-vacuum spherical pan called a vacuum-pan (VP). This had the additional attribute of reducing the energy costs in the boiling process and hence offered an additional advantage over the existing technology which boiled the water off in a series of pans open to the elements (OPS) except for a roof to shield the boiling process from the rain.[5]

It is in this transition from open to vacuum pan boiling that the major technological differences arise. This is because there is an inherent engineering relationship involved in processes occurring within spheres. Since the ratio of an increase in volume to an increase in circumference is only 0.6, there are intrinsic scale economies in larger-scale plants. Hence, beginning from a crushing capacity of about 200 tonnes of cane per day

106

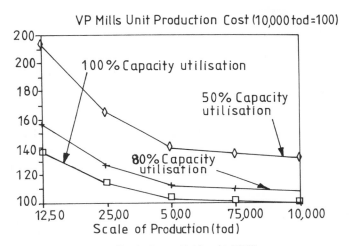

VP Mills Unit Production Cost (10,000 tod = 100)

Source: Compiled from Tribe (1989)

Figure 5.2. *Scale economies in VP plants (10,000tcd = 100)*

(hereafter tcd) in the mid-nineteenth century, the most technologically efficient plants now crush in excess of 20,000tcd. The extent of scale economies arising in VP production is shown in Figure 5.2, from which it can be seen that the major scale economies are realized in plants crushing around 10,000tcd. However, as is to be expected, because these plants tend to be highly capital intensive, the costs of sub-optimal capacity utilization are high.[6]

Yet although these very large-scale mills, benefiting from all the economies of scale inherent in processing industries, are clearly the most technologically efficient plants, they account for only a minority of global sugar production. There are a number of reasons for this (some of which will be considered in detail later in this chapter), amongst which the following are the most important:

• the market may not be large enough to absorb the output of a large plant running at full capacity, and local production costs will often be higher than prices received on the world market (that is, unless they fall within one of the various preferential quotas) making exports disadvantageous;
• the managerial problems involved in large-scale production are very complex. For example, a 10,000tcd plant will involve the delivery and

107

Table 5.1. VP sugar factories with capacities of less than 1,000tcd (excluding China)

Country	Number of factories	Capacity range
Angola	1	700
Argentina	1	700
Bangladesh	1	300
Burma	4	50–600
Colombia	1	400
Costa Rica	12	300–800
Dominican Republic	1	500
Ecuador	3	150–900
Grenada	1	500
Guatemala	3	50–450
Guinea	1	400
India	35	500–982
Indonesia	1	900
Japan	13	360–950
Mali	1	400
Mexico	4	600–950
Nepal	1	500
Nicaragua	1	600
Pakistan	1	550
Paraguay	4	200–800
Peru	2	300–450
Philippines	1	478
Rwanda	1	150
Sierra Leone	1	400
Spain	3	300–600
Thailand	2	50–982

Source: Hagelberg (1989).

off-loading of a 10-tonne truck every 90 seconds, round the clock. Failing to co-ordinate this effectively can have high costs, for if cane is left to stand its sucrose content diminishes rapidly. The larger the plant, the greater the extent of these managerial hurdles;

- the production of adequate supplies of cane on a regular and predictable basis may not be possible. Experience shows cane shortfalls are more likely in rain-fed agriculture (especially in sub-optimal ecological zones), where unstable pricing regimes prevail, where soil degradation is occurring and where smallholder production is prevalent. One or more of these conditions often prevail in many developing country environments, making large-scale plants more difficult to operate;

- there may be many diseconomies of scale in large-scale plants, especially those which are outside of the plant itself — lack of adequate infrastructure may require the construction of new roads, large agglomerations of full-time estate workers may require new houses and poor industrial linkages may make the maintenance of sophisticated large-scale plant difficult.

Consequently, many countries which have committed themselves to VP technology are unable to provide the conditions under which these scale economies can be realized, and have had to settle for plants of much smaller capacity than the optimal 10,000tcd size. There are around 100 plants in 25 countries which operate VP mills of less than 1,000tcd capacity (Table 5.1). In addition, in China in 1983, 148 sugar factories were of a capacity of between 500–1,000tcd, and 169 factories had capacities lower than 500tcd; indeed, only 42 out of the 359 Chinese cane sugar factories had a capacity of more than 1,000tcd. Until very recently, Indian planners aimed at VP plants of 1,250tcd as the optimal plant size for Indian operating conditions. It can be seen from Figure 5.2 that production at these levels involves a more than doubling of sugar production costs. These extra costs incurred in small-scale VP production can be substantial, for even best-practice large-scale plants have difficulty in keeping recurrent production costs lower than the residual 'free market' price at which excess sugar has to be sold, or where supplies can be purchased.

It is in this context that the evolution of small-scale OPS plants can be situated. The processing of sugar cane to provide sweeteners has a history dating back beyond 325BC, originating in the South Pacific and then passing on through Asia to India where the first granular sugars were probably produced. For much of the two subsequent millennia the processing technology remained crude. The cane was squeezed by ox-powered rollers, the juice was boiled in open pans and then left to crystallize in earthen jars for two or three weeks. The separation of crystals was achieved by storing the residue in sacks weighed down with heavy stones for about a week.

The consequence of these rough and ready methods was that crystal formation was poor. Two types of final products emerged: most commonly a thick sticky brown substance called jaggery (panella in Latin America) was produced, involving a combination of both invert (that is, molasses) and non-invert sugars; since jaggery possesses a strong taste and does not dissolve easily, so often granular sugar was produced. But this final sugar was usually discoloured, had a high molasses content and was made up of unevenly sized crystals. Moreover the sugar yield was only about 5 per cent of crushed cane.

The nineteenth century saw the introduction of the first VP mills. Not only were they energy self-sufficient (burning the crushed cane to satisfy their energy needs), but they were also able to obtain a much higher yield of sugar and to produce a more evenly textured product. By the early 1970s these modern VP mills were achieving sugar recovery rates of between 9 and 11 per cent (depending upon ecological zones). Yet the OPS plants had not escaped improvement, initially through the introduction of mechanized centrifuges (replacing the bags weighed down with stones) in the 1920s, and then subsequently through the utilization of sulphitation clarification in the 1950s, which had the effect of increasing sugar yields. By the early 1970s, therefore, the improved Indian OPS plants had achieved a sugar recovery rate of around 7–8 per cent (depending upon ecological zones). At this time they were the subject of economic analysis in which it was concluded that although their capital costs were much lower than the inherently capital-intensive VP plants, this was outweighed by their significantly lower sugar recovery rates.[7] Their continued survival and prosperity — there were over 8,000 small-scale OPS plants producing crystal sugar in India — was said to derive from a policy environment in which small-scale sugar was preferentially treated by comparison with large-scale VP plants.

There is some doubt about the validity of these economic analyses (see pp. 111–13). But whatever their accuracy they were soon rendered irrelevant by two significant technological developments in OPS technology, both occurring in the late 1970s. The first and most significant concerned the boiling stage, where under traditional furnace designs only dried bagasse (that is, crushed cane) could be utilized as fuel. (By contrast, VP mills were able to burn their bagasse directly after crushing.) Consequently, an extensive labour force was required to lay out the crushed bagasse so that it could dry in the sun. This not only required extensive land, but meant also that when it rained the boiling process had to be suspended until sufficient wet bagasse could be dried. A change in furnace type, utilizing a design well-known in the industrialized countries, transformed this picture since crushed bagasse could be fed directly into the furnace without prior drying. The new furnace design also meant a much better control over the boiling process so that the sugar recovery yield increased marginally.

The second major improvement involved a change in basic juice-extraction technology. Previously the OPS plants had utilized a series of roller mills modelled on those incorporated in VP mills. However because they were unable to take advantage of inhibition (in which the remaining juice in the crushed cane is washed out with water),[8] the rate of juice extraction was only about 67 per cent. But based upon an old screw-expeller technology which Indian engineers found in Quebec, a new form of crushing was developed which increased the juice yield to around 72 per cent, close to that achieved by the large-scale VP plants using inhibition. This development had a particularly significant impact in raising sugar-recovery rates.

As a consequence of the introduction of both these two technological innovations, labour and energy costs were reduced, less land was required and sugar recovery rates of OPS mills were increased from 7–7.5 per cent to between 8–9 per cent. This transformed their profitability relative to that of many VP mills, initially in India and subsequently in Kenya.

The choice of technology in India

The improvements to OPS technology were introduced in India in the late 1970s, at a stage in which these small-scale plants were holding their own against competition from the large-scale VP sector. At that time around 10 per cent of all Indian cane was utilized by over 8,000 OPS mills, 30 per cent by the VP sector, 10 per cent for seed and chewing and the remainder by jaggery mills.[9] But merely focusing on relative shares provides an unsatisfactory window into the financial and economic attractiveness of these two families of technologies since they operated under very different legal and pricing environments. On the one hand the OPS were favoured by being able to sell all of their output on the free market, whereas the VP sector was nominally obliged to sell between 60 and 70 per cent of its output at controlled prices of about half the market rate. Yet this handicap was more apparent than real, since many large-scale plants (especially new or expanded ones) were exempt from the requirement to sell the major portion of their output at these controlled prices. In many cases large-scale VP plants were provided with soft loans and state governments were authorized to subsidize cane prices, in some cases by more than 40 per cent. Small-scale OPS plants were also subject to various taxes, usually based upon the size of their centrifuges.[10]

Thus it is no easy matter to determine whether the large-scale VP mills were more or less adversely affected by the policy environment than were the small-scale OPS mills. If older VP mills are considered then OPS is probably favoured significantly by this legislative environment since most of these older plants are obliged to sell a major portion of their output at controlled prices. On the other hand, the newer and larger VP mills are largely exempt from these restrictions and probably fare rather well in comparison to OPS.

These general conclusions need to be substantiated and it is in doing so that it is possible to identify a key component of the macro-economic environment which has affected the development and diffusion of sugar technology in India. The detailed economic analysis is drawn from the production of sugar in northern India, in Uttar Pradesh, in 1982.[11] There the declared costs of production of the large-scale VP sector (based upon returns submitted by these mills, an average recovery rate of 9.6 per cent and an average plant-size of between 1,250 and 1,500tcd) was Rs326.02 per quintal. By contrast, the average costs of production of the unimproved OPS plants were Rs420.86 per quintal for the 100tcd plant and Rs399.02 for the 200tcd OPS plant. Thus even the improved OPS plants appeared to have higher costs of production than the VP mills, at Rs355.96 per quintal for a 100tcd plant, and Rs334.19 for a larger 200tcd mill (Table 5.2).

Yet these initial calculations suggesting higher production costs by the smaller-scale plants do not really provide an adequate basis for comparison. There are two reasons for this. First, although the calculations are corrected

Table 5.2 Relative costs of production: India (Rs per quintal)

	VP	Unimproved OPS 100tcd	Unimproved OPS 200tcd	Improved OPS 100tcd	Improved OPS 200tcd
At market prices, historic capital costs	326.02	–	–	–	–
At market prices, replacement capital costs	395.00	420.86	399.02	355.96	334.19
With same wage rates, replacement capital costs	395.00	441.13	420.86	373.66	347.79

to ensure that both the small- and large-scale mills paid the same prices for their cane, these different-sized mills pay very different wage costs, and taking these into account further exaggerates the cost disadvantage of the OPS sector (Table 5.2); second, an even more significant bias in these costings arises from the undervaluation of capital in these large-scale plants. Capital costings in the 'average Uttar Pradesh VP mills' were based on historic costs. Since most of these VP mills were old, and operated in the context of an inflationary economy, the depreciation of capital costs on historic, rather than replacement, cost severely underestimates the real cost of capital. For example, in these average costs of Rs325.02 per quintal, the estimation of capital costs was only Rs5.86 per quintal. Yet, the replacement cost of a 1,250tcd mill in 1982 was Rs80m, which if depreciated over 20 years (at 10 per cent) and operated at average capacity utilization, should have led to a depreciation charge of Rs70 per quintal. By contrast the calculations of OPS costs of production assumed a full repayment of capital costs on a replacement basis.

Thus, consideration of realistic capital costs transforms the picture of relative profitability. This is largely because under the existing accounting regime, the large-scale mills — most of which are in the parastatal or co-operative sector and heavily depreciated — virtually exclude their primary processing cost from their accounts. This is akin to the small-scale plants writing off virtually all their labour costs.

There is no clear indication of shadow prices in India, so it is not possible to 'fine tune' the discussion of the economic (as opposed to the financial) characteristics of these two sets of technologies. As, however, the economy suffers from recurrent balance of payments problems, has significant levels of unemployment and faces a savings constraint, it is instructive to assess the extent to which OPS and VP mills utilize these primary factors of production. Table 5.3 provides information on the coefficients of production and Table 5.4 estimates the number of workers required and the capital costs involved in attaining 1982 sugar output by utilizing either VP or OPS technology.

112

Table 5.3. Coefficients of production of OPS and VP technologies: India[a]

	Captial/ labour (Rs)	Output/ labour (tons)	Output/ capital (tons/Rs000)
VP	91,954	18.1	0.20
OPS	22,099	6.15	0.28

[a] Calculated on basis of median-sized VP mills of 1,250tcd and 200tcd improved OPS plant.

Table 5.4. Capital and labour utilization and number of plants required to achieve 1982 production levels (5,150,000 tons): India[a]

	No. of Plants	Capital cost (Rsm)	Employment
VP	327	26,160	284,490
OPS	2,682	18,492	836,784

[a] Calculated on basis of median-sized VP mills of 1,250tcd and 200tcd improved OPS plant.

The OPS plants have a much lower capital cost per workplace than the VP mills, offset to some extent by a lower productivity of labour. Yet since their productivity of capital is higher, both technologies can be classified as economically efficient (see Chapter 1). The potential significance of this greater labour intensity and the smaller scale of output of the OPS plants are graphically illustrated if it is assumed that India's total sugar production resulted either from 1,250tcd VP mills or 200tcd improved OPS plants. Instead of 327 large-scale factories costing Rs26,160m and employing only 284,490, production could be spread around a far larger range of sites (2,682), involving the decentralization of economic activity and allowing farmers in areas with limited acreage available for cane to benefit from cash earnings from this crop. An extra 552,000 people would be employed in the processing sector and there would have been a saving of investment of almost Rs8,000m. To be set against this is the fact that more land would have been required, since the sugar recovery rate from cane is lower in OPS plants than in VP mills. It is just such a trade-off which makes it difficult to determine unambiguously which is the appropriate technology.[12]

The choice of technology in Kenya

Sugar production began in Kenya in the 1920s, with two relatively small-scale VP plants. One was established in the less ecologically favourable coastal region, the other in the more hospitable Western area. After Independence in 1964, five new plants were established in the Western part of the country and production grew rapidly. For a time (between 1978 and 1981) domestic production exceeded demand, but thereafter a fall in production and a continued rise in consumption led to a growing need for importation (Figure 5.3). Two small-scale OPS plants were established in the 1970s, one in 1974 and the other in 1977. Both failed. In large part this was due to the sub-optimality of the equipment which was chosen. But one of the plants was also established by a farmer's co-operative and was subject to poor managerial control. However, at the beginning of the 1980s a modern OPS plant was established and this continued to thrive, expanding production right through the decade. Its performance forms the basis of comparison between large- and small-scale sugar production in Kenya.

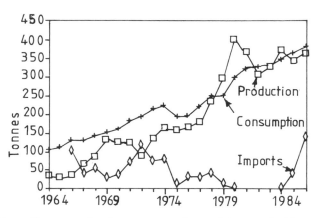

Production, Consumption and Imports

Figure 5.3   *Sugar production, consumption and imports in Kenya*

Explaining the fall in sugar production in the 1980s, key decision-takers involved in the formulation of sugar policy argued that six factors were especially important:

- inadequate arrangements for crop financing
- drought in 1980–1 and 1984
- poor research efforts
- lack of effective and co-ordinated extension services to farmers

114

- inappropriate high costs of new investments and financial structures
- high financial costs to sugar companies resulting from the devaluation of the Kenya Shilling, since some costs necessitate the expenditure of foreign exchange. (Nyongeza and Mbuthia, 1989)

These explanations suggest a *prima facie* case in favour of the smaller-scale OPS technology since, given the capital intensity of the VP mills, they are more likely to make intensive use of foreign exchange. Moreover some of the other explanations (such as uncoordinated extension and the inappropriate financial structures of these large-scale plants) suggest that there might have been some diseconomies of scale. Was this indeed the case, and does it suggest an important role for small-scale OPS technology in Kenya's sugar sector? In order to assess this it is necessary to take a more detailed look at the cost and production structures of these two types of sugar processing technology in Kenya.

In mid-1982, when this research was conducted, the structure of Kenyan sugar prices was as follows. Ex-factory selling prices were KSh3,600 per ton. In addition to this there was an excise duty of KSh1,000 per ton, a Kenya National Trading Corporation (KNTC) levy of KSh690 per ton,[13] a wholesalers margin of KSh116 per ton and a retailers margin of KSh344 per ton. The final retail selling price was thus KSh5,750 per ton. This controlled retail price was highly sensitive to political pressures since sugar was a basic foodstuff. So, too, was the price offered to cane growers, who comprised a politically vocal rural constituency. Thus, over the years, the margins available to sugar processing were squeezed at both ends. As a consequence, none of the VP mills, including Mumias, the largest and most efficient VP mill crushing 7,000tcd, could operate at a profit.[14]

Unlike the modern OPS plant currently operating (which is owned by an Asian citizen), the two earlier OPS plants had been established by indigenous African citizens. Their political influence had led to an important price concession, absolving them from selling sugar through the KNTC and thereby saving them from paying this levy. This concession granted to small-scale sugar plants remained on the statute books, so that the modern OPS plant established in the early 1980s continued to benefit, receiving an ex-factory price of KSh4,335 per ton compared to the KSh3,600 per ton obtained by the VP mills. At this selling price the costs of production in this small-scale OPS plant were such that as long as its sugar recovery rate was greater than around 7.5 per cent, it could be profitably operated (Figure 5.4). Only if a recovery rate in excess of 9 per cent was achieved — which was at the upper end of feasibility for this small-scale plant — could the OPS technology continue to run profitably at an ex-factory price of KSh3,600 per ton. But, as has been shown, neither could any of the VP mills realize profitable production at this price, even though their sugar recovery rates varied from 9.3–11.2 per cent.

115

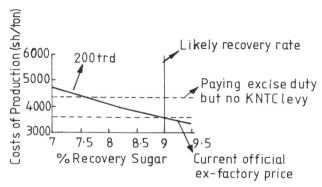

Figure 5.4   *Costs of production for 200tcd improved OPS plant in relation to sugar recovery rate: Kenya*

There is a further factor suggestive of the high relative profitability of this OPS plant. As in India, the VP costs of production grossly underestimated their capital costs. The most efficient VP mill, Mumias, was depreciating its capital on its historic cost of K30m, which was significantly below its replacement cost. These were estimated by a variety of sources to be much higher. Based upon Mumias's own estimates a more realistic figure would have been just over K£100m; on the experience of the recently installed neighbouring South Nyanza plant, the replacement capital costs were just over K130m; and according to World Bank cost estimates, a figure of almost K£300m would have been more accurate. Depreciating these costs at 10 per cent over 20 years provides an additional cost of KSh1,400–5,000 per ton.

In this light it is possible to see that the controlled price of sugar was basically set to enable the more efficient large-scale producers to recover their recurrent costs of production. (By contrast, the small-scale mill was in the private sector and was obliged to produce a return on total capital costs — this issue will be treated in more detail, pp. 129–32.) Hence the incorporation of more realistic depreciation charges in the costings of the large-scale mills would have allowed the small-scale OPS plant, already profitable at an ex-factory price of KSh4,335 per ton, only KSh690 above the official price, to produce at a very significant rate of profit.

Corroboration of the financial attractiveness of this small-scale OPS plant can be obtained from the fact that right through the 1980s it continued to operate profitably. This was a period in which of the VP mills, only Mumias was able to also show a positive bottom line on its balance sheet, despite the fact that none of them actually paid excise tax for most of this period and that they were depreciating capital at historic costs. It was also only the OPS plant

116

which was able to survive if exposed to the winds of market forces since whilst it was wholly privately owned, all of the VP mills were predominantly owned by parastatals, and (except for Mumias) continued to accumulate losses.

Comparing the operation of small-scale OPS plants, it is probable that OPS production is relatively more profitable in Kenya than in India. This is for two major reasons. First, and perhaps this reflects the more recent history of sugar production in Kenya, most of the VP mills have consistently run at less than optimal capacity. Moreover, during the 1980s there was a tendency for the rate of capacity utilization to fall in many of the Kenyan VP mills (Table 5.5). (It is interesting that there was no clear tendency for capacity utilization to be greater for older mills — suggesting a process of learning by doing — nor for the decline in capacity utilization during the first half of the 1980s to reflect the age of the mills.) Second, both VP and OPS plants are produced by the Indian capital goods sector, whereas in Kenya only OPS equipment is made domestically. This means that the ratio of VP to OPS capital costs is very different in the two countries — the installed costs of VP plants are 9.5 times cheaper per unit of crushing capacity in India than in Kenya, whilst the ratio for OPS plants is only 4:1.

Table 5.5. Capacity utilization in the Kenyan VP sector

	Date of establishment	Capacity (tcd)	Capacity utilization (1979–80)	Production 1981	(000 tons) 1985
Miwani	1920s	1,200	67.1	31.0	11.0
Ramisi	1920s	1,530	65.1	8.3	10.8
Muhuroni	1966	1,800	81.1	36.6	38.0
Chemelil	1968	2,235	91.7	51.4	51.8
Mumias	1973	7,000	98.8	168.0	182.0
Nzoia	1980	2,000	97.5	44.0	29.7
SONY	1980	2,000	65.6	29.6	16.7

Source: Kenya Sugar (1981); Interviews; Lone (1989).

The high relative capital cost of VP production in Kenya is reflected in the coefficients of production of the two sets of technologies (Table 5.6). Based upon an estimate of replacement capital costs of £130m for a plant of 7,000tcd capacity,[15] the capital cost per workplace is almost 22 times greater than in the small-scale plant. As is to be expected, since both types of technology are economically efficient, the VP mills have a much higher productivity of labour (nine times as great). Translating these coefficients into the production of all of Kenya's 1982 sugar output, an even more striking policy choice emerges in Kenya than in India (compare Tables 5.6 and 5.3). Instead of three large-scale VP mills,[16] Kenya's sugar production could have been met by 81 smaller plants, employing 21,500 more workers and saving K£241m,

Table 5.6 Coefficients of production of OPS and VP technologies: Kenya

	Capital/ labour (K£)	Output/ labour (tons)	Output/ capital (tons)
VPa	76,471	136	0.015
OPSb	3,497	15	0.023

a Based on performance by the most efficient VP mill in Kenya (Mumias) of 7,000tcd.
b 200tcd improved OPS plant.

most of which was foreign exchange (Table 5.7). Again, as in India, these policy attractions are to some extent outweighed by the greater land-intensity of OPS production although some of the social costs of this are already reflected in the analysis in a greater cost of cane by the OPS plant.

One factor undermining the appropriateness of OPS technology is that per unit of crushing capacity, the OPS plant makes significantly more intensive use of expatriate staff (Table 5.8) than does the largest of the VP mills. To some extent Mumias's ability to do this partly reflects the greater capital intensity of its equipment; it has also benefited from a prior history of VP production in the region which led to the development of a pool of transferable intra-industry skills on which Mumias could draw. By contrast the OPS plant is a pioneering enterprise and this shows in its initial need to employ Indian kharigars to control the boiling process. These skills were rapidly transferred to indigenous Kenyan citizens and this accounts for the early fall in the number of expatriates, down by two-thirds within the first five years of operation (compared to only one-third in the case of Mumias). Thus whilst the evidence is suggestive of a greater expatriate-intensity of small-scale sugar production in the early years, the conclusions are ambiguous.

These considerations of financial and economic performance meet only part of the task of assessing the appropriateness of technological choice. As

Table 5.7 Capital and labour utilization and number of plants required to achieve 1982 production levels (380,000 tons): Kenya

	No. of plants	Capital cost (K£m)	Employment
VPa	2.6	338	4,420
OPSb	81	91	25,920

a Based on performance by the most efficient VP mill in Kenya (Mumias) of 7,000tcd.
b 200tcd improved OPS plant.

118

Table 5.8. Tons of crushing capacity per expatriate employed: Kenya

Year of operation	Mumias	OPS Plant
1	140	17
2	206	25
3	219	33
4	259	40
5	219	50
6	280	67
7	292	–
8	368	–
9	388	–
14[a]	1,750	–

[a] Information for years 10–13 not available.
Source: Derived from Lemmings (1989).

was argued in Chapter 2, social and environmental considerations also need to be taken into account. Unlike the financial and economic analyses which focused directly on the sugar processing, the assessment of social appropriateness is more relevant in relation to the farming of cane.

First, is sugar production an appropriate product? Is it associated with patterns of agricultural activity which have socially adverse characteristics? Second, are particular sets of social characteristics causally associated with the two different types of processing technology? In comparing the characteristics associated with the small- and large-scale factories, it is possible that some of the observed differences arise from factors which have little to do with the processing technology itself. For example, variations in farmer behaviour may reflect the longer life of the VP factories (some dating from the early 1970s) compared to the OPS plant (beginning production a decade later); they may also predate the arrival of cane farming and reflect social and political events in pre-colonial times; or they may reflect the ecological characteristics of the two different regions.

Choice of farming technology
Cane yields appear to be greater for farmers serving the large-scale factories. Makanda compared yields (in tonnes per hectare) in two areas — those serving the OPS plant in Kabras and those providing cane to the Miwani/Chemelil/Muhoroni VP mills.[17] Neither area is as ecologically favourable as the catchment areas for the Mumias/Nzoia mills. Farmers providing cane to the OPS plant obtained an average of 70 t/h on the first crop, 40 t/h on the second and 30 t/h on the third. By contrast, farmers servng the VP mills obtained 80–100 t/h on the first crop, 60–90 t/h on the second and 50–75 on the third crop. But these figures only reflect gross output and account needs

119

to be taken of factor inputs, especially chemicals. Makanda argues that because of the greater input intensity of the farmers serving the VP mills their break-even cane yield (61 t/h) is far higher than that for the farmers serving the OPS plant (43 t/h).[17] He concludes from this that the discounted rates of return are in fact greater for those farmers serving the OPS plant.

A recent survey of farmers producing cane for both the Mumias VP plant and the Kabras OPS plant reaches similar conclusions, namely that the chemical input intensity by farmers producing for the VP mills is far higher. But the data which emerge from Table 5.9 also point to three other relevant developments: first, whilst in the Mumias area the cane farmers appear to be more 'progressive' than non-cane farmers (defined by the use of chemical inputs), the opposite is true in the Kabras area (the potential significance of this will be considered below); second, cane farmers in general tend to make greater use of more capital-intensive ploughing than non-cane farmers; third, farmers serving the OPS plant made more intensive use of ox-ploughing than those producing cane for the VP mills.[18]

Table 5.9. Input use by farmers in Kabras and Mumias catchment areas (percentage of farmers)

| Input | Mumias (VP) | | Kabras (OPS) | |
	Cane farmers	Other farmers	Cane farmers	Other farmers
Manure	61.1	63.3	88.6	77.1
Fertilizer	100.0	20.2	45.7	52.1
Pesticides	12.6	8.2	8.6	16.7
Owning ox-plough	26.8	12.8	54.3	43.8
Owning tractor	2.1	0	2.9	4.2
Hiring tractor	19.5	5.5	17.6	4.2

Source: Derived from Lemmings (1989).

These conclusions on the greater labour intensity of the OPS farmers are confirmed by Makanda's comparison between the Kabras farmers and those serving the Miwani/Chemelil/Muhoroni complexes. He found that not only did a lower proportion of Kabras farmers use chemical inputs but also that, when they did, they tended to do so in significantly lower doses. The VP mill farmers also made much more intensive use of mechanized ploughing. In addition, Makanda identified the greater labour intensity of cane production compared to other crops — 1,746 person hours per hectare compared to 325 person hours per hectare for maize. Cane production in general, and production for the OPS plant in particular, contributed very significantly to employment generation in an area which has had a long-term problem with unemployment.

Inequality in land holdings

The transition from communal to individual land tenure systems began in the late 1950s, so that when cane farming was introduced, it was against a background of private property rights. In the early years of the Mumias complex (1970–75), there was a five-fold spurt in land transactions but the significance of this should not be overestimated since only 2 per cent of total land in the Mumias catchment area was affected.

A comparison of land distribution between the areas growing cane for the large-scale Mumias VP mill and the small-scale Kabras OPS plant shows different patterns (Table 5.10). Average farm size in the Mumias area is greater than that in the Kabras region. Within these two areas, cane farmers tend to have larger farms than non-cane farmers, and the degree of land inequality in the Mumias area, as well as the difference between cane and non-cane farmers, is much greater than in the Kabras region.

Table 5.10. Average farm size (percentage of farms)

Farm size	Mumias (VP)		Kabras (OPS)	
	Cane farmers	Non-cane farmers	Cane farmers	Non-cane farmers
<1	6	28	8	18
1–2	24	43	43	35
2–3	27	17	17	15
3–4	12	3	13	13
>4	31	9	19	19
Av Farm Size (ha)	4.00	1.59	2.74	2.35

Source: Lemmings (1989).

Class formation These patterns of land holdings suggest an interaction between cane farming and class formation — cane farmers tend to hold larger plots than non-cane farmers. But at the same time the degree of inequality is significantly higher in the areas growing cane for the VP mills. Insofar as the concentration of land holdings is an indication of the process of class formation, there would appear to be a correlation between the introduction of cane and the growth of social differentiation. What is less clear, though, is whether within this, the production of cane for large-scale factories involves an even more rapid process of class formation. Is it this which reflects the greater inequality of land holdings in the Mumias area, or is it rather that the Mumias mill has been operating for a longer period of time? If the latter explanation were to hold, the degree of inequality may continue to increase in the Kabras area.

Class formation is not only to be reflected in the growth of capital holdings, but also in the development of wage labour. As has already been indicated, cane is more labour intensive than other crops. A hectare of cane requires approximately 1,746 person hours of labour a year, but the average family in the Kabras area is only able to provide 2,960 hours a year.[19] If more than one hectare of land is devoted to cane, then the hiring of labour will be essential. If seasonal labour demands are considered, then even a 1-hectare sized holding will require the employment of wage labour. Two-thirds of the Mumias cane farmers hired labour, compared to only one-third of the non-cane farmers. In the Kabras region the figures were less differentiated (52.9 versus 47.1 per cent). It is interesting that the average wage paid on cane farms in both areas was greater than that paid by non-cane farmers. In addition, average wage rates were higher in the Mumias region than in Kabras. The wage premium on cane farms in Mumias was much higher for males than for females, suggesting that the labour market in the formal sector (predominantly employing males) was far tighter in Mumias than in Kabras.

An analysis of the degree of involvement in other businesses corroborates the conclusion that cane and sugar production tends to be associated with a process of class formation.[20] Whereas 75 per cent of Mumias cane farmers had other businesses, the proportions for other groups were as follows: 25 per cent for non-cane farmers in Mumias; 14 per cent for cane and non-cane farmers in Kabras. Interestingly, a high proportion (36 per cent) of workers at the Mumias factory also owned other businesses, the bulk in trading. Only a few were involved in small-scale maize mills, knitting and workshops.

Nutrition and social welfare

It is often argued that when peasant farmers become involved in cash crops such as cane, they neglect the production of subsistence crops such as maize and beans. This is associated frequently with a switch in the balance of intra-family power. Women have been responsible traditionally for the control of food crops, and men for cash crops. The switch from one to the other is said to be associated with the purchase of durable consumer goods by men, or investment in low-yielding education, both at the expense of family welfare.

Certainly the data provided by the detailed surveys of Makanda, Odada et al. and Lemmings show many of these phenomena. The growth of cane production has clearly occurred at the expense of food crops for direct consumption. Both Makanda and Odada et al. suggest that this is 'irrational' since the returns from cane farming are in fact lower than those from food crops. Makanda argues that farmers continue to expand cane production because they are unaware of the opportunity cost of money. If the delays in receiving payment for cane are taken into account, he argues, then the discounted net present value of cane production is lower than that of maize and beans. But this analysis is based upon a valuation of alternative crops at officially gazetted market prices. In reality, however, rural markets function imperfectly and the actual returns obtained by farmers are often at variance with the official prices. The 'irrationality' of these peasant farmers is thus less clear and in fact the proportion of cane and non-cane farmers buying no food shows little difference in either the Mumias or the Kabras areas. The major differences lie between Mumias (between 56.5 and 55.9 per cent of farmers not buying food) and Kabras (34.3 per cent of cane farmers and 31.3 per cent of non-cane farmers).[21]

The accretion of material goods within and between the two areas shows some differences, though. In Mumias, cane farmers tend to have larger and more permanent housing and a significantly higher proportion own bicycles, radios and watches.[22] By contrast, not only are these possessions less prevalent in the Kabras area, but there it is the non-cane farmers who tend to have more material possessions. As to the gender balance of power, Lemmings shows that in Mumias there has been a shift of decision-taking towards males, and that this has been far greater in cane-growing households than on other farms. No such drift is discernible in the Kabras region.

In so far as education is concerned, a familiar pattern emerges (Table 5.11). Families in the Mumias area are more likely to send their children to secondary education than are those in the Kabras region. And within Kabras, non-cane farmers tend to invest more in their children's education than do the cane farmers.

Table 5.11 Percentage of children attending school

Education	Mumias (VP)		Kabras (OPS)	
	Cane farmers	Non-cane farmers	Cane farmers	Non-cane farmers
Children older than 20 years				
School enrolment	87.8	78.5	87.5	86.7
Secondary education	57.4	46.3	36.3	50.0
Children between 15 and 20 years				
School enrolment	98.5	89.9	100	97.9
Secondary education	50.5	27.6	12.9	35.4
Children between 10 and 15 years				
School enrolment	98.1	81.9	96.9	94.0
Secondary education	7.8	2.4	0	0

Source: Derived from Lemmings (1989).

From these various indicators of social development it is not clear that the introduction of cane in these regions is associated with a reduction in welfare. Reported cases of malnutrition in the sugar areas are not particularly high, but this may be a misleading indicator. For one thing, much malnutrition may go unreported; for another, it is probable that the real consequences of malnutrition will be found in families displaced from their land by sugar farming and now living elsewhere — but no tracer-studies on these migrants have been undertaken. It would seem, then, that the fears that the introduction of cane farming would have a negative impact upon welfare appear to be misplaced. Given the relative prices prevailing for different food crops the incomes accruing from cane growing are sufficient to enable the purchase of adequate food. Even if Makanda is correct in arguing that the rewards from growing food crops are greater than those arising from cane, this does not rule out the basic nutritional viability of cane farming in either of these two regions. Overall welfare thus seems to have benefited in real terms from the introduction of cane.

Environmental issues

Not much is known about the long-term environmental impact of sugar production in Kenya. As with all monocropping it is likely that if it is sustained for a substantial period of time, soil nutrients will be adversely affected. Two different types of farming systems can be identified and these are likely to be associated with different environmental impacts. One involves the utilization of chemical inputs, the use of tractors for ploughing and the use of fallow land and crop-rotation. The likely long-term environmental impact of this farming system will be negative as sustained mechanized ploughing is more likely to lead to the erosion of topsoil, chemical residues build up and nutrient degradation becomes an increasing problem.

Most of these factors suggest that the farming systems associated with the small-scale OPS plant are less environmentally damaging than the larger farms producing for the VP mill. As has been shown (pp. 119–20), they have a lower propensity to utilize chemical inputs and mechanized ploughing. Moreover, the extent of monocropping is greater, with 22 per cent of the Mumias farmers devoting more than 5 hectares to cane compared with 15 per cent of Kabras farmers. In addition, farmers in Mumias devote an average of 45.9 per cent of their land to cane compared to only 24.9 per cent in Kabras. However, neither the Mumias or the Kabras farmers have extensive fallow land (7.8 and 6.4 per cent respectively), and the percentage of fallow land in non-cane farms is much higher (13.2 per cent in Mumias and 14.2 per cent in Kabras).

To sum up this discussion of social and environmental impact, four major conclusions emerge:

- the overall impact of cane production has a number of positive features. It is associated with substantial cash incomes, increased education and a growth in material possessions. Increased malnutrition does not appear to be prevalent;
- there are some negative features, notably the increasing utilization of chemical inputs and mechanized ploughing;
- the degree of these negative characteristics varies, being found in greater extremes in farms serving the Mumias VP mill. In some cases, such as

growing gender imbalances and land inequality, the negative features are confined to Mumias cane farmers and are not evident in the farms serving the small-scale OPS plant;

- there appear to be important differences in the balance between cane and non-cane farmers in the two regions. In Mumias the more 'progressive' farmers (reflected in the use of chemical inputs and in investment in education) are involved in cane production, whereas in Kabras it is the non-cane farmers who are both more 'progressive' and richer. No clear explanation exists for these differences, but it almost certainly reflects different patterns of social and political history in the two regions.

AT, sugar and macro-policy issues in Kenya

A number of important issues are raised by Kenya's experience with sugar production, many of which can be generalized to other DC environments. They all reflect a focus on AT which transcends the choice of technology at a plant level but which is essential in the development and diffusion of AT at a sectoral, regional and national level.

Sugar as an appropriate product

The Kenyan economy has often been characterized as one of the most successful in sub-Saharan Africa, with an annual growth in per capita incomes of 1.9 per cent from 1965–85. This was achieved despite having one of the highest recorded rates of population growth. But the economy is not without its problems. Like many other DCs, Kenya saw its growth rates decline precipitously during the 1980s; since at the same time the deficit on the balance of payments widened, long-term debt also grew, from 27 per cent of GNP in 1970 to 58.5 per cent in 1985.

Associated with these developments in the economy has been a steady growth in unemployment and underemployment. In 1985 the Kenya Government issued a Sessional Paper in which it estimated that the proportion of the labour force unemployed had risen from 7.1 per cent to 14.6 per cent between 1976 and 1984. Even before the 1980s slowdown, detailed studies had estimated that at least 33 per cent of rural households and 15 per cent of urban (and thus more than 30 per cent of all households) were living below the poverty line. Much of the rural poverty is centred in the western part of the country. Income and wealth distribution is also highly skewed. A study of income distribution in the early 1970s showed Kenya as being the fifth most unequal DC for which data were available and, by all accounts, inequality has widened since then. Land inequality, too, has worsened, even amongst smallholders.[23]

It is in this context that macro-policy towards AT in general, and the sugar sector in particular, has to be formulated, a context in which foreign exchange is in great shortage, a high growth rate is essential to feed the

125

population, and unemployment is a major factor underlying a relatively skewed pattern of income and wealth distribution. It is also a situation in which there are strong regional variations in social welfare, the richest area being in the centre of the country and the poorest regions in the north and the west.

The sugar sector has probably received greater investment than any other single sector in the economy and consequently its role in these developments needs to be questioned. Even if all of Kenya's sugar production had occurred in VP mills running as efficiently as Mumias, the cost of this investment (in 1982 prices) would have been K£350m, much of which was in foreign exchange. Add to this the cost of infrastructure, which as a rule of thumb in these large-scale plants is 50 per cent of fixed capital costs, and the cost increases to K£525m, equivalent to around $825m. Most of the investment decisions were made in the context of world prices being lower than the recurrent costs of sugar production, even in ecologically favourable regions such as Western Kenya.

So, one possible package of policies towards appropriate technology would have been to consider domestic sugar production as an inappropriate product. Some sugar could have been imported at the prevailing world prices and use of artificial sweeteners such as saccharin and aspartame could have been stimulated. Although these synthetic products would have to be imported, their foreign exchange cost per unit of sweetening is undoubtedly lower than the foreign exchange input in sugar production and although they may well have adverse medical impacts, the poverty indirectly associated with the production of sugar is in aggregate terms possibly even greater. (This is because the land and other resources freed from sugar production could have been put to better use in other sectors, perhaps helping to swell food production.)

One of the keys to the desirability of this policy package is whether world sugar prices will continue to be lower than the recurrent costs of production. If not, then there will obviously be costs to giving up domestic production in an ecologically suitable environment. Policy-makers would have to consider whether the risks of a sustained increase in world market prices are high. For if they are, it would be difficult to withhold a basic commodity such as sugar from the domestic market and the foreign exchange costs may be severe. Buying sugar during periods of global shortages involves paying high prices and the political pressures to encourage domestic production may be irresistible. Moreover, given the structure of world prices in many crops, where much production is subsidized, so that world prices are determined by residual factors rather than costs of production, the position in other crops may be little different to that of sugar. In other words, the use of border prices to determine the appropriateness of domestic food production, a procedure essential to the social welfare economics approach to the evaluation of AT, may not in itself be an adequate methodology for assessing appropriateness.

But there is another, and probably more persuasive, objection to a policy package which sees sugar as an inappropriate product in Kenya. This relates to the regional distribution of income where the Western region suffers from relative poverty. Table 5.12 considers the rates of return to farmers from a variety of alternative crops in the regions growing cane for the VP mills. It is quite clear from this that at least in some areas of the sugar belt (and even on farms furthest from the mills which have to pay higher transport costs) cane is a highly profitable crop. On these figures, only tea provides higher returns. Moreover, the unfavourability of cane in comparision to the intercropping of maize and beans is overstated since rural markets for these crops function imperfectly and many maize farmers do not obtain the prices which the Ministry of Agriculture and Livestock uses to calculate these relative returns; by contrast cane prices are effectively controlled. One other potential crop excluded from Table 5.12 is coffee. Arabica coffee can be grown in all of the sugar belt areas (although not necessarily on the same farms) and the even higher value robusta coffee can also be grown in Mumias. Returns from coffee, were it to be grown in this region, would exceed even those of tea.

Table 5.12. Gross annual margins per hectare (KShs)[a]

Crop	Nzoia	Mumias	Chemelil	Muhoroni	Miwani	SONY
Sunflower	947	947	947	947	947	947
Tea	55,089	55,089	55,089	55,089	55,089	55,089
Maize and Beans	3,910	3,910	3,910	3,910	3,910	3,910
Zone A Cane	5,591	5,288	5,268	2,235	2,414	1,646
Zone B Cane	5,180	4,832	4,865	4,810	2,110	1,313
Zone C Cane	4,769	4,376	4,462	4,386	1,807	981
Zone D Cane	4,409	3,977	4,109	4,015	1,541	789

[a] Zones refer to distance from the mill. The greater this is the higher the deductions for transport by the mills.
Source: Odada et al, 1986.

The problem for Western Kenya is that these two high-yielding crops, tea and coffee, are predominantly grown for the world market. Global over-supply has led the producers of these crops to reach agreements with each other and with the major consuming countries which limit production in order to maintain the level of prices. Each supplying country therefore has an agreed quota. For historical and political reasons, the Kenyan quota has already been distributed to other regions of the country, especially to Central Province and Rift Valley growers.[24] This is one of the factors explaining the relatively high levels of per capita income in these two provinces.

In the absence of the political will to redistribute tea and coffee quotas from growers in these provinces to farmers in the Western Province, one of the country's poorest regions, cane is one of the few substitute crops available which yields high returns. Indeed the development of the sugar industry in Kenya must be seen more as a form of regional income distribution than one of maximizing economic growth. It is this context that the 'social impact' of cane-growing can be considered. As shown above, despite a general prejudice against cash-cropping, cane growing is generally associated with beneficial development patterns, and there are important reasons why sugar is an appropriate crop for the Western Region of the country.

Welfare economists are unlikely to agree with this conclusion. They would argue that based on the border prices of alternative crops, the most efficient cropping pattern should be chosen and the resulting economic surplus be redistributed to poorer regions. Not only is it unclear whether surplus would be significantly maximized by growing other crops (since it is possible that the border prices of other crops are also below production costs), but the mechanisms for redistributing incomes, especially between regions, are not well developed in developing countries such as Kenya.

If these conclusions are accepted, two issues remain: how much sugar should be produced and which technology should be utilized? The first is difficult to answer. Granted there is a place for sugar, primarily as a way of redistributing income regionally. But should this be extended until domestic demand is satisfied? Already cane-growing has saturated the most ecologically favourable areas (Mumias, Nzoia and Chemelil) and moved into less favourable regions. One response might be to allow sugar production to expand in small pockets with relatively low incomes (as Kabras used to be), subject to certain ecological constraints. This is a slippery path and it is not clear where the logic of this extension of sugar production should end.

The second question is much easier to answer. On the basis of earlier analysis, there is little doubt that the small-scale OPS technology is much more appropriate. It provides higher financial and economic returns, and the social and environmental factors associated with its introduction appear to be at least as favourable, if not more so, than those arising from production by VP mills. An associated policy issue is whether, given prior investments in inappropriate large-scale VP mills, it would be more economical to rehabilitate or expand these rather than to install new small-scale OPS capacity. A priori this would appear an attractive proposition. Yet the figures do not bear this out. Between 1986 and 1988 $15m was spent on the Muhoroni plant, raising capacity from 1,800–2,400 tcd. This works out at a capital cost of $25,000 per ton of crushing capability. Yet a newly installed 200 tcd OPS plant (in 1989 prices) would only cost $2m, a capital cost of $10,000 per ton of crushing capacity. Despite this the Kenyan Government will have spent almost $100m in rehabilitating three large-scale VP mills between 1986 and 1990.[25]

Various combinations of small- and large-scale plants lend themselves to policy implementation. Where the economic and social infrastructure exists, such as at Mumias, large-scale VP may be encouraged and new cane growing areas could be opened up by small-scale OPS plants. This would avoid the costs of excess capacity at underutilized VP mills. Either these small-scale OPS mills could subsequently be converted to VP production, or they could be decommissioned and moved to virgin areas. A further possibility suggested by a senior manager of Booker McConnell (the major TNC operating in DC sugar production) is for the juice extraction process to occur in a series of small-scale mills and then be shipped in bulk tankers to VP boiling houses. This would make maximum use of the higher technical efficiency of the VP process and simultaneously allow for the economic and social benefits of small-scale production to be realized in crushing and clarifying.

Most of these conclusions are drawn from India and Kenya. Yet, they would seem to have wide application in other DCs. Many other sub-Saharan African economies have also seen low rates of capacity utilization in their VP mills. In Tanzania, for example, only 46 per cent of capacity is utilized, necessitating extensive sugar imports. The costs of rehabilitation are also high — the Kagara VP mill, with an installed capacity of 2,000 tcd, is estimated to need an investment of over $75m.[26] Neighbouring Uganda, too, shows potential for small-scale OPS production. Since the ratio of VP:OPS capital costs in many of these economies is likely to show a similar pattern to that of Kenya, rather than India (see p. 117) there is every reason to believe that small-scale sugar offers great potential in other DCs.

Modes of ownership

Earlier analysis of both India and Kenya showed that the major factor allowing the VP mills to dominate was their effective writing-off of capital costs. This occurred since either they did not depreciate investments at all or did so at historic, rather than replacement, costs. The rationality of this procedure for plant which has already been installed is clear — as long as recurrent costs are covered, fixed investment costs can be considered as 'water under the bridge' (the phrase used in many cost-benefit analysis text books). But for new, *ex ante* investments, there is no justification for this and it is striking that TNCs have withdrawn from investments in sugar production in many DCs. Instead they have managed to appropriate their returns through management contracts: in the mid-1980s, the government owned 92 per cent of the SONY plant which was managed by the Metha Group; Muhoroni was 74 per cent state-owned and was also managed by the Metha Group; Mumias was 71 per cent owned by the state, with most of the rest being held by parastatal banks — Booker McConnell owned only 4 per cent of the equity, but had a management contract; Chemelil was also managed by Booker, but without any equity stake; and Nzoia was almost wholly state-owned (97 per cent) and managed by Technisucre, a French TNC. In India, too, most of the VP mills were owned by parastatals and those in the private sector were mostly heavily depreciated and had effectively written-off capital recoupment charges.

By contrast, in both India and Kenya the small-scale OPS plants were in the private sector. New investors are required to recoup their investments, including those in fixed capital. However, even if they were not doing so, unit capital costs are a much smaller proportion of total costs than for the capital-intensive VP plants, and they would thus benefit less from depreciation at historic costs. For these small-scale plants a similar form of subsidy would be some institutional mechanism allowing them to write-off their labour costs. But clearly no such solution is in sight so that under existing regimes of ownership, these small-scale plants remain severely disadvantaged.

A second 'mode of ownership factor' which arises in the case of sugar concerns the political underpinnings behind state support for different types of technologies. The emphasis given to the sugar sector in Kenya reflects the nature of the internal political coalition after Independence in 1964. At that stage the state was dominated by Central Province interest groups who furthered their position by ready access to the capital city and links with TNCs. The rural constituency in Central Province was partially satisfied by the distribution of tea and coffee quotas. In these circumstances national unity had to be maintained by providing opportunities to those in other regions and it is in this context that the high relative price of cane was established. After the political transition in 1978, Western interests were increased in the state and this largely explains the continued expansion of the sugar belt.[27]

Political factors were also evident in early investments in OPS technology. Two occurred in the 1970s — initially by one of the first indigenous industrial capitalists, and the second by a politically vocal farmers' co-operative in the Kakamega area. This immediately resulted in a price concession to the small-scale plants (see p. 115), a statute which remained on the books even after their demise. This allowed the Asian-owned modern OPS plant established in 1981 to thrive but it benefited from the historical accident of prior indigenous citizen-owned investments rather than from any specific concern for AT by the state. Because there were no aspirant politically influential indigenous citizens interested in small-scale sugar production, no additional concessions were made available to encourage the choice of AT.

Thus it is that the future of AT in the sugar sector in Kenya, as well as in other sectors, probably hinges more on the emergence of a group of aspirant indigenous capitalists than on any intrinsic value of the technology. The horizons of indigenous capitalists are now beginning to extend in Kenya, and plans are under foot for at least one other OPS plant, to be owned by a farmers' co-operative. It is not a coincidence, therefore, that for the first time the Kenya Sugar Authority is beginning to consider more sympathetically the logic of small-scale sugar production.

A final ownership consideration poses a particular dilemma for the AT movement. As was argued in Chapter 1, there has been a long-running debate in the AT movement about the social context in which AT diffuses. The experience of small-scale sugar in both India and Kenya is relevant to this controversy. In India the technological improvements in OPS were being diffused in the first instance through a group of industrialists linked to a right-wing political party which had campaigned against land-reform. In Kenya not only is the $2m investment in OPS technology clearly beyond the resources of those which the AT movement targets for assistance, but its diffusion is associated with the extension of land inequality, the growth of wage labour and the emergence of rural capitalism. Are these the objectives explicitly or implicitly favoured by the AT movement?

This is not a simple dilemma to resolve, but it is worth bearing three mitigating factors in mind: first, in the context of viable economic opportunities in the Western region of Kenya, the choice is probably between dynamic capitalism and static peasant commodity production, between higher absolute levels of income with inequality or greater equality and lower living standards; second, some would argue that the transition to a basically more equitable form of social organization is contingent upon the prior extension of capitalist social relations; and third, there remains the regional problem. Even if Western Kenya abdicated from sugar production and was able to remain a region of relative equality, the absence of a high-yielding cash crop would make the province significantly less affluent than other areas of Kenya. Inequality would thus be heightened, but at an inter-regional rather than intra-regional level.

None of these ownership-related factors is either specific to India or Kenya. All find ready extension in other sectors and other countries. As argued in Chapter 1 there has been a hegemonic attitude towards industrial policy which has favoured investments in large-scale capital-intensive technologies. In many DCs this has led to uneconomic production costs, so that ownership has tended to retreat into state hands,[28] where it has been all too easy to write-off capital costs, often by depreciating on an historic, rather than replacement basis. In these circumstances, many small-scale labour-intensive investments have been undermined.

Whether or not all investments by the state necessarily lead to the choice of inappropriate technologies depends on the social and political basis of state power, and the mode in which state investments have occurred. The experience of brick production in Tanzania (Chapter 4) and cement production in China (Chapter 7) makes it clear that state ownership can indeed be associated with the introduction of ATs. Similarly the political power of different groups of a country's population (for example, those with regional or ethnic power bases) often affects the choice of technology. In Nigeria, it led the Federal Government into the absurdity of supporting an automobile assembly plant in Kaduna, many miles from the coast and with poor infrastructure. Knocked-down kits of automobiles were being air-freighted into the country for assembly!

One generalizable conclusion here is that unlike Asia, Africa seems to lack a domestic political constituency whose interests are extended through the choice of small-scale technology. For this reason the panoply of state support and price interventions tends to be geared towards the mobilization of large-scale inappropriate investments, despite their demonstrated failure. In these environments the idea of AT is often received with some hostility. By contrast, in many parts of Asia a ready constituency emerges in support of small-scale industry.[29] And as for the dilemma of producing 'by or for the masses', this has been considered in Chapter 5 (pp. 101–3).

Time, resources and the institutional context for technological development
Although small-scale sugar production has a long history, the systematic attempt to improve OPS technology is of relatively recent origin. It was only after the mid-1970s that resources of any significance were addressed to meeting the technological problems of this sector and after the death of M K Garg in 1985, much of this pioneering momentum came to an abrupt halt. Many of the earlier adverse judgements on OPS were based on the unimproved technology and failed to recognize the potential for enchancements.[30] It is fortuitous that Garg and the Appropriate Technology Development Association (ATDA) in India did not make the same mistake.

A similarly static assessment of early VP technology in the mid-nineteenth century would probably have been drawn to a comparable conclusion about its relative performance. It took at least 30 years for VP technology to become a cost-competitive form of processing and a century before its full potential was realized. Beet-sugar technology also involved many years of effort and its recovery rate rose from a negligible percentage in 1799 to just over 5 per cent in 1836 and to around its present optimum (17 per cent) only in the first decade of the twentieth century. Moreover, studies of technological developments in other sectors show a similar timespan.[31] The Japanese and Koreans took around six decades to develop their textile industries and the recent Japanese prowess in the automobile sector involved seven decades of production and at least four decades of concerted effort. Thus, capturing the potential of an AT such as OPS may often involve a long timespan and a broad canvas for policy-making.

This is not to say that the time taken to develop this technology was as short as it might have been. To the contrary. The technologies involved — a furnace design used for over a century in the West and an obsolete molasses screw-expeller from Quebec — were drawn from the shelf of available technologies. The sums involved in the technological development — less than $1m (in 1989 prices) — are trivial by comparison with the potential economic and social impact of the improvements, for sugar processing vies with textiles as being the most important industrial sector in many DCs. The investments involved are also trivial by comparison with the sums invested in other sectors. For example, the European and American automobile industry (the largest sector in the IACs) sank $120bn in the decade after 1976 to upgrade product and process technology.

Yet the returns to this negligible developmental expenditure on small-scale sugar technology have been great and offer significant potential. They have changed the balance of profitability against the large-scale VP mills in some DC environments. Moreover there remains plenty of room for further improvement, not just through the accretion of minor improvements on the sugar recovery rate, but also with respect to fuel efficiency and labour productivity. Why, then, are the larger TNCs not moving into this sector?

There are in fact few TNCs with significant sugar operations in DCs. Most of the larger traditional firms such as Booker McConnell and Tate and Lyle have diversified out of sugar, have moved into beet or have concentrated on sugar distribution. In a few isolated cases they have maintained their involvement in the form of management contracts, as in the case of the relatively successful Mumias mill in Kenya. A number of factors has contributed to their retreat from direct equity and production:

- domestic pressure has forced out the TNCs in a sector where the technological barriers to entry are perceived to be slight[32];
- there has been a gradual squeeze on processing margins. In many countries governments have been confronted with conflicting pressures in setting the price structure for sugar — the necessity of keeping the consumer price of a basic foodstuff low, and the political pressure from the commercial farming lobby for high growers' margins (both are evident in India and Kenya). The consequence has been a generally low rate of return for sugar processing and a tendency for much of the ownership to lie in the public sector. This is not uncommon in basic goods industries which are subject to these scissors-like pricing pressures;
- central management has great difficulty in appropriating this surplus, although in theory the quantum of profit from many small factories may be greater than that arising in a single large factory. (A similar pattern was observed in Chapter 3 in relation to bakeries.)

Faced with the absence of the major institutional developer and diffuser of new technologies, the vacuum has been filled by the NGO movement. The ATDA in India is an NGO, as is the ITDG which has provided almost $500,000 to fund the sugar programme. But these inputs have been inadequate and this has slowed both the development and diffusion of an AT which offers considerable potential to many DCs. The inputs required may be trivial by comparison with those seen in other sectors, but they are large for NGOs. A similar picture emerges with respect to small-scale cement technology where the AT offers significant potential but remains relatively underdeveloped (see Chapter 7). Less than $1m has been invested in

133

improving this technology and it appears to have further potential. But none of the major NGOs is keen to risk the investment of a further $500,000 since 'large projects' such as these appear to be outside their remit.

A second problem faced by these NGOs is that they are not driven by the 'Schumpeterian motor' in the same way as are private sector firms.[33] The search for technological rents is not endogenized in their survival and they thus lack the urgency to make developments quickly, and then to diffuse them widely. The NGOs have to satisfy their funders, many of whom are private individuals. For this they need to demonstrate rapid results, and a direct beneficial impact on alleviating rural poverty. The $2m projects such as sugar and cement are not as easily defensible to this clientele as are microprojects such as grain-milling and baking.

Finally, few of these NGOs have the political muscle to change the incentive system in favour of AT development and diffusion. The policy steps required to give sugar processing ATs a fair run, most significantly a realistic costing of capital, are not within the persuasion of NGOs. Until a political constituency emerges to support such a change in policy regime, there is probably a limit to the successful diffusion of ATs.

As was made clear in Chapter 1, the call for the wider diffusion of AT is not confined to DCs. Many of the problems associated with inappropriate technology are also to be found in the IACs. Therefore before turning to the role played by states and markets in the diffusion of AT, it is first desirable to consider some of the broad trends emerging in the richer countries which are relevant to the development and diffusion of AT.

CHAPTER 6

The economics of small: AT in the industrially advanced countries

As pointed out in Chapter 1, the problem of technological appropriateness cannot be limited to DCs or to the concern with rural poverty. It has a much wider relevance and the AT movement continues to flourish in the industrially advanced countries. Moreover, as was argued in Chapter 1, the three branches of the AT movement — environmental, social and economic — had common origins, representing a response to the degradation of a particular mode of global economic growth. Indeed, two of these branches — those concerned with social and environmental appropriateness — first found their expression in the IACs. So notwithstanding the primary focus of this book on the problems of alternative technology in the developing countries it is also illuminating to consider briefly its role in the First World.

While it is possible to focus on all three of the dimensions of appropriateness in the IACs, only the economic is discussed in this book, and this is considered only in relation to the question of optimum scale. As was seen in Chapter 1, since the mid-nineteenth century there has been a preoccupation with bigness in the IACs. The logic of this is now increasingly being examined, and the 'economics of small' are becoming more apparent. This focus on small-scale is merely an examplar of the more general need to consider the nature of technology in the IACs.

It is important to note that the social appropriateness of technology is also being questioned in the IACs, for example in relation to the optimal pattern of work-organization. The organization of work in the mass-production era emerged over a period of many decades. It involved the specialization of tasks and hence the polarization of skills. Supervisory tiers of management were introduced and information flowed downwards, from the top of the managerial hierarchy to the detailed worker at the bottom. This form of work-organization was alienating and increasingly came to be associated with conflict on the shop-floor, absenteeism, poor quality and often expensive products. This has been referred to as the 'degradation of work'.[1]

But market conditions have begun to change, and the basis of competition in global markets is altering from the mass-production era's emphasis on price to one in which product innovation and performance are paramount. In a context in which price was the major determinant of competitiveness, labour could be seen as a cost which had to be minimized. But when flexiblity, innovation and quality become important, labour must be seen as a resource. Consequently the most efficient firms are moving from this

135

inherited pattern of work-organization to one which emphasizes multi-tasking and multi-skilling, and gives substantial autonomy back to the detailed worker. Whilst in itself this does not necessarily optimize the quality of working life, it does represent an improvement over the patterns prevailing in the mass-production era. It also provides plenty of scope for attempts to enhance further the quality of working life.

These issues of social appropriateness will not be considered here.[2] But it is important to note their emergence as a major policy concern in the IACs, since it illustrates that the introduction of socially appropriate technologies need not necessarily be associated with a loss of competitiveness. To the contrary, there are reasons to suppose that many socially inappropriate technologies are outdated and can only be operated at the risk of reduced competitiveness. These developments provide an important potential boost to the AT movement in the IACs, although there is not much evidence that AT activists have yet grasped their significance.

Similarly, the neglect of environmental appropriateness in this book does not arise because it is irrelevant to the problems of IACs. Indeed, concern with these issues is currently probably higher on the political agenda than at any previous stage of history. The greenhouse effect — resulting from the simultaneous production of carbon dioxide (most of which results from the use of carbon-based fuels in the IACs) and destruction of oxygen-producing forests (most of which lie in the DCs) — is rapidly coming to be recognized as a major environmental hazard whose solution necessarily lies in co-ordinated international action. Acid rain is harming animal and plant life. It arises not only from the inappropriate use of energy-intensive technologies, but also from the particular technologies which are utilized in the production of energy.[3] The reduction of the ozone layer probably results from the utilization of noxious chemicals (CFCs) in refrigerators and aerosols and this is likely to have untold environmental and health consequences. And inorganic chemicals continue to build up in the environment, resulting both from energy-intensive agricultural production and from industrial effluents.

There has been progress in some areas and more environmentally benign technologies have been introduced. For example, the utilization of energy seems to have grown more efficient since the 1973 oil-price shock — the ratio of oil use in the OECD countries (in tonnes per $1,000 of GDP per capita) fell from 0.29 in 1973 to 0.18 in 1988. Yet even these levels of fuel-use appear to be too high for a sustainable environment. Moreover they partly result from energy-intensive and polluting industries moving to the DCs — both Korea and Taiwan increased their oil-consumption by more than 20 per cent in 1988 alone.[4]

Consequently there are grounds for concern regarding both the environmental and social appropriateness of the technologies utilized in the IACs. But s nce this book is primarily concerned with the problems of DCs, we have only limited scope for considering the problems of the IACs. This will be done by concentrating on economic appropriateness and, in particular, on the issue of the optimal scale of operations.

The emerging concern with diseconomies of scale

Schumacher was by no means the first to be concerned with the problems of large-scale organization and production. Yet his 1973 book *Small is Beautiful: A Study of Economics as if People Mattered* played a major role in concentrating attention on this issue. His personal background had been as a senior economist in Britain's state-owned National Coal Board which for many years had pursued scale economies in organization and production. Schumacher was first sensitized to the problems of scale by the NCB's attitude to the problems of pneumoconiosis, a lethal disease of the lungs associated with coal-mining.[5] Instead of recognizing the self-evident health consequences of coal-mining, the NCB chose to defend itself rigorously and to fight (and subsequently win) the legal argument on technicalities. In saving itself relatively small sums of compensation (£2–3m), Schumacher believed that the NCB had ceased to concern itself with people. More importantly, he believed that such uncaring attitudes were not exceptional but were an inevitable consequence of the organization's scale.

Thus modern economies, believed Schumacher, are on a 'collision course with nature'. At the root of the problem, he argued, was the widespread assumption of unlimited resources and the unrestricted carrying power of nature. This had led modern society to act as if material production could be equated with satisfaction and happiness. As a result, technologies that were seen as maximizing output were considered optimal. For this collision path to be avoided, an alternative set of technologies is required:

> In industry, we can interest ourselves in the evolution of small-scale technology, relatively non-violent technology, and technology with a human face, so that people have a chance to enjoy themselves in new forms of partnership between management and men. (Schumacher (1973) pp. 17–18)

In this plea Schumacher encapsulated all three branches of the modern AT movement — the environmental, the social and the economic. For him the key to understanding the problems of modern technology and the design of alternative paths lay with the problem of scale. This affected the environment since

> Small-scale operations, no matter how numerous, are always less likely to be harmful to the natural environment than large-scale ones, simply because their individual force is small in relation to the recuperative forces of nature. (Ibid. p. 31)

It also affected economic performance, as

> production from local resources for local needs is the most rational way of economic life, while dependence on imports from afar and the consequent

need to produce for export to unknown and distant peoples is highly uneconomic and justifiable only in exceptional cases and on a small scale. (Ibid. pp. 53–4)

Finally, the social costs of large-scale organization are clear to all (except, that is, to economists):

> Most of the sociologists and psychologists insistently warn us of . . . [large-scale organization's] inherent dangers — dangers to the integrity of the individual when he feels as nothing more than a small cog in a vast machine and when the human relationships of his daily working life become increasingly dehumanized, and dangerous also to efficiency and productivity, stemming from ever-growing Parkinsonian bureaucracies. (Ibid. p. 225)

Schumacher provides a ringing plea for a new attitude to life and a new form of technological progress, one which would emphasize smallness rather than 'giantism'.

> I have no doubt that it is possible to give a new direction to technological development, a direction that shall lead it back to the real needs of man, and that also means *to the actual size of man. Man* is small, therefore, small is beautiful. To go for giantism is to go for self-destruction. (Ibid. p. 148)

This plea of Schumacher, to the extent that it has been heard in the world outside of AT, is largely a moral one. Human beings ought to encourage a greater use of small-scale technology and organization because it will improve the quality of life and because large-scale production is environmentally unsustainable. If this means a loss of material output, then it is is a sacrifice worth bearing. But this normative reading of Schumacher too often ignores a further strand of his argument, that is that the ever-growing commitment to largeness was economically inefficient. However, he believed that the costs of scale were largely realized in the form of external diseconomies. By that he meant that the real costs were not borne by the direct producers but by society at large.

It is in this consideration of the economic costs of scale that important developments are beginning to emerge. Increasingly, scale is not seen as a necessary concomitant of economic growth, but rather is recognized as a factor — perhaps the factor — which reduces its rate. Moreover, no longer are the costs of scale only reflected in external diseconomies, they are now increasingly being experienced by the direct producers themselves. A touchstone of the importance of these new trends is to be found in their discussion in the business literature. This is relevant because this body of opinion is not concerned with the ethical or social characteristics of scale, nor with external diseconomies, but merely with its impact on the rate of economic growth. Here it is increasingly common to find a disillusion with mass production and large-scale organization. The perspective of the flexible specialization school (briefly considered in Chapter 1) is gaining increasing importance. Piore and Sabel consider the 'limits of the model of industrial development that is founded on mass production' and the 'production of standardized commodities' (1984, p. 4) and review the 'recent historiography of technology [which] clearly documents the vision of automatic machine production as a structuring principle of Anglo-American, particularly American, technological developments' (p. 45). The root of contemporary economic problems is thus traced to the coming to dominance of large-scale, automated mass production in the mid-nineteenth century which, especially in the US and the UK, forced out small-scale craft-based production. Piore and Sabel argue that those countries such as Italy and Japan which have maintained this small-scale flexibly-oriented craft sector are the ones which have come to dominate and it is the mass-production economies which are now in relative decline.

Another indicator of the growing awareness of the economic costs of large-scale technology can be found in a best-selling book by Tom Peters.[6] In the early 1980s he had co-authored an account of 12 of the most efficient US corporations,[7] only to find that within a short space of time, many of these exemplars were facing severe economic difficulties. Facing up to this, Peters offers a critique of 'the American perchant for giantism' and the associated obsession with quantity, rather than quality:

> Big, not best, has always been the American calling card. In fact, I bet you can't drive more than seventy-five miles in any direction, from anywhere in the United States, without running into a 'biggest in the world' of some sort. Wide-open spaces and an apparently limitless frontier set it all in motion . . .
> This all-American system — long production runs, mass operations — paid off with victories in World Wars I and II, and cemented subsequent US economic dominance. But we won World War II with *more* tanks and planes, not, in general *better* ones. (Peters, 1987, pp. 15–16)

By contrast the Europeans (except the British) maintained their tradition of product excellence. More pertinently, Peters pointed out that the Japanese challenge has been underwritten by its continual commitment to the virtues of smallness. He notes

> the unique Japanese passion for smallness, in a world where the advantages of smallness seem to be fast eclipsing the once generally perceived value of giantism. (Ibid. p. 18)

Interestingly, Peters quotes at length from a Korean scholar (author of a book entitled *Smaller is Better: Japan's Mastery of the Miniature*) to show the prevalence and historic depth of smallness in Japanese culture.[8]

The brunt of Peters's argument is that giantism is neither efficient nor innovative. He cites evidence from a variety of industries that large-scale plants have often failed to realize the supposed productivity gains arising from scale economies in production. Similarly, there is little evidence that large multi-plant firms display superior performance to their single-plant rivals. The new drive towards flexible production also appears to be facilitated by smallness of plant size. In relation to innovation he also casts doubt on the advantages of scale and quotes the distinguished authors of *The Bigness Complex* who argue that 'the smallest firms produced about four times as many innovations per R&D dollar as the middle-sized firm and 24 times as many as the largest firms' (Peters, pp. 23–4). In fact only 34 per cent of all major innovations in the US come from firms employing more than 10,000 people, despite their much larger share of overall US production.

Yet although there is obviously evidence of a move towards smaller scale in production and organization, in many sectors there is a simultaneous tendency towards a growth in scale. It is important therefore to try and understand some of the reasons why there has been a sudden interest in smallness as opposed to giantism. This will help in defining a series of relevant policy issues: on balance, will the post-1980s trend towards small-ness outweigh the inherited momentum of bigness: are there sectoral biases in the economics of small; and are there different dimensions of the economies of small? In the discussion which follows attention will be given to a variety of technological and organizational trends which affect economies of scale. Most of these are only emerging as important trends in the early 1990s and have not yet had a wide impact on scale. The discussion which follows, therefore, is only suggestive of the sort of issues which are affecting the optimality of scale, mostly (but not exclusively) reversing the historic trend towards greater concentration.

The nature and determinants of scale economies

Some relevant concepts

The discussion of economies of scale has a long tradition in economic theory, beginning in the nineteenth century when fixed and indirect costs were first emerging as important elements in production. Given that the underlying factors determining scale economies have inevitably changed over this long time period, it is not surprising that scale has become a somewhat ambiguous concept. Pratten's general definition in a well-known study of the early 1970s is pitched at the most general level and begs the complexity of scale: 'Very crudely economies of scale are reductions in average costs attributable to increases in scale. They can be defined, most readily, in relation to plants'.[9] Similarly, in the 1930s Viner distinguished between the long- and short-run cost curves. The latter consisted of the envelope of the former: 'The long-run cost curve shows the lowest possible cost of producing at any scale of output after all possible adaptation to that scale has taken place', whereas '[t]he short-run cost curve traces out the relationship between the average costs of production and the extent to which plants are utilized'.[10] This, too, provides only a general description of scale economies and is of limited insight into an exploration of their cause.

These classic views on economies of scale are restrictive because they both refer to only one dimension of scale, that of plant-size. But this is only one type of scale economy. In the analysis which follows, three different dimensions of scale are discussed, informed by Silberston's illuminating distinction between time periods, products and units.[11] The reason why the classical theories of scale economies conflated these three dimensions is that hitherto they have tended to increase in concert — an increase in one was generally linked with an increase in the others. With respect to plant scale, there is much evidence that as the size of the plant increases, so unit costs of production have historically tended to fall.[12] Whilst in principle smaller efficient plants could be built, in reality these have been neglected in favour of enhancing the efficiency of the larger ones. In many sectors, therefore, small-scale plants are no longer to be found, and this has been one of the 'windows of opportunity' which the AT movement has begun to explore. At the same time as this has occurred so there has been a consistent tendency for the concentration of ownership (reflecting firm-size) to increase. In the UK the proportion of net manufacturing output accounted for by the hundred largest enterprises rose from 16 per cent in 1909 to 24 per cent in 1935 to 38 per cent in 1958 and to just over 40 per cent in 1970. Concentration in the USA rose in a similar manner over this period (although to a lesser extent), that is from 22 per cent in 1909 to 33 per cent in 1970.[13] And product economies of scale increased as standardized output was produced for ever-larger markets. The simultaneous increase in these three dimensions of scale reached their ultimate logic in the production of 'world products' by 'world firms' (that is, TNCs) in 'world factories'.

A number of different reasons have been adduced to explain the tendency for a consistent increase in these dimensions of scale. Pratten lists seven as being of particular importance:

- indivisibilities such as the minimum effective levels of scale of particular sets of machinery
- economies of increasing dimensions; for example when volumetric increases are greater than those in surface area (see pp. 144–5)
- specialization of labour, machinery and suppliers
- economies of massed resources, that is, 'the operation of the law of large numbers' which diminishes risk and facilitates smaller inventories
- the ability to utilize superior technologies, for example, in the transition from batch to flow production
- learning arising as a consequence of larger size and longer experience, and
- the ability to control markets to reduce uncertainty and optimize producton

It is significant that although Pratten (and others, including Silberston) also list a series of diseconomies of scale — notably getting to the edge of

Figure 6.1. *Scale in production*

Woodward's classification	Nature of activity
A *Discrete products*	
Unit- and small-batch production	⌈ Production of units to customer requirements Production of prototypes Fabrication of large equipment in stages ⌊ Production of small batches to customers' orders
Large-batch and mass production	⌈ Production of large batches ⌊ Mass production
B *Dimensional products*	
Process production	⌈ Intermittent production in multi-product plant ⌊ Continuous flow production in single product plant

Source: Adapted from Woodward (1965).

technical knowledge, control loss with large managerial numbers, in labour relations and in distribution [14] – until recently these have been given little prominence in the analysis.

Another important gap in emphasis in these classic studies of scale economies is their lack of systematic distinction between different types of industries. In so far as particular types of scale economies have technological roots, and in so far as these underlying technological parameters are now changing, this is a significant issue. Here it is the industrial sociologists and engineers who have offered useful concepts, distinguishing between two types of process and various types of industrial organization (Figure 6.1). The process difference is that between the production of discrete (sometimes called integral) products, that is those products produced as individual separate items, and dimensional products (produced in units of volume, capacity and weight). The relevant industrial organization difference is that between very specific, 'bespoke' products, and those made in almost infinitely large numbers. While this suggests a continuum of possibilities, it tends to find expression in production systems which are geared either towards one-off/small-batch production, or to mass production. These industry differences have direct relevance to changing parameters of scale, as will become clear in later discussion (pp. 148–154).

In assessing the likelihood of emerging changes in the determinants of scale, it is useful to elaborate briefly on the views of Pratten and others and to flesh out the discussion on three of the major determinants of scale economies: the distinction between direct and indirect costs; scale economies in process industries; and the evolving dominance of the mass-production ethos. These are chosen since in one way or another they are all being affected by the new production technologies and organizational forms to be discussed below (see pp. 149–151). As the discussion proceeds, the implications which these changing determinants have for the three dimensions of scale will be highlighted.

Direct and indirect production costs

Direct production costs are inputs such as machinery, labour, energy, raw materials, components and buildings. Some of these costs are variable, in the sense that they are generally used in a constant relation to output; that is, any increase in output requires an equivalent increase in these inputs. Raw materials, components, labour and energy are generally the major elements of variable costs.[15] The second major constituent of direct costs are those which are lumpy and fixed, especially machinery and buildings. Although these items are directly used in production, they have to be accounted for whether the plant is in operation or not. Clearly the greater the degree of their utilization, the lower unit costs will be, and this category of fixed, direct costs is one of the main determinants of plant economies of scale.

A number of factors will determine the rate at which these fixed costs are utilized. Assuming that sufficient demand exists, unit fixed costs will be minimized if machine downtime is kept to the lowest possible level. This will be determined by the constant availability of adequate quality components and raw materials and by the reliability of the machinery itself. Perhaps more importantly, machine downtime is kept high if changeovers are limited, since the constant resetting of machinery will lead to production losses. Here there tends to be a link between high fixed capital costs, large-scale plants and undifferentiated final products.

If direct production costs (and, more specifically the fixed elements of direct production costs) are one of the major underlying factors for plant economies of scale, indirect production costs are crucial to the emergence of firm economies of scale. These indirect costs comprise activities which lie in the background of actual production. Whilst they are not generally used up in the process of physical manufacture, if they are not sustained at some general level, then the enterprise as a whole will not be able to function competitively. Historically, a limited number of indirect production costs have stood out in significance: the most important has been R&D such as

143

that involved in long-run product improvement and development, and this clearly varies in importance between sectors; a second indirect cost of importance is management, not so much the detailed (junior) management of line production (which is more like a variable cost), but more the overall strategic planning activities of middle and senior management; third, is the function of raw material and component acquisition, storage and management; and the final major indirect element of total costs is that of sales and marketing.

These distinctions between direct and indirect, and between fixed and variable costs provide insights into the technological underpinnings of scale economies. Production processes which require a great deal of time to reset for different product specifications (such as that involved, for example, in changing patterns of weaving looms) will in general be associated with the need to specialize production, and hence necessarily involve the production of particular products, generally on specialized lines or in specialized plants. On the other hand, those process and product technologies which make heavy use of indirect inputs (for example, they may require a great deal of marketing, or be very technology intensive) will provide scale economies for large firms who are able to spread these costs over a large number of plants. As will be seen later, the trend over the past century has been for both of these categories to grow simultaneously, and so have plant- and firm-scale economies. The extent to which product-scale economies have been dominant has tended to reflect the problems involved in resetting machinery which, as will be seen, is not only a physical and technical issue but also one affected by the underlying management philosophy.

The process industries

A distinction has been drawn between dimensional and discrete products. The former was defined in relation to the constancy of its output-specification. Often, this category of dimensional products is conflated with the less-easy-to-define category of process industries since these industries most generally produce uninterrupted flows of output. The problem is that this apparent flow in process industries may, on detailed inspection, comprise different batches, and this will have implications in the production processes for the resetting of machinery specifications. Hence Woodward (1965), who was primarily concerned with the nature of productive organization, felt that the clearer distinction was to be made between dimensional and discrete industries, rather than between process and non-process industries.

What then are process industries, and do they have inherent scale economies in production? As their name implies these industries can be most easily characterized in terms of the necessary completion of chemical reactions in production. This requires a carefully controlled environment — the process may be completed in either a continuous form (with a constant flow of inputs and outputs) or in the form of separate batches. It is out of the necessity to control chemical reactions that scale economies in production arise, and this appears to be directly related to the inherent nature of volumetric space.

Briefly, controlled production requires enclosed containers; the geometry of volumes is such that increases in internal capacity do not occur in the same relation as increases in external surface — in fact the relationship of change in surface area to volume is around 0.6. Over the years process plant engineers noted a rule of thumb that as they doubled plant capacity, so construction costs only tended to increase by about two-thirds. They have come to refer to this as the '0.6 rule', based on the understanding that in these industries volumetric processes are dominant.[16] Here it is possible to see a close internal dynamic to plant economies of scale in production. The degree of product-scale economies is unrelated to this '0.6 rule' but instead reflects the ease with which particular processes can be switched to different batches. Firm-scale economies are also variable in the process industries, depending upon the intensity with which indirect costs are involved. It should be said, however, that process industries tend to be highly technology intensive, and in fact it was to meet the needs of one of the first process industries, that of sugar, that the first school of chemical engineering was established in Audobon in the USA in the nineteenth century.

The mass-production ethic

The ethos of mass production is now overwhelmingly dominant in most of the IACs. Despite the fact that batch production continues to play a prominent role in modern industry, Charlie Chaplin's unforgettable experience with the automated production line and the dentist's chair in his film *Modern Times* continues to dominate most of our perceptions of production in the modern factory.

Whilst the mass-production line was first developed in the nineteenth century in the USA in the armaments, cigarette and canning industries, it became the dominant production technique only in the early twentieth century.[17] This was as a result of two major factors: the growth of the school of 'Scientific Management' (largely following the precepts of F W Taylor) which was closely bound up with the professionalization of engineering and the establishment of the Society of Mechanical Engineers in the USA in the 1890s; and the demonstration effect of Henry Ford's mass-production line, and the consequent stimulation of consumer demand and supplier industries. That this form of production reflected the unique characteristics of the US, heavily conditioned by a shortage of labour and the relative absence of a craft tradition, became shrouded, so that the belief that mass production equalled efficiency was almost universal. It became the 'ideal type', the model to be pursued by all industries even if they were ultimately constrained by the small-batch nature of demand. So instead of factories striving to reduce

145

changeover costs and increase the flexibility of small-batch production by producing near the final market, the alternative of specialization via production in dedicated lines became dominant. The inevitable consequence was the growth of large-scale factories at the site of least production cost, and the shipping of output to the site of final demand. In the most recent period, this specialization has occurred on a global scale, with 'world factories' producing components for assembly elsewhere.

A particular set of organizational patterns associated with this mass production ethic involved the specialization of production. In relation to factory layout it led to functional patterns of production organization in which particular types of machines (such as welding) and processes (such as assembly) were grouped together. Work-in-progress traversed the shop-floor in a confusing and higgledy-piggledy path as raw materials were transformed into final product. In terms of work-organization, management followed the principles set out in Adam Smith's description of pin production. Individual labourers were tied to minutely specified tasks in the belief that they would become more dexterous at them, and that the time involved in changing from one task to another would be minimized. At the same time the work was increasingly deskilled to minimize wages and the power which workers might have to disrupt production.[18] Detailed control over the work-process was taken away from the line-worker and given to supervisors — the line was to be kept working at all costs, even if this meant faulty products. The cost of rectifying these at the end of the production line was considered to be less than the costs of interrupting production. (It was these factors which led Schumacher to rail against the inhumanity of contemporary working life.) Inventory lines were to be kept full, just in case anything were to go wrong, and suppliers were subject to the same organizational forms — in order to squeeze costs to a minimum, dual-sourcing and arms-length relationships were preferred.

Scale economies in the era of mass production

These three underlying determinants of scale, considered together with differences between industries, make it possible to identify more clearly the particular characteristics of the scale economies which have come to dominate over the past century. Figure 6.2 relates the growth of scale economies in the three major forms of production organization — small-batch discrete products, large-batch discrete products and process industries — with the three most important dimensions of scale economies — product, plant and firm. It can be seen from this that with the exception of much of small-batch production (where product scale is limited by the nature of final demand or technological factors — See p. 158), scale economies have tended to rise coterminously. Not only have undifferentiated products come to be the norm, but so have individual production lines and plants. The consequence

146

Figure 6.2. *The technological trajectory towards scale economies over the past century*[a]

Dimensions of scale economies Type of industry	Product economies of scale	Plant economies of scale	Firm economies of scale
Small-batch discrete products	static	varies by sector, but generally static	varies by sector, but generally static
Large-batch discrete products	growing	growing	growing
Dimensional industries	growing	growing	growing

[a] These are 'ideal types', representing central tendencies. There will obviously be variations, reflecting sectoral specificities, differences in corporate strategy and some differences between countries.

has been that most factories have been too specialized to meet the immediate market and final output has been shipped to distant places. Significantly this has often occurred when there are no inherent technological reasons why plants should produce on a large scale.[19] Product life-cycles have tended to be long enough to recoup these heavy expenditures on large-scale and dedicated production lines. Finally, partly because of the homogenization of final demand (representing heavy indirect expenditure by large firms in taste creation) and partly because of the growing R&D intensity of technological progress, firms have become increasingly large, such that a relatively small number of TNCs now dominate global manufacturing production.[20]

This drift towards the large scale has of course had important implications for the Third World. The development of 'world factories' has simultaneously had positive and negative effects: it has been to the advantage of those selected NICs who have had a role to play in international specialization, but for other DCs this has made production for export more difficult. In so far as local markets are concerned, the small size of their markets has often been in sharp contrast to the minimum effective levels of scale in many sectors, making it difficult to achieve low-cost production. This has had manifold implications: in the agricultural sector the absence of local production of implements, fertilizers and so on has inhibited the growth of output; linkages for the continued development of the modern industrial sector have been restricted; and the pattern of unevenness of development within many DCs, favouring concentrated production in enclaves at the expense of decentralized development, has been exacerbated.

Factors inducing a change in optimum scale

A large number of analysts now acknowledge that since the early 1970s the IACs have begun the process of transition to a new pattern of growth. As explained in Chapter 1, this represents a departure from the pattern of economic and social development which emerged over the past century, especially since 1945. Naturally, as with any attempt to characterize such a complex terrain, there are a number of different views on the nature and significance of these changes. There is also some difference of views on what constitutes the 'new order'. Nevertheless there is fairly widespread recognition of a number of the more important components of transition: a change in market preferences from standardized to differentiated products; the introduction of new forms of managerial orientation and work organization; the diffusion of systemic electronics-based automation technologies; and the development of new forms of inter-firm linkages.

All of these have important implications for optimality in each of the dimensions of scale. It is relevant, therefore, to consider this in somewhat greater detail, beginning with a discussion of consumption patterns, organizational factors and flexible manufacturing technology. Since these changes are only in embryonic form, conclusions can only be drawn at a general level.

New preferences in consumption

As Henry Ford showed, by producing standardized products, and selling them in a standardized form to 'standardized customers', production costs were lowered and markets were expanded. But as the basic needs of consumers were satisfied, and as incomes rose in the IACs, so consumers became more demanding. Moreover, as market conditions became more competitive, producers played an active role in fostering consumer dissatisfaction with unchanged products. As a result, the last two decades have seen a significant change in consumer preferences in the IACs. Price is now less important than quality and novelty.

This trend towards what is called 'niche markets' is not confined to final consumption goods such as autos, garments and consumer electronics. It also applies in intermediate products such as steel and chemicals. In both of these sectors differentiated products — special steels and fine chemicals — have become the areas of highest growth.[21] In microelectronics as well raw processing power — 'the most bits for a buck' — is giving way to greater flexibility and programmable microprocessors are the areas in which the greatest technological rents are to be earned. Applications Specific Integrated Circuits (ASICs) are considered to be the wave of the future.

These changes in consumer preferences often demand matching alterations in the technology of marketing. The 'supermarket' principle, which has been widely applied not just to foodstuffs, is being threatened by the growing

148

differentiation of consumer preferences. Thus in both the UK and the US (where the principles of mass production are most firmly entrenched) sales of garments in large stores are being undermined by the development of specialist retailers. The attempt to apply these supermarket principles to other sectors, such as banking, appear to have had little success and firms such as Merrill Lynch have retreated from earlier plans to introduce 'one-stop financial supermarkets'.[22] As will become clear below, these changes in consumer preferences have not occurred autonomously and have been facilitated, and often fuelled, by simultaneous changes in production philosophy and technology which have made it possible to widen customer choice.

New forms of managerial orientation and work organization

The gains appearing to accrue from the introduction of mass production were phenomenal. Take the case of Henry Ford's early attempts to restructure his production system. In the case of magneto assembly, what had previously taken a single person 20 minutes was split into 29 operations with 14 persons assembling 1,335 magnetos in 8 hours. This represented a more than four-fold increase in productivity. The same principle was extended to the chassis assembly line, progressively reducing the labour content from 12.5 to 1.5 hours over six months.

So the principles of mass production were forged: factories laid out on a functional basis, dedicated lines, homogeneous output, just-in-case inventories, deskilled labour, specialized job-tasks, and control by supervisors. This was then extended to production in general with the expectation that the principles would be widely applied. The fact that this was not to be the case, and that in most of the engineering sector in the IACs around two-thirds of production occurred in small and medium batches, was generally swamped by the belief that mass production had triumphed. Where this was not the rule, it became one of the primary functions of management to redesign the organization of production so that the principles of mass production could be brought into operation.

But after a long period of growth this system ran into difficulties. It proved to be unwieldy, and required stable social environments which became impossible to maintain. It also became very costly. For example, the idea that tasks should be specialized led to quality control being relegated to the end of the production line. With complex and costly products, the ex-post rectification of errors proved to be very expensive. Moreover goods were often of a shoddy nature and were not sensitively attuned to changes in consumer taste patterns. (The experience of the US TV and auto industries is especially relevant here.)[23] Often, also, the functional layout of factories meant that work-in-progress was 'lost' for long periods. One British company reorganizing itself found that under the old system of functional layout, metal took 13 weeks to get through the plant (for a total processing time of less than 16 hours), travelling 3 kilometres in the process and involving the production of significant numbers of defective components.

Japanese 'total competition', in production technology and managerial efficiency, came as a devastating blow to this organizational paradigm. With the attempt to match Japanese quality, and then to reduce inventories, a managerial revolution began to sweep through Western industry in the late 1980s, beginning in the semiconductor industry. Just-in-time became the catch-phrase, quality circles were introduced, single-union agreements with flexible work practices were increasingly negotiated and suppliers were cajoled to co-operate. What is especially important is that after the initial misperception that 'Japanese work-practices' could be introduced into old-established systems in a series of discrete steps, Western management has come to realize that the real lesson to be learnt from the Japanese is the systematic and inter-related nature of these organizational changes, and the virtues of nimbleness and flexibility. These features of managerial orientation represent a profound change from the old mass-production order.

In order to achieve this flexibility, the central tenets in the mass-production system have to be overturned. Factory layout has moved from a functional basis to production manufacturing-cells, each of which possesses the range of machinery required in production. (The results of this reorganization have been striking — the British firm described above reduced its work-in-progress from 13 weeks to 12 days, with the metal travelling 80 metres rather than 3 kilometers and the defect rate being significantly lowered.) Instead of focusing on long runs of homogeneous output, the emphasis must be placed on frequent and rapid changes in product. This requires multi-skilled workers. In the pressing of body panels for autos, for example, the die-changing has traditionally been done by a specialized cadre of workers, and this has contributed to the time taken to change the tools. In the new mode it requires the same workers to operate the presses, to change the dies and in some cases to undertake elementary maintenance and repair tasks themselves. It also means that workers must become more actively involved in the production process and that they must be given some degree of control over it. This is especially relevant for quality control, since 'zero-defect' inventories are a prerequisite for just-in-time production.

These and other factors represent a fundamental reorientation of managerial perspectives, overturning a professional culture forged over nearly a century. There is no doubt that it is permeating rapidly, and that together with the introduction of flexible new electronics-based production technology, it will have a profound effect in transforming the inherited mass-production paradigm. At the same time, as shall be seen, it will have major implications for scale economies in production.

The significance of microelectronics-based automation technologies

It was not simply a clever phrase designed to capture the attention of the public that led Henry Ford to offer a Model T Ford in any colour as long as it was black. There were inherent technological reasons why this product specialization was desirable, and this was due to the desire to minimize downtime. The importance of this can best be explained through a number of examples. These examples are illustrative also of the interaction between the technological and organizational determinants of scale in production.

In automobile production, parts which are specific to particular models of cars require settings of machines, and these may take time to reset for different models. Take the case of body-panels, which define the outside lines of the auto. In general these are shaped by the pressing of flat sheets of metal in five stages, involving the exertion of between 300 and 500 tons of pressure. The nature of the final shape is defined by the 'dies' which are used. As can be appreciated, in order to translate this high pressure to the metal blanks, these dies are of considerable size and weight. Changing them can be complex and time-consuming — the production line has to be stopped and specialized die-changers called in to perform the task. In the mass-production paradigm this took up to eight hours, involving a considerable amount of idle machinery and workers. Inevitably, therefore, there was pressure to maintain the continuity of production, not just in the manufacture of body-panels but for other components and processes (for example, the colour used in the paint-shops) which were specific to individual cars.

A second example is that of the production of glass containers (such as tumblers and bottles) which involves a series of carefully-controlled operations. A precise amount of molten glass has to be extruded from the furnace into a carefully-positioned mould. The mould has to be manipulated in a series of steps involving the blowing of air into the molten mixture (to determine the internal dimensions of the container) and the formation of the top of the bottle, often requiring the defining of a screw-shape around the rim. These processes require precise control of the temperature of the molten glass, the positioning of the mould, the blowing of the air, the repositioning of the mould, the formation of a screw-top and the transfer of the final product to a moving line for inspection. The production of a different shape of container requires the whole process to be brought to a halt — it takes about two hours to change the moulds and to reset the timing of the machinery. As can be appreciated this manual resetting can only be approximate in a situation in which precision is vital and the consequence is generally that production occurs through a series of iterations. As a rule of thumb it is reckoned that machine downtime is around eight hours, two of which are for resetting and the remainder for iterative resetting. Not only are machines idle — the furnace requires refiring (for which fuel-use is disproportionately high) and waste products are produced during the iterative resetting of machinery.

151

A third example of the role which downtime played in reinforcing plant- and product-scale economies is that of steel rolling. Steel is made from molten material which is then produced in a series of final shapes to meet the needs of customers. This may involve flat sheets (used in body-pressing in the auto industry, as described above), bars or coils. Of course each of these forms has different tensile characteristics as well as different thicknesses, lengths and so on. In the case of the rolling of bars this involves the reception of molten metal and a series of rolling sub-processes during which the ultimate shape is produced. Changing the final specification requires the stopping of the rolling plant (and sometimes also the furnace) and the resetting of each of the stages of rolling. Again, as in the case of glass containers, the resetting is done manually and an iterative process is consequently required before acceptable output is produced.

From each of these examples it is possible to see the roots of scale economies in production. Changeover costs are substantial, involving machine downtime and spoiled output and the need to dedicate production to a particular product. In the case of automobiles, the general rule of thumb by the late 1970s was that plants had to produce 250,000 of the same cars a year, generally involving two separate lines, to reach the bottom of the cost curve. In the case of glass containers, production costs were minimized when machinery was dedicated to the production of a single type of container. The industry's ideal was a glass-forming machine producing a single type and size of container which was fed directly into a bottling plant situated on an adjacent site. Steel rolling occurred in specialized lines, often dedicated to the production of a single specification of metal. In each of these cases the minimum size of the line was set by the minimum scale economies involved in a particular sub-process, so that the inherent technological characteristics involved in body-pressing, for example, dictated that it would not be optimal to press less than a particular quantity of panels. Thus two sets of machines pressing 125,000 panels of the same type per year would cost less than 250,000 sets of machines producing one panel each per year. It was this factor that led to the definition of the optimal size of the assembly plant as a whole.

The link between these technological characteristics and the inter-firm division of labour is thus manifest. Bottles, cars, metal, beer and other products were each manufactured in a dedicated large plant in order to minimize costly machine downtime. Then, because in most cases the immediate market was too small to absorb this scale of output, the final product was shipped to consumers, even if they were at the opposite end of the world. Once this was being done, it was logical to locate the plant at the point of lowest labour-cost — perhaps using female labour in the Third World — especially as the abundantly available energy and state-provided communications infrastructure meant that communication costs were relatively low.

It is here that the significance of microelectronics-based automation technologies is to be found. Their flexibility and precision mean that many of the changeover costs which have underlain scale economies can be substantially reduced, and can sometimes even be eliminated. Consider, for example, the case of the glass-moulding machine described above. In the pre-electronic era, the precise timing mechanism consisted of a heavy metal cam, with a series of protruding switches each of which activated individual sub-processes. This was the type of mechanism incorporated in the musical-boxes of old, in which a rotating drum ('cam'), with protruding fingers, depressed extended metal 'notes'. In the same way that changing the position of the fingers on the drum produced a different tune, so changing the position of the activators on the cam affected the timing of the sub-process in the glass-moulding machine. With electronic controls the resetting of the activators is not just immediate, but also exact, so that downtime is reduced to mould changeovers; and there is little spoilage after resetting. The electronic timing mechanism is a small box — it used to require a reinforced floor, capable of holding a heavy rotating drum without distortion. In steel rolling new electronic controls are being introduced which make it possible to continually and precisely adjust the pressure exerted on the rollers and to rapidly change their size. Consequently, it is relatively easy to change the specification of the metal being rolled and plant flexibility is significantly enhanced. In autos new flexible die-changers allied to new work practices (which have in fact been more important) have cut changeover times from around eight hours to less than ten minutes. This has significantly reduced the cost of moving production from one model to another.

Increasing attention is now being given to the introduction of these flexible microelectronics-based automation technologies in a wide range of sectors. Whereas in the mass-production era automation was largely confined to dedicated production lines producing many variants of a single product, the reduction in changeover times (and the increase in precision) is now allowing the automation of medium- and small-batch production. It is also allowing mass-production lines to produce a wider range of products, in smaller batch-sizes. The technologies are still evolving and include flexible transfer lines (which allow for the alternative routing of work in progress), flexible machining cells (FMC, allowing for the machining of different parts), flexible manufacturing systems (FMS, involving the machining and assembly of different parts), and computer numerically controlled machine tools (CNC, individual stand-alone machines).

The relationship between these various flexible technologies and the extent to which they allow for the manufacture of many different types of parts produced at different scales is illustrated in Figure 6.3. It is instructive to compare these choices with the 'hard automation' of the dedicated production line.

Before considering the implications which these developments in flexibility have for the dimensions of scale, it is necessary to note one other emerging

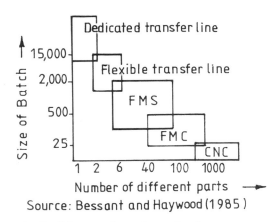

Source: Bessant and Haywood (1985)

Figure 6.3 *Options in flexible manufacturing technology*

characteristic of the diffusion of microelectronics. This concerns the increasing importance of systems in automation technology, reflecting a combination of the introduction of similar machine-logic devices and convergent technologies.[24] The common use of digital electronic control devices in a wide variety of individual machines (ranging from word processors, through computer-aided design to numerically controlled machinery and testing equipment) allows them to be easily interconnected. For example, machine controls can easily be specified in the design stage, and at the same time the information can be used for stock control and publicity brochures. Convergence arises because of the common technological solution to the processing of information and its transmission between different workpoints. The consequence is that together with the drive towards flexibility, technological progress in the IACs is being geared to the reaping of systematic gains, rather than to increasing the productivity of individual stand-alone machinery. This has important implications for the viability of small-scale production in the capital goods industry in DCs.

Implications for the dimensions of scale

Thus the 'normal' pattern of technological and organizational change which characterized economic growth in the IACs for many decades has begun to change. Some of this results directly from technological change, such as the introduction of electronically controlled automation technologies whose flexibility provides opportunities to switch production between products and so reverse the tendency towards greater scale. Other changes appear to have

154

their primary origins in the domain of organization, such as changes in factory lay-out and in the nature of work. Yet other changes manifest themselves as social phenomena, but in part result from the possibilities opened up by new organization and technology. Consumer preference for more diversified products (which is inherently descaling of product runs, and often also has descaling implications for plant size) is an example of this.

Although these changes are still at an early stage, they are becoming increasingly pervasive. Their relative importance is likely to vary between sectors. Is it possible, therefore, to predict the likely impact of these changes on the three dimensions of scale? Given the embryonic nature of these developments, the discussion which follows will only really be suggestive of the likely pattern of descaling. For reasons which will be discussed, the degree of uncertainty is particularly high in relation to changes in firm economies of scale.

Implications for plant size

Not all of these developments have descaling implications, for in some sectors opposite trends are to be found. It is important therefore to separate out these two divergent trends in plant size. Before doing so, it is necessary to digress briefly into a discussion of definitions.

Plant size is an ambiguous concept and can be reflected in a variety of indicators — numbers of workers employed, the physical size of the plant, or the units of output produced in a given period of time. Each of these criteria raises an important concern. With the rapid capital-intensification of production, a falling or static labour force may at the same time be associated with a major increase in plant output. The same is true of the physical size of the plant and here it is interesting that one of the largest Japanese automobile-components firms has adopted a policy to reduce the average physical size of its plants by 3 to 5 per cent per year and to hold the size of the labour force constant. Simultaneously, through the use of new flexible electronics-based automation technologies it plans to increase output. It has adopted this strategy because it believes that 'smaller factories are happier factories' and therefore that this will facilitate higher productivity and better quality production.

The most common interpretation of plant size probably refers to the rate of output in a given period of time, and here an especially important conundrum arises for developing countries. Consider the notional case of the steel rolling mill described above, producing, say, 50,000 tons of steel per year. In the mass-production paradigm, there would be a series of plants situated around the country, or the world, each specializing in a single specification of rolled steel. In no single region would the local demand be sufficient to absorb the total output of each of the plants, so the result would be a complex transport system distributing the output around the affected

155

regions. But with the introduction of the new flexible equipment, each of these plants might be able to produce five different specifications of the steel, either divided through the year into five sets of 10,000 tons, or in any combination of product specifications. In these circumstances, the local market would be able to absorb this diversified output, and there would be a much reduced need to export the final product. But is this a reduction in plant size? On the one hand the plants still produce 50,000 tpa each, so there has been no change. On the other hand, the flexibility of these plants means that it is now possible to introduce a new, flexible plant into a region (say a developing country with small markets) producing a range of products for the final market where previously the total market for any one of these types of output would have been too small to justify production unless a considerable proportion of output were to be shipped to other markets. In this sense, insofar as it could be said that scale economies prevented decentralized production in the old paradigm, it would appear that the new technologies are descaling in nature. However the impact of this new flexibility on plant scale might be described, there can be no gain-saying its overall effect on the location of production.

Reductions in plant size Broadly speaking therefore, it is possible to distinguish two different components of diminishing plant-economies of scale. The first is where plant size is falling in absolute terms, involving fewer people being employed, smaller physical size or reduced output. This is indeed occurring. For example, one of the major producers of pumps for the semiconductor industry currently serves the global market from a single plant; it is now setting in train a process whereby production will be split into three (and possibly in the medium-term, four) different plants. One will serve the east coast of the US, one the west coast and one Europe and Japan. (This latter plant may itself be divided into two, one being set up in Japan.) Interestingly, this transition to what the firm describes as a flexible manufacturing strategy involves a combination of both new electronics-based machinery and new managerial practices. It does not yet envisage the introduction of flexible manufacturing systems, which are widely recognized as being technologically immature. The second component of changing plant-scale relates to the mix of output. Here, as was seen in the case of steel-rolling, the scale implications are to be observed in physical space, relating to the economics of location rather than the absolute size of individual factories.

In addition to these technical determinants in each country and industry there are a series of macroeconomic factors which also have an important bearing on optimum plant size. The power-generating industry is an important example of how changes in the legislative environment complement technological factors and lead to a reduction in optimal plant size.[25] Traditionally this sector has been seen as a natural monopoly and in many countries is served by a large nationalized utility. In many cases these utilities have suffered from the same fixation with 'giantism' as Schumacher observed of the British National Coal Board. Large-scale plants generating 600 MW to 1,000 MW and costing billions of dollars have been constructed on the assumption of a rapid growth of demand. Yet whereas demand growth in the IACs used to average 7 per cent a year in the 1950s and 1960s, it fell to around 3 per cent during the 1980s and the likely future growth will be in the region of 1 per cent. Thus, as demand increments get smaller, very large-scale power stations will necessarily face idle capacity until demand catches up with these large increments in supply. High interest rates have also been seen to increase the cost of this idle capacity, while new technologies have emerged which reinforce the virtues of small-scale production. These include cogeneration (using waste heat to generate electricity), which can be operated to satisfy the needs of individual manufacturing plants, and combined-cycle gas turbines which are reliable, relatively cheap, quick to build and allow for a choice between different machines, thus enabling utilities to reduce their risk.

Perhaps, more importantly, changes in the legislative environment have also had an impact. Small-sized plants tend to be less disruptive and are thus less prone to delaying public enquiries. In the US the Public Utilities Regulatory Policy (Purpa) of 1978 was enacted to encourage energy saving by allowing small-scale cogeneration plants to sell electricity to the public utilities at the same price (the 'avoided cost') as it cost the utilities to produce the electricity. One decade later 3,720 small-scale Purpa generators produced more than 62,000 MW of power, equivalent to 9 per cent of the US's generating capacity (or the whole of the UK's).[26] Thus in the US these Purpa generators and a range of new investments in plants less than 200 MW are becoming of increasing importance. Similar trends seem likely to emerge in the UK as its power utility is privatized, although the extent to which smaller-sized plants flourish will depend on the precise provisions of the legislation.

The demise of the nuclear power industry in many countries, especially the US and the UK, is a particularly telling example of the dangers of giantism. Held to have great economic advantages, these large-scale generators have suffered not only from environmental hazards, but also from unanticipatedly long gestation periods. Consequently, and in view of their very high capital costs, they have proved to be highly uneconomic — in the UK their unit generating costs in 1989 were approximately three times those of thermal power plants, and the programme of expanding the number of nuclear power plants was brought to an end.

Increases in plant size Earlier in this chapter, a matrix was constructed (Figure 6.2) in which the three dimensions of scale (plant, product and firm) were set out in relation to types of industry (small-batch discrete products, large-batch discrete products and dimensional). It was argued that where it was possible to specialize production, large-scale plants resulted because changeover costs could be reduced. But three types of industry have avoided these growing scale economies. The first are those industries in which demand is by its nature heterogeneous, specified for the needs of individual customers. The major industry encountering differentiated demand is that producing capital goods where plant and equipment are often fabricated for individual users or for a small group of firms. By contrast, the intermediate goods industries (cement, steel, semiconductor components), the primary sectors (minerals and agricultural products) and the consumer goods sectors (with some exceptions discussed below) fit into the category of large-batch, standardized (and hence automated) production.[27] A second example of heterogeneous demand is the handicrafts industry where the individualization of each product is an important product-attribute and large-scale production is ruled out almost by definition. The third industry in which small-scale production has predominated is where automation was prevented for technological reasons. This has been the major factor limiting the growth of large-scale production in the garments, shoes and leather goods industries since it has hitherto proved to be nearly impossible to automate the assembly of limp materials.

It is in the category of small-batch production that the new flexible electronics-based technologies are having a major impact. Essentially, in the pre-electronic era the customization of final output was achieved by using highly flexible and generally cheap machine tools, with machine specifications continually being reset manually. The consequence has been that for much of the time — 70–95 per cent by one estimate in the USA[28] — machinery stood idle. Since these capital goods were relatively cheap, the costs of this low utilization rate could be contained and the barriers to acquisition were low. By contrast, the automation of small-batch production involves the introduction of costly equipment; and plants in these sectors become large to justify the investment. (This represents an increase in the fixed component of direct production costs discussed in earlier sections — see pp. 143–4.) Here it is possible to observe a plant-scaling tendency in production, in direct contrast to the descaling tendencies discussed above. This involves not just the enlargement of the scale of plants, but also the diversity of products, since these new electronics-based flexible technologies work best with 'families of parts', that is when utilized to manufacture products which are similar to each other.

These developments create considerable problems for the capital goods industries in the Third World. These small-scale workshops will come under increasing competitive pressure, both in global and domestic markets. The continued viability of groups of such enterprises, such as the well-known Oklah industrial estate outside Delhi which is renowned for its small-scale production of machine-tools for world markets, must be open to question. Additional pressures on these small-scale plants will be exerted by the advance of systematic technologies in the IACs. Here it is the capability to provide the whole package of capital goods, integrated through the widespread use of electronic control systems, which will determine competitive survival in the future. There are reasons to believe that the mechanical engineering industry will evolve in the same way that process-plant construction has come to be dominated by large integrating firms offering turnkey plants. This has already begun to emerge in the IACs. In the automobile industry, for example, production lines for engine manufacture used to be put together by the auto firm itself buying individual capital goods from a variety of small-scale firms. By the late 1980s they were acquired as a package, assembled by specialized large-scale capital goods firms.

A similar process of plant enscaling is beginning to occur in the garments industry, and this is of course a major problem for small-scale enterprises in developing countries. The final assembly of the limp cloth is still difficult to mechanize, although much progress has been made on the automation of in-plant materials transfer and stock control. Over the past decade major changes have been made in the pre-assembly phase, with the introduction of computer-controlled design, grading and cutting technology. This replaces a process which used to be undertaken manually with a drawing board, cardboard and a sharp knife. From a modest almost purely labour-intensive process, the industry is being increasingly transformed by the diffusion of new pre-assembly equipment, costing up to $500,000. This increase in the fixed component of direct costs is thereby forcing plant-scale economies into a sector which has traditionally been small scale in nature. Similar trends appear to be occurring in the case of the shoe industry.

The effects of these developments on DCs, especially those with low per capita incomes, are likely to be adverse. Textile, garments, shoes and leather products account for between one-third and one-half of all Third World manufactured exports, and for a much higher proportion in the lower income countries. In most cases production of these products has taken place in small-scale plants. The potential employment implications are significant here, since according to one estimate, around 10 million people are directly and indirectly employed in the textiles and garments industries alone in developing countries.[29]

Implications for product scale
The precision and flexibility offered by new technologies and by changed managerial perspectives is leading to major changes in the pattern of product technology, both with regard to the variety of products being offered, and the lead-time with which they are produced. In most cases the consequence is one of descaling, with product runs being shorter and time-horizons reduced. These effects are being felt across almost all industries. Some examples should give a flavour. In the garments industry, the size of production runs is declining and, simultaneously, the number of seasons is increasing and quality is being upgraded. In part this reflects an innovative response to

escape competition from low-wage DCs. But it is being facilitated by new electronics technologies, especially in design, cutting and grading, and new forms of organization and management. New computerized equipment saves not only labour and cloth, but also time in the calculation of different-sized patterns and the cutting of cloth, and allows for a substantial increase in the variety of designs which can be produced. The new information technologies also allow for a more rapid response to changes in market demand.

These new automation technologies have been used by the Italian firm Benetton to develop a rapid-response system to production organization. Widespread use is made of networked electronic point of sales terminals in all their shops throughout Europe. This information system is linked to inventory control in one of the most automated warehouses yet built. This is so flexible that before the goods are delivered their labelling and price tags are made out in the language and currency of the country in which they will be sold. Computer-aided design equipment is linked to this careful control over marketing trends so that it is possible to adjust rapidly to the minutest change in demand, adjusting colour-shading, or product mix, or developing new designs as appropriate. Production itself is undertaken by a large number of independently owned sub-contractors who receive regular instructions and design updates from the Benetton offices. This system represents one possible direction which the flexible manufacturing paradigm may take and illustrates many of the points which have been made above (pp. 151–4). It shows firm-scaling characteristics, in that through these innovations (which have required extensive indirect production costs) Benetton's share of the Italian knitwear and jeans market rose from 1.8 to 6.8 per cent between 1978 and 1982. It also shows some plant-descaling characteristics in production since Benetton has introduced an extensive system of small-scale subcontracting.

In the automobile industry, the introduction of the new electronics technologies has led to a rapid shrinkage in the time required for model development. This used to take 6–8 years but has recently shrunk to 2–3 years. Much of this is due to the use of computer-aided design (CAD), a technology with widespread application in other sectors. It also follows from the flexibility of production equipment — in the case of the British Rover Group's engine plant which was completed in 1989, the development lead-time for the new K-series engine was halved since it was no longer necessary to first build and test the engine before the (dedicated) production line was constructed. Because the new technology is flexible, it was possible to begin constructing the production line before the engine design was complete, with the confidence that any of the design changes required could have been incorporated in the final plant.

The Japanese have become the major exponents of these product-descaling strategies in the automobile industry (and other sectors). Figure 6.4 illustrates their relative performance in a number of important areas of scale. In

160

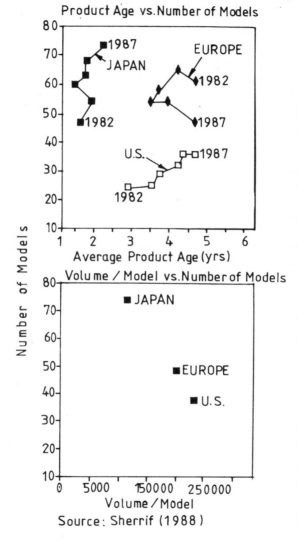

Figure 6.4.   Product economies of scale and economies of scope in the automobile industry

Figure 6.4a it can be seen that compared to other manufacturers, their product-age is much lower (reflecting a decrease in product-development lead-time) and the number of variants which they offer is much larger. From Figure 6.4b it is clear that this is not a consequence of their higher output allowing greater product diversity in large-sized production runs, but directly because their model product scale is much lower than the volume producers in Europe and the US.

These examples not only reflect reductions in product economies of sale, but also show the interaction between changes in plant and product-scale factors. This has especially important implications for developing countries. In both the garments and the shoe industries, the economics of location are dictating that production occurs near to the final market. At the same time, in the garments, shoes, consumer electronics and automobile industries the increasing incidence of protectionism means that the politics of production are reinforcing this change. This is shown graphically in the case of two Hong Kong garments firms which have relocated from their home base to the UK,[30] and have done so by using the most modern automated equipment. In part this is to get access to the European market, but it also follows the need to be able to respond rapidly to market changes. Similar trends are evident in the automobile industry.[31] Ultimately, apart from those particular sectors where automation is leading to an increase in plant scale, the effect of these product-descaling factors is likely to be felt on both product and plant scale, with a larger number of factories being built around the globe, each designed to meet local demand with flexible production associated with rapid changes in product.

Implications for firm-scale economies
In order to understand the significance of the changes occurring in firm-scale economies, it is necessary here to refer to the earlier differentiation drawn between direct and indirect costs of production. The larger the fixed component of direct costs, the more significant were plant economies of scale. On the other hand the larger these indirect costs, the more substantial were the 'economies of massed resources', that is, firm economies of scale.

There is a variety of indirect costs underlying production, of which four stand out in importance:

- R&D
- middle and senior management
- the acquisition of inputs
- the marketing and sale of outputs.

Of these, there is no special reason why the third and fourth items should be changed by the new technological and managerial systems sweeping through the IACs. In the case of middle management, there is now considerable speculation (and some evidence) that computerized information technologies reduce the need for intermediate levels of management.[32] Another factor militating against the growth of firm-scale economies is the tendency of large firms to be more bureaucratic and for innovation to be greater in new small firms. It is not clear how culturally specific this tendency is, since whilst it has been of considerable importance in the US, the rapid rate of innovation in Japanese and Korean firms seems to have occurred within very large (and growing) combines. In addition, Siemens, the largest West German firm, seems in recent years to have become the dominant European innovator in many sectors.

But these firm-descaling factors must be set against the simultaneous increase in the research-intensity of production and the growing market-intensity of sales. By the late 1980s these had speeded up considerably and became one of the most important characteristics of modern production. As such they dwarf the scale-diminishing implications of a reduced role for middle management. There are a variety of different ways in which this growth in R&D and marketing intensity are finding expression in the expansion of firm economies of scale. One immediate impact is that it is strengthening the role being played by TNCs in many sectors. This is becoming especially important in the chemicals and agricultural sectors as the biotechnology revolution is beginning to penetrate production. One recent study provides evidence for this and forecasts a major trend towards the appropriation by these TNCs of technological advance in agriculture.[33] Another expression is the growing power of global brands in determining market-share, in DCs as well as in the IACs.

But there are also other ways of diffusing indirect costs which do not have the same implications for firm-scaling. One possibility arises from the ability to swap technology, although this often involves TNCs. This is now an entrenched phenomenon in the global electronics industry in which technology licensing is induced less as a reason to maximize revenues from technology generation than as a means of obtaining access to the technology of rivals.[34] It is a process also sweeping through the aerospace, military, automobile and commercial vehicles sectors and is likely to become equally important in all other sectors in which the technological intensity in production is growing. Candidates here include the garments industry, of especial relevance to small-scale firms and household producers in developing countries.

Co-operation between small firms who share indirect costs of production is another alternative to the growth of large firms. This is probably at the most advanced level in what has come to be called flexible specialization.[35] In this, small firms collaborate and share those indirect costs such as marketing, design-intelligence and R&D which underlie the growth of large firms. This has become a particularly prominent form of organization in parts of Italy where *consorzia* have developed, facilitated by new forms of legislation. These groupings of small firms have enabled Italy to become the world's largest net exporter of shoes, garments and furniture. In footwear the average size of firms is 17 employees (as against 110 in the UK); in furniture it is 5.8 and in garments 5.5.[36] Similar types of co-operation are to be found in West Germany. In Cyprus, the government reversed a long-running strategey aimed at encouraging the growth of large firms, and adopted one in which *consorzia* of small firms (modelled on those operating in Italy) are being encouraged.[37]

A related aspect of these developments in firm-size is the belief that co-ownership may be especially productive in relation to the new organizational and work forms which are emerging. (The discussion by Schumacher and other thinkers in the AT movement concerning the possibilities for co-ownership and the virtues of small business become relevant here.) The production lines being pioneered in Sweden and Japan reverse the historic tendency for control to be taken away from the production worker, and in many plants the line-worker has the ability to close down the line if he/she notices something untoward happening. In the context of the conflictual relations between management and labour which have emerged in the older IACs it is difficult to conceive of this autonomy being returned to the line-worker without extensive disruption occurring in production. (In Japan it is possible because the quasi-feudal social relations which exist there seem to inhibit workers exercising this control in contradiction to the wishes of management).[38] It is arguable that the only way in which the more 'democratic' western IACs can successfully institute these new forms of production is through the introduction of a more participative system of ownership and management.

In Figure 6.5 these emerging changes in economies of scale are summarized and contrasted with those which developed in the mass-production era. In relation to products, there appears to be a reduction in scale in the large-batch discrete products and the dimensional industries, but an increase in scale in the small-batch discrete products industries. In relation to plant size, scale economies are reducing in the large-batch discrete products and the dimensional industries, and rising in small-batch production. By contrast firm economies of scale seem likely to increase in each of these three major categories of industry, unless there is a more widespread movement towards interfirm networking (as in the Italian *consorzia*) or technology swapping.

Changes in scale and appropriate technology in the Third World

Modern industrial society appears to be poised at a transition from a highly specialized production system in which the emphasis has been on giantism towards a more systemic and flexible paradigm. It is not yet clear how extensive these changes in scale will be, nor how these might be distributed between sectors, regions and countries. In part this uncertainty arises from

Figure 6.5. *The three dimensions of scale in the change from mass production to flexible production*[a]

Dimensions of scale	Product		Plant		Firm	
Type of Industry	Mass production	Flexible production	Mass production	Flexible production	Mass production	Flexible production
Small-batch discrete products	static	growing	static	growing	static	growing
Large-batch discrete products	growing	falling	growing	falling	growing	growing
Dimensional industries	growing	falling	growing	falling	growing	falling

[a] These are 'ideal types', representing central tendencies. There will obviously be variations, reflecting sectoral specifications, differences in corporate strategy, and some differences between countries.

the inherent lack of predictability of these developments and in part because we are still at the early stages of this process of change; it also reflects the fact that social and political processes will be involved in determining the course of future events. As such there is no unique scenario which will unfold, nor is there a single pattern of social organization which will encourage the emergence of a more rational and humane system. Indeed it is precisely this latter factor which opens the space for policy action in the AT movement. Alternatives do exist, and it is important that they be shaped in socially meaningful ways.

From the point of view of the Third World the need to shape these emerging technologies assumes even greater importance. This is not just because many developing countries face an urgent need to improve the living conditions for the mass of their populations, but also because the new paradigm offers particular opportunities for development, especially in so far as it reduces the scale constraints to production. Moreover, because many developing countries have not had decades of commitment to the outmoded mass-production paradigm, they may well be able to make the transition to a new order more successfully than can the mature industrial economies of North America and Europe. The underlying changes also pose some threat. Left to market forces in the IACs the Third World's historic pattern of dependence on inappropriate technology may continue.

There are four major areas in which descaling holds promise for AT in the Third World:

165

- to meet the needs of the modern sector, where continued economic growth is being hindered by underutilized capacity and by shortages of material inputs. High minimum effective scales of production in the context of small markets have led to monopolistic market structures and unequal patterns of development, while the capital intensity of these inappropriate large-scale technologies has exacerbated the already serious employment problems prevailing in many economies;
- especially in so far as the urban poor are concerned, more appropriate modern-sector technologies may cheapen wage goods and perhaps expand employment;
- descaled technologies might improve the prospects for the local manufacture of inputs, with linkages not only to the modern sector in the urban areas, but also to the agriculture sector where the mass of the population is to be found;
- and new possibilities are being opened up by emerging technologies, such as in the case of the micro-hydro plants whose sudden viability is almost wholly explained by the development of electronic switching mechanisms. Basic needs may be met in previously unanticipated ways.

It is helpful therefore to put together these various types of concerns of the AT movement in the LDCs with the emerging trends of the new paradigm, conscious that there is no unique form which will necessarily emerge. This is done in Figure 6.6 — the columns relate to the emerging changes in the dimensions of scale, the rows to some basic concerns of the AT movement. It is clear that in general the expected reduction in plant size in the mass-production industries is beneficial to the cause of AT in developing countries since it encourages local production. Conversely the growth in plant economies in the small-batch industries is generally adverse, especially in relation to the capital goods sector (perhaps producing inputs for agriculture). Greater product flexibility and shorter production runs not only mean reductions in plant size, but also open new possibilities for tailoring goods to meet local needs and tastes. In the case of the expected growth in firm-economies of scale, the general effect is, as expected, negative for AT, especially if (local) small firms tend to choose more appropriate techniques than (foreign) large ones — but this will of course vary between countries and probably also over time.

This chapter has considered the prospects for AT in the IACs by focusing on emerging changes in economies of scale. After many decades in which there seemed to be an inexorable drift towards ever-increasing economies of scale, the picture has now become more complex. In many sectors, especially those mass-producing discrete products, optimum plant size is falling and product runs are becoming smaller. Economies of scope are substituting for economies of scale and this presents exciting prospects for more disaggregated

166

Figure 6.6. *Likely changes in the dimensions of scale and their implications for appropriate technology in the Third World*

	Changes in scale in the dimensions of			
	Plant size		Product	Firm size
	falling in large-batch industries	growing in small-batch industries	falling	growing
Industrial development in modern sector	positive impact on economic growth	negative as local production hindered	positive as more possibilities	negative if large firms/TNCs choose inappropriately or repatriate profits
Wage goods for the low-paid	positive as local production	positive as goods cheaper	positive if for low income goods	negative if large firms/TNCs choose inappropriately
Intersectoral linkages (incl. for agriculture	positive as local production easier	negative as local production hindered	positive as more possibilities	negative if large firms/TNCs have fewer linkages
Wholly new possibilities (i.e. technological blending)	positive as local production easier	negative as capital goods industry is less viable	positive as new products are developed	negative if large firms/TNCs do not relate to local needs
Balance of payments	positive as local production easier	negative as local production hindered	positive if more local production or exports	negative if large firms/TNCs import more or export less
Encouragement of small-scale or co-operative ownership	positive as entry barriers lower	negative as entry barriers higher	neutral	negative by definition

units of production and therefore for a decline in the optimum economic scale of social organization. (The social optimum has been lower than the economic optimum for some decades.) It is not surprising, therefore, to find that the business community has begun to question the trend towards giantism and to see the economic benefits of smaller scale which Schumacher and others identified many years back. It is also not only in the IACs that the economic benefits of this descaling are apparent and, if anything, DCs are likely to benefit from this even more.

At the same time as there are tendencies towards descaling in some dimensions and in some sectors, enscaling factors are being injected into others. This has particularly deleterious implications for DCs, especially those who rely on low wages for their comparative advantage. In addition, whilst both product and plant economies of scale may in general be reducing, two of the major factors underlying firm-scale economies (that is, R&D and marketing) not only shows no sign of diminishing but, if anything, are likely to increase further. These growing indirect costs may either be met by a further growth in firm-concentration or by more co-operation and networking between small- and medium-sized firms. There are no inherent technological reasons why large-scale firms should win through.

There is thus no inevitability about the positive outcome of these changes. Clearly they are suggestive of a generalized tendency towards descaling and for this reason the overall impact is likely to be beneficial. What is less evident is the extent to which these new technological opportunities will diffuse and at what pace. One possibility is that left to market forces alone, the prospect of profits will induce rapid innovation. But this may not necessarily be the case. Moreover, the inadequacy of the market mechanism may not be confined to these changes in economies of scale. These factors are considered in the following chapters.

CHAPTER 7
AT, states and markets

The formulation of policies to encourage the development and diffusion of AT cannot be seen outside of wider policy discussion. Over the past decade there has been a vibrant debate about the nature of development policies in general. 'Neo-liberal' theorists have accused development economists and development policy of being excessively 'statist', ascribing too dominant a role to government in the process of economic development. Considered briefly, this recent neo-liberal critique can be reduced to five central tenets.[1]

- the primacy of economic over developmental considerations is asserted and it is argued that it is better to have more unequal shares of a large cake, than equal shares of a small cake. It is considered axiomatic that there is a trade-off between growth and employment-maximizing and/or redistributional policies;
- high rates of economic growth are thought to lead to a trickle-down of benefits to the population at large;
- growth is said to be maximized in the context of perfectly functioning markets for both physical inputs (such as labour, capital and raw materials) and for services;
- it is claimed that state intervention is characterized by 'rent seeking behaviour' in which state employees utilize their control over quotas, concessions and other policies to extract a non-productive rent from producers and consumers. State failure is considered to be endemic;
- however imperfect markets tend to be, market-failure is considered preferable to state-failure. The response to market-failure should not be a larger role for the state, but a drive to reduce market imperfections.

A number of policy conclusions are drawn from these neo-liberal tenets, amongst which two are particularly relevant to this discussion of AT: policy should be geared to maximize the operations of markets, especially by bringing factor prices in line with opportunity costs; and state intervention should be minimized and private entrepreneurship maximized. If these policies are adopted, it is argued, then appropriate products will be chosen and these will be produced with appropriate technologies. Thus 'factor markets will be cleared', that is unemployment will cease to be a problem, and the pent-up demand for (often imported) inappropriate goods will be exhausted.

Much of the discussion in preceding chapters has been relevant to this policy debate. In each of the three case-studies considered — bakeries, bricks and sugar — both state-failure and market-failure have been prevalent. But the existence of state interventions detrimental to the development and diffusion of AT can not necessarily be taken to give support to the neo-liberal paradigm's assertions. For even in cases when markets do function effectively, ATs do not necessarily flourish. Optimal policy will therefore necessarily involve a mix of market allocation and state intervention. The concept of an 'AT-enabling state' is particularly helpful here. One problem in these policy discussions is that there is often a tendency to generalize illegitimately between different sectors and countries and over time. Particular policies may be appropriate in some environments and not in others, and universal prescriptions thus should be avoided.

Market prices, government regulations and opportunity costs[2]

There are a number of respects in which economic opportunity costs are not reflected accurately in market prices or in government regulations affecting resource allocation. These can be conveniently classified into three groups: those affecting factor inputs, especially capital and labour (since land is relatively unimportant in non-agricultural activities and this book is exclusively concerned with non-agricultural activities); those affecting other non-factor inputs, such as raw materials and intermediate inputs; and product distortions which relate to the competitiveness of an enterprise's output.

A variety of government policies may affect these factor, input and output markets, exaggerating the difference between market prices and opportunity costs. Haggblade, Liedholm and Mead classify these into the following groups:

- trade policies, including quotas, tariffs, subsidies, foreign exchange rates and other foreign exchange controls
- monetary policy, including interest rates and banking regulations
- fiscal policies, involving both government expenditure and revenue
- labour policies, such as minimum wages, social security and public-sector wage policy
- the control of output prices for both consumer and producer goods; and
- direct regulatory controls, including licensing, monopoly privileges and environmental controls.

Estimating the magnitude of these policy distortions, as well as their economic impact, is not an easy task: what prices would really prevail if markets were to function perfectly; how can the quantitative impact of non-price interventions (for example, limiting imports through controls over volume, rather than through tariffs) be measured; to what extent can the differences in the price of particular factors be explained by variations in quality (for example, do varying wages paid by small and large firms reflect variations in the quality of labour employed)?

Cognizant of these methodological difficulties, Haggblade, Leidholm and Mead assemble evidence from a variety of developing countries. With respect to wage differentials, they conclude that in general 'the empirical evidence seems to support the contention . . . that the extent and magnitude of labour market distortions are generally rather small' (p. 16). In Asia there is no clear evidence that small and large firms pay different wages, whilst in both Africa and Latin America studies suggest that small firms benefit by paying wages approximately 20–30 per cent lower than those of large firms. Capital price distortions are adjudged to be much more significant. Whilst large firms generally obtain finance at low or even negative interest rates, the median rates of interest paid by small-scale industry in a range of DCs exceeded 40 per cent.[3] Although large enterprises tended to pay higher taxes than small-scale firms, they were more likely to obtain export finance.

Their evidence concerning price distortions in a range of DCs where reasonably comprehensive information exists is summarized in Table 7.1.[4] This shows that for the countries concerned, distortions of the price of capital tend to exceed those of labour, and hence to favour the large-scale capital-intensive firms.

Table 7.1. Policy-induced factor price distortions in large and small non-agricultural enterprises in selected DCs (expressed as the percentage difference in large firms' costs relative to small firms')

| Country | Period | % Difference in labour costs | % Difference in capital costs due to | | | |
			Trade Regime	Interest Rates	Taxes	Total Capital Distortion
Asia						
Hong Kong	1973	0	0	0	0	0
Pakistan	1961–4	0	−38	−44	+22	−60
South Korea	1973	0	−5	−35	+10	−30
Africa						
Ghana	1972	+25	−25	−42	+26	−41
Sierra Leone	1976	+20	−25	−60	+20	−65
Tunisia	1972	+20	−30	−33	na	na
Latin America						
Brazil	1968	+27	0	−33	na	na

na not available.
Source: Derived from Haggblade, Liedholm and Mead (1986).

These factor-price distortions are often complemented by a series of other government policies which adversely affect small-scale industry, and thus the development and diffusion of AT. Foreign trade regimes tend to provide large-scale industry with high effective rates of protection, whereas small-scale firms suffer from negative effective protection. Export finance is differentially available to large-scale firms and although small enterprises often benefit from fewer controls on their activities (for example, being freed from minimum-wage legislation in many countries) they are also often affected by other regulations (for example, on location) which affect their survival adversely.

The Haggblade, Liedholm and Mead study also reviews attempts to compute the consequences of these distortions. Unlike the IACs where the effect of market distortions on reducing output is limited (estimated at around 1 per cent of GDP), some studies suggest that the output loss in DCs may be much higher, ranging from 6–16 per cent. Output loss leads to (an unquantifiable) loss of employment, a dulling of agricultural growth (because of the greater linkages between small enterprises and agriculture), a reduction in exports and a tendency to reinforce income inequalities.

Some of these conclusions should be treated with care. For example, the estimation of overall output loss (said to vary from 6–16 per cent of GDP) is particularly suspect and rests on macroeconomic analyses of disputed validity. On the other hand, there is no doubt that the balance of distortions is heavily weighed against the development and diffusion of AT, as has been shown in each of the three case-studies presented in Chapters 3–5. This is particularly so in Africa and Latin America, rather than Asia, and follows from the political coalition in these two continents between large-scale capitalists, foreign investment and the state (see Chapter 8).

Consequently it is no surprise that the adherents of the neo-liberal perspective have pushed for a realignment of factor prices in the belief that this will lead to a more efficient allocation of resources, and hence to greater prospects for AT. The problem with this policy response, however, is that it is too limited. In focusing on the freeing-up of markets, it addresses only part of the difficulties faced in the development and diffusion of AT. Market forces alone are unlikely to lead to a significantly greater role for AT since there are a range of other factors which influence its development. Some of these have already been considered, especially the problems associated with technological development. In both the cases of small-scale sugar (Chapter 5) and cement (this chapter), the types of capital goods firms in existence are concerned with meeting the needs of large-scale producers. Left to market forces alone, OPS sugar technology and small-scale cement technology would not have been developed. Similarly, the types of entrepreneurs who are likely to utilize ATs are often not adequately trained to do so, and market forces provide little opportunity for their nurturing.

Many similar points about the inadequacy of a market-based response could be made at a general level, but it is only at a concrete level that they can be validated. Therefore it is helpful to focus in more detail on a particular country's experience (Botswana) since it has largely attempted to follow a set of policies designed to induce the choice of more appropriate technology by influencing market prices, and by reducing the capital constraint to innovation. What forms have these market incentives taken and have they led to the development and diffusion of more appropriate technologies?

The market solution and the diffusion of AT in Botswana[5]

Between 1960 and 1982, Botswana's GDP growth rate (12.8 per cent a year) was almost twice as high as that of any other African country. There were a number of sources of this growth. Reflecting Botswana's geostrategic importance, there has been a relatively large inflow of aid which, at $126 per capita a year in 1986, was the highest in Africa. However, little of this growth can be attributed to the agricultural sector which was gripped by drought through much of this period. Indeed the volume of agricultural production actually fell at an annual rate of 2 per cent from 1970–84, and the share of GDP contributed by agriculture fell from 34 per cent in 1965 to 6 per cent in 1985. The discovery and exploitation of copper and nickel and (especially) diamonds have had the most significant impact on Botswana's economic progress and the share of the minerals sector in GDP rose from 7–41 per cent between 1965 and 1985.

Manufacturing growth has also been important, although beginning from a tiny base. Between 1965 and 1980 it grew at 12.5 per cent a year, and although this fell sharply to 5.8 per cent a year between 1980 and 1985, it still exceeded the average of 3.5 per cent a year for sub-Saharan Africa. But growth in this sector has trailed that of minerals so that the share of manufacturing in GDP fell between 1965 and 1985, from 12 to 8 per cent.[6] Lewis and Sharpley calculate that in the most recent decade, approximately 48 per cent of manufacturing value added accrued from the growth in domestic demand, a further 37 per cent from import substitution and 14 per cent from production for foreign markets.[7]

This economic performance might sound like a confirmation of the market-oriented paradigm. After all, here is a country which in the midst of economic decline in sub-Saharan Africa saw a remarkable rise in GDP and a sustained increase in manufacturing value added. This occurred in the context of macroeconomic and industrial policies which explicitly favoured private rather than state ownership and which concentrated government intervention on short-run subsidies and price-adjustments rather than longer-lived protection or direct involvement in production. In the face of these achievements it might seem churlish to question the extent of this 'success'. But the fact is that there are a variety of reasons to suggest that this manufacturing progress could have been better, and that the technologies used could have been considerably more appropriate. There is also evidence that much of the progress which did occur was the result of factors other than those which the policy-makers believed were influencing industrialists. A

173

detailed consideration of this evidence can be found elsewhere.[8] Here the discussion focuses on the success of attempts to induce the choice of appropriate technologies through changing factor prices, reducing capital constraints and affecting the composition of units.

The Industrial Development Policy (IDP)

The IDP was published in 1984. It was designed to promote the government's major planning objectives of furthering economic growth and independence, diversifying the economy away from minerals and cattle and achieving these objectives in the context of 'social justice'. The explicit aims of the IDP were to create productive employment for citizens, to train citizens for jobs with higher productivity, to increase the GDP accruing in Botswana and to citizens, to diversify the economy and to promote industrialization in rural areas. The heavy emphasis on citizenship as a theme of industrial policy arises from the particular dependence of the economy on non-citizens — it was calculated in 1980 that about 10 per cent of gross national income accrued to non-citizens in the form of employee compensation, with as much again accruing as operating surplus of expatriate-owned enterprises outside the mining sector.[9] Although not explicitly linked to the diffusion of AT, there was a general presumption that citizen-based enterprises were more likely to be small in scale and to utilize more ATs.

Anxious to minimize the role of the state in industrialization, three basic principles were enunciated: the first was the 'Government's belief that a free enterprise, market-oriented system for this sector is both efficient in producing goods and services and economical in the use of scarce administrative capacity'; second, the sectoral emphasis was to be the utilization of the country's natural resources and the establishment of linkages with the major sectors of the economy (mining, government and agriculture); and, third, recognizing the divide between citizens and non-citizens, assistance to the large-scale sector would predominantly take the form of incentives, whereas the small-scale sector would be additionally assisted with extension services. It was also believed that the two major obstacles to investment by citizens were the lack of equity capital and the absence of long-term financing.

The Financial Assistance Policy (FAP)

FAP was the major instrument chosen to implement these general principles of industrial policy. Its focus lay with the creation of productive employment, that is, the creation of jobs with no output traded-off. The *numeraire* for assessing 'productive' was the border price of imports and exports, and the scheme was limited to the production of goods which either substituted for imported items or could be exported. (This is the same methodology involved in the estimation of sugar as an appropriate product in Kenya — see Chapter 5.) Large-scale mining and cattle production, the areas of historical comparative advantage, were excluded from the FAP. The only service inputs which

174

were included were 'linking industries' which provided a marketing function to 'productive' enterprises, and relevant repair and maintenance. The FAP scheme made a clear distinction between small-scale enterprise (SSE) and medium- and large-scale enterprise (MLE). The scheme for SSE was initially limited to those enterprises with a capital investment of P10,000 (subsequently raised to P20,000) and was confined to citizen owners. The MLE category was also subdivided between medium- and large-scale enterprises and was open to non-citizens as well.

The SSE scheme provided a grant to those enterprises which had a reasonable expectation of future financial viability at market prices. The grants were primarily for capital equipment (excluding motorized transport), although some leeway was provided to cover raw material (but not working capital) costs. The value of the grants were computed as the lesser of either P2,000 per job created or 40 per cent of the investment costs, with a further 10 per cent for female-headed firms and an additional percentage (on a sliding scale of 10–30 per cent) to encourage location in distant rural areas. Thus a male-headed small urban firm would receive a maximum grant of P4,000 (subsequently raised to P8,000) if he created two (subsequently four) additional jobs, whereas a female-headed enterprise in the far west of the country would receive P8,000 (subsequently P16,000) if a minimum of four (subsequently eight) new jobs were created.

This SSE scheme was predominantly seen as a sop to growing political pressure by citizens for participation in industry. It was thus designed to be a once-and-for-all grant (although there existed a loose infrastructure for extension services) and to be simple to execute and administer. By contrast the scheme for MLEs was considerably more subtle.[10] It consisted of two alternative grants:

Automatic Financial Assistance (AFA) Subject to the enterprises obtaining a manufacturing licence (involving a judgement by the Ministry of Commerce and Industry of profitable market opportunities), three types of financial assistance are unconditionally available to new enterprises: a *tax holiday* (100 per cent in years 1 and 2, 75 per cent in year 3, 50 per cent in year 4 and 25 per cent in year 5);[11] an *unskilled labour grant* (covering only citizens, and defined as below a specified wage-rate), reimbursing 80 per cent of wages in years 1 and 2, 60 per cent in year 3, 40 per cent in year 4 and 20 per cent in year 5; and a *training grant* to citizen employees covering 50 per cent of off-site costs in approved institutions for 5 years.

Case by Case Financial Assistance (CFA) The CFA grant was offered to both new and expanded enterprises, subject to a series of constraining limits. Both the unskilled labour grant and the training grant available for AFA were extended to CFA firms. In addition they were eligible for two additional grants: a *capital grant*, with a maximum of P1,000 for each projected job

175

(subject to maxima, depending upon location);[12] and a *sales augmentation grant* of 8 per cent of sales revenue in years 1 and 2, 5 per cent in year 3, 4 per cent in year 4 and 2 per cent in year 5.

Two overall limits were set on these CFA grants, relating to the benefit accruing to Botswana and to Batswana citizens. For each project an economic return had to be computed over a 5-year period, shadow-pricing unskilled labour at 50 per cent of wage costs, all imported and exportable inputs and outputs at 110 per cent of market prices, excluding training costs and financial transfers and deducting foreign capital inflows and financial outflows. Only those projects with an economic rate of return of 6 per cent or more would be funded. The second overall limit for CFA was that the total assistance provided should be the lesser of 50 per cent of the value added accruing to Batswana citizens over 5 years or a percentage of unskilled wages plus training costs over 5 years.[13]

All this sounds horrendously complicated, especially in a country in which administrative capacity is weak. But, procedurally, a CBA was programmed into the Ministry of Finance and Development Planning's microcomputer and data were entered, based upon the submission of individual firms, which had received prior evaluation by the relevant Ministry. This computer program automatically printed out both the firm's private internal rate of return, the economic rate of return as outlined above and the effect of the constraining limits on grant allocation.

Thus both the IDP and the FAP were concerned primarily with stimulating general industrial development. But recognizing Botswana's problems of unemployment and regional and gender inequalities, specific price-biases were built into these policies to encourage the utilization of labour-intensive technology, regional decentralization and the growth of female-headed businesses. Domestic value added was also encouraged by allowing its extent to constrain the overall quantum of financial support. Moreover, both the IDP and the FAP were cognizant of the 'composition of units'. By limiting some of the incentives to citizens (but only in the SSE scheme), it was not only hoped to increase domestic incomes, but also to influence indirectly the choice of technology. Administrative efficiency was also recognized and the scheme was designed to make minimal demands on state personnel. Rent-seeking behaviour, it was hoped, would thus also be avoided. It was believed that market incentives would be the most effective way of achieving these ends. Price responsiveness in entrepreneurial behaviour was thus an underlying assumption of these policies and the major constraint on innovation was assumed to be finance. Finally, it was assumed that technological capability either existed in Botswana or could be purchased on the market. Therefore, by reducing the capital constraint on innovation, it was believed that industrial development of an appropriate kind would result.

Thus beyond changing price signals to the private sector, little ongoing role was allocated to the state in a policy framework designed not just to

encourage industrial growth, but also to further the diffusion of labour-intensive technologies utilizing local resources.

The IDP and the FAP in practice

The overall pattern of loan commitments and disbursements   There are a number of features of the overall pattern of grant distribution which have a bearing on subsequent analysis:

- By the end of 1987, there had been a total of 1,926 grant commitments. Of these, 718 were to SSEs, 284 to CFA, 70 to AFA and the balance to agriculture. A significant number of these commitments were made in the very early years of the scheme.
- It was projected that 14,941 additional jobs would be created from these grant commitments, equivalent to an average of 2,500 per year. In reality, many fewer were created — about 50 per cent of the projected total for SSEs, 31 per cent of CFA grants and 63 per cent for AFA. In total, therefore, about 4,500 additional jobs were said to have been created under the aegis of the FAP over five years. This contrasts with total additional employment in the 'formal sector' of 5,500 jobs in the same period.[14]
- These grants involved a commitment of over P55m, of which P19m was disbursed by the end of 1987. Of these disbursements, nearly half went on labour subsidies, and approximately 15 per cent to each of capital grants to SSEs, capital grants to CFA enterprises and to sales augmentation. Grants to training and counselling were miniscule. Over one-third of these disbursements could not be fully justified in terms of FAP rules. This was due to various forms of fraudulent claims, including the provision of capital grants on projected jobs which never materialized.
- Of funds disbursed, the cost per workplace created was P14,690 for CFA grants, P2,064 for AFA and P1,608 for SSEs.
- About 60 per cent of CFA grants went to citizen-owned enterprises. This proportion remained fairly stable over the first five years of the scheme, was concentrated in lower technology sectors and predominantly involved non-indigenous citizens of European or Asian origin. None of the AFA grants went to citizen-owned enterprises. The SSEs were wholly citizen-owned, almost all by indigenous citizens.
- Only in the SSE sector was there evidence of a wide regional distribution of grants. There was also little evidence of an increase in female-headed enterprises.

The functioning of FAP at a disaggregated level

In itself these aggregate figures are not very illuminating and in gauging the success of the IDP and the FAP it is necessary to determine how the development and diffusion of ATs were affected at a more disaggregated level.

The SSE programme The context of small enterprise development in Botswana is one of an indigenous population which has predominantly subsisted off cattle production. Over the past few decades a significant proportion of the male labour force, especially in the southern section of the country, has worked as migrant labour in the South African mines; but this provided little opportunity for the growth of entrepreneurship or for the acquisition of industrial skills. The pool of small-scale entrepreneurs is therefore shallow and rural incomes are low. Moreover, incorporation within the South African Customs Union provides little protection from large-scale South African industry and this has inhibited the growth of small-scale industry. The pressure emanating from this sector for the introduction of a scheme such as FAP has nevertheless been one of the most significant political developments in Botswana in recent years and the pent-up demand for FAP grants was substantial. To a large extent this accorded with government objectives to increase the diffusion of AT since it was (correctly) expected that most of the SSEs would use labour-intensive technologies and produce for local consumption.

The effective freeing of the capital constraint on small-scale industry unleashed a flood of enterprises, more than half of which were in knitting and sewing, mostly providing school uniforms. Yet in the absence of effective marketing surveys, overcapacity was rapidly reached; this was exacerbated by competition from South African suppliers. Moreover, despite the relatively simple tasks involved in these small-scale sectors, the technological and managerial capability of most of these small entrepreneurs was pathetically inadequate for the task at hand. Their rate of failure has thus been significant. It is illuminating here to quote the views of a 1984 survey of these small-scale FAP recipients:

- projected employment among the 33 businesses for which such data were available was 98, with actual employment totalling 91 jobs, about a third of which were at best half-time. Employment in about half of the projects was strikingly fluid, with personnel and time commitments in a state of constant flux. One-quarter of the businesses used family labour regularly, reflecting the close affinity between business and family affairs . . .
- Only 10 per cent of the owner-operators felt that they were operating at a loss, but in perhaps one-quarter of the businesses, other sources of family income seemed to subsidise the FAP endeavour. Half of those interviewed claimed that they reinvested in the business, but some of them may be confusing working capital with reinvestment. About 25 per cent of owner-operators failed to distinguish between sales and profit. The most frequently perceived primary constraint was adequate markets (13 businesses), followed by lack of adequate inputs (7) and lack of capital (6). (Isaksen *et al.*, p. 60)

178

This 1984 evaluation of SSEs identified a variety of explanations for this failure rate. The major problems were due to poor entrepreneurial background, poorly-functioning markets, excessive competition and the absence of technological capability. Even those entrepreneurs who reported a shortage of capital as the major constraint could be analysed as suffering from an absence of underlying capabilities, but as seeing their problems in terms of a lack of adequate investment. The 1984 evaluation thus concluded that from the policy perspective, what these enterprises needed most was extension services and effective marketing surveys. Neither of these services was available on the market.

Four years later, little had changed except that these same problems had got worse. When in early 1988 the National Institute of Research sent enumerators to visit FAP small-scale projects which they were assured were in existence, only 73 per cent could be located after four visits and few could be classified as either being thriving or representing full-time production. The 1988 FAP Evaluation aimed to interview grantees still in operation but was only able to locate around half of all the sample. Of the ones which they were able to interview (which must be deemed to be the relatively 'successful'), less than two-thirds had created any additional employment over five years. With the exception of a few cement-block manufacturers (where the technology is simple, markets are assured and producers are protected by the high transport-to-value ratio of their product), most were in a parlous state. They encountered a variety of problems of which the following were most significant: absence of an identified, competitive market segment (38%); poor management skills (34%); shortage of working capital (31%) (which can easily be seen as an expression of general problems); inability to obtain inputs at a price to enable competition with imports (24%); shortage of work-space at affordable rents (21%); inadequately skilled workforce (14%), and problems with technology (10%). Once again, as in 1984, none of these deficiencies could be rectified by purchasing goods and services on the market.

Changing factor choice At the heart of FAP lies the creation of productive employment. This was designed to occur through two separate, but linked processes. The first involved the stimulation of new enterprises (which because of the labour subsidy were more likely to be profitable in sectors which were inherently labour-intensive) and the second encouraged labour-intensive technical choice. This latter outcome was promoted through the temporary correction of market forces by subsidizing unskilled wages, on a declining basis, over a period of five years.

The effects of this labour subsidy on the choice of technology have been marginal. Of the 19 MLEs investigated during the 1984 appraisal of FAP, only one enterprise was identified in which the subsidization of labour led to the choice of a more labour-intensive technology (in packing). Even in this enterprise the owner planned to mechanize this sub-process as the labour subsidy ran out, and indeed had done so by the time he was revisited in 1988. In two other cases the 1984 appraisal identified firms which were utilizing their FAP grants to mechanize activities which were previously undertaken in a labour-intensive mode. The 1988 appraisal found a slightly higher incidence of an adjustment in technology choice (that is, five out of 38 enterprises visited), but once again the majority of these enterprises planned to mechanize these sub-processes in the future when the labour subsidy expired.

The conclusion, therefore, is that the choice of technology is affected by a range of influences which may be more important than relative factor prices. Two linked explanations emerge from these evaluations of technical choice within FAP. First, process choice was often determined by product requirements. The example of brick manufacture (Chapter 4), which was assisted by FAP, is relevant here since the decision to meet the demand for high quality facing-bricks necessitated the mechanization of processing. The second factor limiting the choice of more appropriate technologies was the nature of entrepreneurship stimulated by FAP. Given that the policy provided financial support rather than assistance with entrepreneurial training and technological choice and development, the only entrepreneurs really able to take advantage of the system were expatriates and non-indigenous citizens. By culture and experience these entrepreneurs were hooked into capital- rather than labour-intensive technologies. The temporary subsidy of labour costs offered by FAP was clearly inadequate to influence their desire to utilize 'modern' technologies and to minimize the use of potentially disruptive labour.

Technocratic decision-makers vs proactive planners One of the objectives of the FAP scheme was also to be administratively appropriate and in the context of a severe skill shortage it was designed to 'run on auto-pilot', being easy to administer, requiring little discretionary decision-making and embodying transparent rules. There were two reasons for this approach. The first was that it reflected a shortage of skilled evaluators. But perhaps more importantly, the progenitors of the scheme were fearful of creating rent-seeking behaviour — hence the insistence on trans-parency and, with the exception of the very large-scale scheme, providing automatic access to grants. The instrument used to calculate available grants was social cost-benefit analysis, incorporated within a personal computer. [15] (This social cost-benefit analysis is the methodology recommended by the social welfare economics approach towards the measurement and determination of AT — see Chapter 2.) 'Evaluating staff', either in line ministries or in the Ministry of Finance and Development Planning, effectively enter data provided by applicants and read off the results. In isolated cases where interviews with applicants suggested a lack of entrepreneurial capability or bad faith, grants were refused or scaled-down but this procedure was 'unconstitutional', although never legally tested.

This system of evaluation has been associated with a significant degree of free-riding, that is, entrepreneurs obtaining grants for ventures which they would have undertaken anyway. There were a number of explanations for this. First, FAP was designed to help citizen-entrepreneurs at the margin. Yet there is a large area of entrepreneurial rent between the marginal and the best-practice applicants, and the modal applicants were nearer the best-practice than the margin. Second, this system of technocratic evaluation is conceptually flawed and naively assumes the efficacy of technocratic decision-making procedures.

There is much to this latter explanation. For example, soon after the FAP scheme was introduced, a number of the largest accounting firms managed to 'borrow' or replicate the cost-benefit program on their own computers. Prospective applicants then began their journey at the accounting offices which played around with the data in their applications until the 6 per cent economic rate of return criterion was met and the constraints on the total grants were minimized. Such procedures make a nonsense of this technocratic and reactive approach to industrial policy. Unless the line ministries are provided with some form of sectoral expertise which enables them to realistically judge the validity of claims on prospective sales, labour utilization, input availability and cost, and so on, the system lends itself either to a series of 'unforced errors' or fraudulent application. Such expertise would also have allowed line ministries to assist entrepreneurs directly, given the non-availability of expertise on the market.

What is at issue here is the fundamental role implied for the state in the process of industrial development and the development and diffusion of AT. It is not that state personnel are necessarily incapable of making professional decisions, but rather that the IDP and the FAP had no intention of promoting such capabilities within the state. Since many of the key 'knowledge inputs' into production, such as market surveys, marketing expertise and entrepreneurial training, were not available through the market-mechanism, the absence of such professional and proactive capabilities in the state was sorely felt.

Promoting technological capabilities and indigenous citizen entrepreneurship The IDP commits policy towards promoting citizen development. This latter perspective finds expression within FAP in a number of forms — the small-scale scheme is confined to citizens, and the extent of the MLE grant is limited in part by the value added accruing to citizens. The problem is that not all citizens are indigenous Batswana and many are fairly recent immigrants from Asia, South Africa, Zimbabwe and the UK. Whilst the FAP scheme makes no distinction between the origins of citizen-applicants,

181

the political pressure for the programme as a whole almost exclusively emanates from the indigenous community. Indeed, there has been a perceptible increase in the pressure for assistance to indigenous citizens. The experience of the FAP scheme has been such as to justify this orientation for it has highlighted the efficiency gap between marginal indigenous citizens' enterprises at the one extreme, and non-indigenous citizens and foreign investors at the other. Moreover, and this is evident not only in Botswana, indigenous citizens are more likely to be involved in small-scale production and to utilize labour-intensive technologies. Thus, eschewing moral and political issues, the nationality of entrepreneurship is an issue of considerable policy importance in the diffusion of AT.

The FAP assumes that imperfections in the supply of entrepreneurial and technological capability can be overcome through the provision of finance enabling entrepreneurs to buy these services on the market. This assumption falls down in two major respects. First, these capabilities cannot be purchased. For example, technological capability is cumulative in nature — it takes some measure of protected development (almost certainly more than the five years infancy implicit in the FAP scheme) before entrepreneurs are able to face up to market forces. Second, to the extent that some elements can be obtained on the market, there are few suppliers of these 'productive services' in Botswana.

These entrepreneurial and technological weaknesses are prevalent in the medium- and large-scale industrial sector as well as in the small-scale sector. The 1988 appraisal of 39 FAP-funded MLEs identified the following most general problems: shortage of suitably skilled workforce (33 per cent); shortage of working capital (a surrogate for general problems of competitiveness) (31 per cent); shortage of appropriately priced inputs to allow for competitive production with imported final products (27 per cent);[16] and absence of a clearly-defined market-niche (27 per cent). Once again these problems are unlikely to be solved by more efficiently functioning markets.

An illustration of the important role played by non-market inputs can be found in a brief case-study of the largest indigenous citizen-owned business in Botswana. Whilst it does not directly address the question of a labour-intensive technology, it clearly illuminates the problems which arise in all technological innovation. Founded and managed by a woman, it used FAP finance to expand from a small tailoring business to employ around 100 people, manufacturing garments for schools and government. Yet the provision of this finance alone has proved disastrous, since the owner lacked the experience and technological capabilities to manage such a relatively large enterprise efficiently. The result has been a growth in corporate and personal debt and, at various times, bankruptcy has loomed. Most recently the enterprise was saved by technical expertise provided by the Swedish Development Agency which effectively substituted for help which could, under a different policy regime, be expected to emanate from government. Briefly, the situation was one in which the system used for cutting patterns from sheet cloth was suboptimal — wastage was around 20 per cent (in a context where, even in efficiently run factories, material costs are around 50 per cent of ex-factory prices). The Swedes provided access to a computer-aided design and grading system which provided a new set of patterns which reduced material wastage to 5 per cent. Without access to this type of expertise, there would be no hope of this enterprise, or any other similarly sized local firms, continuing to survive in a competitive environment. But only one Botswana firm, owned by a non-citizen and exporting garments to Zimbabwe, has been able to identify and purchase this computerized equipment and even then there must be doubts about whether it can utilize this effectively without external technical assistance. Probably almost as important, the Swedes also provided assistance with the layout of the plant and production scheduling. In addition, both the owner-entrepreneur and some of her key staff were provided with training in Sweden.

What this brief case-study does is to show that the problems of promoting indigenous citizen entrepreneurship do not easily lend themselves to market solutions. These offer little hope of addressing the problem since the very absence of these technological capabilities is in itself a source of ignorance about what should be bought in the marketplace.[17] Various forms of practical assistance are required in building both managerial and technological expertise and, moreover, this is a task which is bound to take longer than the five years infancy implicit in the FAP scheme.

Coping with economies of scale There are various scale-related problems facing a small and relatively poor economy such as Botswana: the domestic market frequently appears to be too small to allow local enterprises to realize scale economies in production; when this does occur it might allow for only a single producer and may hence involve the pervasive growth of monopolies; and enterprises may be too small to finance important indirect production costs such as marketing and R&D. On the other hand, even in the IACs (see Chapter 6), smallness is not without its own advantages, not the least of which is that it encourages (but does not necessitate) flexibility in orientation, it undermines bureaucratic structures of managerial control and it makes competition possible.

Thus the policy challenge facing Botswana is to minimize the costs and to maximize the benefits of smallness. Indeed, the transition from large-scale inflexible production to smaller-scale flexible production noted in Chapters 1 and 6 offers significant opportunities to Botswana and other small countries. Two sets of reorientation are immediately apparent. The first concerns the necessity of re-educating the business community and state officials away from their fixation with large-scale production. A good case in point in Botswana relates to the production of bricks where current proposals to build a very large-scale factory will exclude the prospects for a number of smaller-scale plants (Chapter 4). The second is to provide some mechanism whereby Botswana firms, which are small by international comparison, can find some way of sharing indirect costs of production. Here the case of the garments industry is particularly apparent. Botswana possesses significant opportunities in a number of markets, but to take advantage of this will require access to computer-aided design and grading equipment (costing in excess of $200,000), market intelligence on future patterns and marketing itself. The Italian garments industry has shown that all of these indirect inputs in production, as well as the shared-utilization of computerized equipment, can be done on a common basis but that these common services require the stimulus and co-ordination of an effective state mechanism.[18]

So far, with the exception of government provided accommodation and technical support in the industrial estate schemes,[19] the Botswana Government has left it to the market to provide a stimulus for this sharing of common facilities and services. The same is true of the provision of productive services where, aside from accounting and legal services, precious few of these productive inputs have yet emerged.

Skill-creation and the labour market The IDP recognized that one of the primary constraints limiting industrial development in Botswana was a shortage of adequately trained workers. Consequently a training grant was built into FAP, covering half the costs of off-the-job training for citizens in institutions licensed by the Ministry of Education. Yet of the P18.9m disbursed between 1982 and 1987, a mere P81,787 was allocated under this heading. Given the severe skill-constraint in the economy, this element of financial assistance has clearly not served its purpose.

In searching for an explanation it is once again clear that the market is an imperfect mechanism for transmitting the allocation of resources towards dynamic comparative advantage. In part this is because the decision-takers themselves are not aware of their own limitations, a point which can be illustrated by the extent to which 'worker efficiency' was said to vary amongst a sample of the largest employers in Francistown, the second largest town. Six enterprises were visited whose managers had had operating experience in Zimbabwe/South Africa/elsewhere. They were asked to rate the performance of their workforce, and responded as follows: 60 per cent of Zimbabwe and 30 per cent of South Africa (textiles); 25–30 per cent of Zimbabwe (furniture); 90 per cent of Zimbabwe, 75 per cent of South Africa and 50 per cent of Germany (textiles); 50 per cent of Zimbabwe (textiles); 80 per cent of Zimbabwe (bakery); and 100 per cent of Zimbabwe (ceramics).

All of these enterprises were foreign owned and managed, all utilized a common pool of labour and three were in the same sector. Yet it is striking that there is such a high variation in their estimation of relative 'worker efficiency'. Indeed what this reflects most of all is in fact a variation in 'management efficiency'. The absence of indigenous supervisory skills was also mentioned by other firms, only one of which had made a conscious attempt to train its workforce. It had also made recourse to the market for this training and after a considerable search it identified the Institute of Development Management (a parastatal) to run a supervisory course. Three months after the contract was signed and ten days before the course was due to start, no word had been received from the Institute, so the course was cancelled.

What emerges, then, from the experiences of these various firms is an absence both of the demand for relevant training (reflected in part by low worker-productivity) and of the supply. Allowing market forces to correct this structural imbalance clearly holds little prospect of success.

The FAP and the market-oriented solution

It is clear that there are distinct prospects for expanding the manufacturing sector in Botswana particularly in production for foreign markets. One source of optimism is Botswana's unique access to a variety of markets, especially to the USA through the Generalized System of Preferences scheme (GSP), and through the EEC's Lomé Convention. This provides particular incentives for South African and Zimbabwean firms establishing affiliates in Botswana to take advantage of this market access. Another positive feature lies in its attractiveness to 'exiles' from both its southern and northern neighbours. Botswana has a relaxed and non-racial atmosphere which is in sharp contrast to the situation in surrounding countries. And, of course, as long as the mining sector continues to grow and the easy stages of import-substitution remain unfilled, there is also the possibility of expanding production for the domestic market. Given high unemployment, and gender and regional inequality, these objectives are the best method for the widespread diffusion of appropriate technologies.

But to take advantage of these opportunities Botswana has to be able to overcome some of its disadvantages, of which its remoteness, poorly-developed supplier industries (including services), its lack of infrastructure and its low technological development are most apparent. The question raised here is whether the policy prescriptions implicit in the neo-liberal perspective lend themselves to policies which enable these opportunities to be grasped. More specifically, what role does the FAP play in furthering growth and structural change in Botswana's manufacturing sector?

In discussing these issues it is helpful to consider briefly the extent to which Botswana's recent industrial policy has reflected or diverged from the framework set out by the market-oriented approach. In the following respects it can be regarded as being in harmony with neo-liberal theory:

- primacy was given to private sector development and wherever possible, state ownership was avoided;

- public infrastructural goods were provided at opportunity cost and were not subsidized;
- attempts were made to correct for market failure by subsidizing labour and penalizing the use of foreign exchange;
- protectionism was largely avoided, so where support was given, it was provided in the form of subsidies rather than tariffs;
- quantitative controls were not employed and price-signals were used in preference;
- support to the private sector was provided on a temporary basis in order to discourage inefficiency and permanent infancy;
- border-prices were utilized as the basis for assessing social welfare.

Nevertheless there were also some key areas in which industrial policy diverged from the market-oriented paradigm:

- Some state ownership did exist, especially in meat processing. It is significant that this was the major sector of manufacturing growth, especially of exports.
- Local ownership was favoured, largely through confining the SSE scheme to citizens. In addition, the constraints on overall grant provision were based on domestic value added accruing to citizens.
- Female-headed entrepreneurs were favoured in the SSE scheme, as was regional decentralization in the whole programme.
- A tax holiday was provided in the AFA grants to MLEs.
- Preferential purchasing was made available through a sales augmentation scheme.

Despite these areas of divergence from the neo-liberal framework, by comparison with industrial policies implemented in other countries (including many IACs) Botswana's policy framework can be considered to be a relatively faithful reflection of this ideology. Moreover, to the extent that the programme departed from the neo-liberal schema, prices were the primary mechanism used to encourage a shift in resource allocation. So how can the programme be judged?

At an overall level, performance was very good. But it would seem that this was due to the growth of the mineral sector, import substitution and the overall attractiveness of Botswana in the context of regional instability and the *dirigisme* policies adopted in neighbouring countries. More specifically, the success of Botswana's industrial policy in changing the choice of technology appears to have been limited. The price-inelasticity of demand for labour limited the success of altering factor prices, and because of the gap between citizen and non-citizen technological capabilities, the degree of rent ('free riding') inherent in the system was high. In addition, because the MLE scheme was open to all-comers, potential productive opportunities have been blocked for emergent indigenous citizens, storing up political tension for the future and potentially blocking the accretion of indigenous technological capability,[20] and reducing the use of ATs. In both the small-scale and larger-scale sectors, the provision of finance tackled the wrong sort of market failure — the FAP scheme intervened in capital markets, rather than technology and productive services markets. In neither of these latter cases can market failure be overcome through price reform.[21] Consequently, the rapid diffusion of new SSEs was associated with a high degree of entrepreneurial failure and some significant immiserization in rural areas; many MLEs operated with high degrees of X-inefficiency. The period of infancy recognized by FAP (five years) was too short for indigenous citizens to develop the requisite technological capabilities. And, consequent upon these various shortcomings of the FAP policy, significant industrial opportunities appear to have been neglected, especially in production for foreign markets.[22] More relevantly, there was little evidence of a shift towards the use of more ATs.

The question is whether these undesirable consequences of industrial policy could have been avoided, and if so, how? Broadly speaking, two alternative approaches can be envisaged. On the one hand, minor changes could be made to bring Botswana's industrial policy even more closely in line with the neo-liberal schema. Primarily, further attempts could be made to redress market failure, for example by bringing wages more in line with opportunity costs (that is, close to zero). If this proved to be impossible, then the subsidization of wages could be extended beyond five years. (This labour-subsidy, targetted at market failure, is distinct from the infant industry argument and there is no theoretical reason why it should have been temporally limited.) The favouring of indigenous citizenship could be phased out, tax holidays could be removed, preferential purchasing abolished and more rigorous attempts made to privatize the few enterprises where state ownership existed.

Yet in view of the problems faced by Botswana's industrial sector, it is dubious whether these steps would have had the desired effect. The transition to more flexible 'niching' strategies which is a key component of contemporary external competitiveness (see Chapter 6), especially in garments production, seems to be beyond the reach of existing entrepreneurs and there are no market-based institutions providing this form of stimulus to local industry. Similarly, the sharing of overhead costs which would allow smaller-scale Botswana enterprises to maximize the benefits of smallness by sharing design and marketing and by taking advantage of new flexible technologies almost certainly requires state co-ordination. Moreover, the long-run accretion of technological capability does not seem likely to arise from providing conditions for greater short-run profitability. And with respect to ATs, greater emphasis has to be given to assisting entrepreneurs by informing them of the range of technological choice available, assisting them in the acquisition of technological capability, upgrading managerial control of production, training the workforce and stimulating local repair and maintenance capabilities. This is especially relevant for indigenous citizen entrepreneurs, who are more likely to use ATs.

For these and other reasons, it would therefore seem that for Botswana to grasp its market opportunities, a strategic capability is required in the state. Yet as was made clear in earlier chapters, some forms of state intervention may create more harm than good. This state capability has to be appropriately focused since in a small economy such as Botswana, and one with such a severe skill-constraint, some form of sectoral targetting will be essential. State policy also needs to be geared to the challenges of the modern world, rather than to the inflexible dogma of earlier *dirigisme*.

Small-scale cement production: the role of state policies

The evolution of small-scale cement technology illuminates the importance of state policy in the diffusion of AT in a different context to that of Botswana. In this case it involves a role both for the district state (that is, at the commune level in China) as well as the central states' attitude towards product specifications. Since the experience of the two countries which have given most attention to small-scale cement (India and China) is of potential significance to a range of IACs it is instructive to first discuss briefly the role of the cement industry at a global level, paying particular attention to DCs.

Cement in the world economy

The move from hunting and gathering to settled agriculture and habitats necessarily involved the construction of durable abodes. The traditional method of construction, compacted earth, laths and earth or stone blocks, made no use of cementitious materials and it was only fairly recently that modern binding materials were introduced. The first recorded use of mortar (that is involving a mixture of sand and cementitious materials used to bind blocks or stone) was in Egypt. The Greeks and Romans developed the use of lime as a basic raw material input, but all these mortars suffered from the twin flaws of not setting when wet, and only having structural properties on the external surface.

The introduction of various silicaceous materials such as volcanic ash and burnt clays solved both of these problems, leading to the development of what has come to be called hydraulic limes. The initial use of these in the Roman empire, in which the best quality volcanic earth was drawn from Pozzuoli, has led to the generic term for these materials as *pozzolana* mortars. These allowed for the construction of thinner walls, arches and domes since they had better structural qualities. Because of their hydraulic properties, they could also be used in the construction of baths, canals and drains.

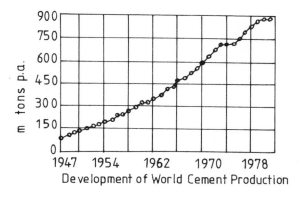

Source: Feichtinger et al (1983a)

Figure 7.1.   *The development of world cement production (m tons)*

Pozzolanic hydraulic mortars then fell into relative disuse until the early part of the industrial revolution when the renewed need for buildings with structural properties led to their reintroduction. In the 1850s portland cement[23] became widespread. This involved the sintering of inputs at a temperature of around 1400–1500⅓C. Initially the process was undertaken on a batch basis in a vertical kiln which is much like the lime kilns still in use. Subsequently there was a series of significant technological developments, the most notable being the introduction of rotary kilns at the turn of the twentieth century.

For a number of reasons, cement has probably now come to be the most ubiquitous of modern building materials: it is transportable and easy to use; it has high structural integrity and is consequently an essential ingredient in many constructions; its raw materials are widely available; and alternative materials such as wood and steel are often in short supply.[24] Whilst there is a variety of specialized cements in use, the overwhelming share of global cement production is that which at a minimum conforms to the specifications of ordinary portland cement.

As with most global industries it has been the post-Second World War period which has seen the greatest surge in output, as is evidenced from Figure 7.1 below. Growth in production was continuous between 1947 and

189

Share of World Production   Global Output (m tons)

Source: Feichtinger et al (1983b)

Figure 7.2.   *The change in relative shares of world cement production, 1950–83*

1974, rising from around 50m tpa to over 700m tpa. The general downturn in
the global economy in the early 1970s saw the first major reversal in trend and
despite a minor upsurge in the latter 1970s (mostly due to the continued
increase in Third World production) the growth curve flattened. If the long-
run 1947–82 trend is maintained, then it is likely that global cement
production will be around 1.25bn tons in 1995.

This growth in aggregate global production masks important differences
between countries. Although no comprehensive econometric studies have
been undertaken, it would appear that the income elasticity of demand for
cement is high at low levels of per capita incomes and low at high levels of
income.[25] Circumstantial evidence for this is provided by Figure 7.2 which
shows (on the left axis) the share of total global cement production and (on
the right axis) total annual cement production in tons. From this it is clear
that not only is the share of the industrially advanced countries falling, but so
is the absolute level of production. By contrast in most DCs (represented in
Figure 7.2 by Taiwan, S. Korea, Brazil, India and Mexico) the production of
cement continued to grow even through the 1970s. The Eastern European
countries, too, showed a significant increase in production.

There are a number of reasons why the growth of cement production in
DCs was so much higher than that of the industrially advanced countries. In

190

the first place their overall growth rates were substantially higher than the IACs through the 1960s and 1970s, but this in itself explains only a small proportion of the variation. A second, and probably the most substantial reason, is that at low levels of per capita incomes infrastructural investments are especially important. These include not only railways and roads but also public and private buildings such as hospitals, schools and houses. Indeed in the Third World the overwhelming proportion of cement is used in the manufacture of concrete blocks for housing and low-level buildings, whereas in the IACs it is mostly used where structural integrity is required, such as in highways and high-rise buildings. The third major reason why Third World cement production has grown so substantially is due to the substitution-effect in which ordinary portland cement is being used instead of other pozzolanic materials.

Nevertheless, despite this rapid rate of growth in cement production, consumption per capita in DCs tails far behind that of the IACs (Table 7.2). Whereas in 1984 per capita consumption in Italy was almost 682 kgs, the figure for India was only 41 kgs, and although these represent the extreme ends of the spectrum, in general it is the case that such disparities between DCs and the industrialized countries are common. In so far as the DCs are following in the footsteps of the industrially advanced countries, there is likely to be a continued advance in their production capacity and a continuing relative (if not absolute) fall in IAC production. Trade in this industry is small, at around 8 per cent of global production, reflecting the widespread availability of suitable raw material inputs and easy access to production technology. Thus the importance of the cement industry is likely to grow very substantially in the Third World, at least in the next two or three decades.

The choice of technology

The key variation in cement technology concerns the design of the kiln. The development of portland cement in the nineteenth century occurred through the use of kilns which are similar to those currently producing lime. Basically these are stationary vertical shaft kilns (VSKs), operating on a batch basis in which the raw materials are fed in at the top and the burning zone is optimally kept at a depth of about 4ft. The final product (clinker) emerges through a grate at the bottom and is subsequently ground and mixed with gypsum to retard setting, and thus facilitate use.

Towards the end of the nineteenth century these VSKs were supplanted by rotary kilns (RKs), rotating on a horizontal axis. These have three characteristics which have tended to make them the preferred technological choice:

- the quality of output produced by the VSKs is not only more variable than that produced by the RKs (given the batch nature of the process) but, perhaps more important, it is also inherently lower[26]

Table 7.2. Cement consumption per capita, 1913–81 (kgs pa)

	1913	1930	1938	1950	1960	1970	1981	1984
W. Europe	54	90	127	146	289	475	462	417
France	40	125	91	155	289	551	501	393
Germany	98	73	212	200	436	602	475	428
Italy	36	85	95	111	319	603	746	682
E. Europe	21	35	48	86	230	386	509	477
Africa	5	14	18	37	40	59	91	105
Kenya	1	6	4	21	26	24	39	30
Nigeria	1	2	2	5	23	16	91	49
N & S America	63	134	75	153	188	219	242	228
USA	148	222	138	251	299	326	289	332
Canada	178	167	176	210	290	320	339	265
Brazil	3	2	8	14	12	25	73	146
Mexico	8	16	20	54	89	148	255	231
Peru	5	9	21	39	54	84	135	100
Asia	2	6	9	8	35	67	110	133
India	1	2	4	7	18	26	33	41
Japan	10	43	72	48	223	528	659	587

Source: Compiled from Cembureau (1982 and 1985).

- RKs, involving enclosed processing on a continuous basis, are inherently subject to economies of scale (see Chapter 6)
- RKs allow for continuous processes which have become increasingly automated over the decades. From the point of view of management these process-plants are much easier to control than the human-controlled, batch-oriented VSKs.

As a consequence of these factors, RKs tend to be of much larger scale than VKs. The optimum size of plant in the industrially advanced countries begins at around 500,000tpa (1,500tpd). Where markets are proximate (either because of high-density populations near raw material sites, or because of bulk exporting) these plants can exceed 6mta (18,000tpd), as they do in Japan. More typically the need to balance dispersed markets with raw material sites which are invariably distant has meant that most IAC plants are less than 1.3mtpa (3,900tpd). By contrast the VSKs seem to run out of scale economies at a capacity in excess of around 350–400tpd. This is because of problems encountered in loading and unloading the kiln and in maintaining product homogeneity. In India and China most mini-cement VSK plants have a capacity of less than 150tpd. Thus the range in scale of cement technology in these countries is considerably greater than in the case of sugar (Chapter 5).

It is sometimes argued that rotary kilns have a much lower energy efficiency than vertical kilns.[27] Yet, in addition to the doubts cast upon the engineering logic involved in this assertion, many of the large-scale plants have been able to compensate for their energy-loss by using waste-heat to preheat the raw materials before firing; it is this which has come to be known as suspension preheating. In addition, modern variants of RK kilns utilize dry rather than wet-processes and this further reduces their energy utilization.[28]

In the light of these differences between vertical and rotary kilns and between dry- and wet-process RK technology it is instructive to observe their relative fuel efficiencies since they point to the apparent inefficiency of the small-scale shaft-kilns in comparison to large-scale RKs which use modern suspension preheating and precalcinating technologies (although energy is of course only one item of operating costs) (Table 7.3). Even the Indian mini-cement plant under development is more energy intensive than modern RKs. The data show also that both old and new designs of Chinese small-scale VSKs are less energy efficient than their Indian counterparts. An additional important difference between the RKs and VSKs is that in the former process heat is applied in an indirect form, so that a variety of sources can be used including gas, coal, electricity and waste. In the VSKs the fuel is mixed in with the raw materials and there is little flexibility; only particular sorts of coal are suitable.

Unfortunately detailed costings on the choice of technology are not reliable.[29] They do not exist for China, and for India they have been done only on a cursory basis. As in the case of sugar processing (see Chapter 5),

Table 7.3. Approximate energy consumption in best-practice plants

	k cal/kg cement
Rotary kilns	
Dry (long kiln)	860
Wet (long kiln)	1,300
Semi-dry	850
Dry (with suspension preheaters)	790
Indian vertical shaft kilns	
Current	1,100
Potentially	1,000
Chinese vertical shaft kilns	
Old design	1,300
New design	1,160

Source: Interviews; NATO/CCMS–46, 1976; Li Mingyu et al. (1984).

financial comparison in the Indian cement industry is bedevilled by a range of restrictions on price, inputs and outputs. For example, large-scale plants are forced to sell a proportion of their output at controlled prices, to which is added a uniform freight-equalization charge irrespective of the distance of plants from final markets.

After stripping out the effect of all these 'market distortions', the ex-factory price received by the large plants was around Rs784 per ton (1985 prices). At these prices most of the large-scale RK plants were able to run at a profit, but this is only when they depreciate capital at historic and not replacement costs. (Reference to Chapter 5's discussion of Indian sugar-processing shows that this depreciation procedure heavily understates the costs of large-scale capital-intensive plants and thus overstates their profitability.) Detailed costings exist for one 25tpd small-scale plant in Northern India. At an ex-factory price of Rs794 per ton, and operating at 90 per cent capacity, the small-scale VSK plant shows an internal rate of return (IRR) of 13.3 per cent, falling to 10 per cent at an 80 per cent capacity utilization. An enlarged 50tpd VSK plant of the same size was under development and was computed to show an IRR of 14.1 per cent at 90 per cent capacity utilization.

These figures suggest that at Indian factor prices, the small-scale VSK technology is financially viable, particularly if the large-scale RK plants were to depreciate at replacement rather than historic costs. Given its ability to utilize small deposits of raw materials, which are particularly prevalent in Northern India where the largest markets are to be found, and the lower foreign exchange content of the technology, its economic viability is likely to be even more favourable. Although no detailed analysis has been made of its social appropriateness, this is likely to follow similar lines to sugar processing, further favouring the attractiveness of the small-scale technology.

It is likely that these conclusions apply to other countries, and especially to DCs. Many countries have fragmented markets, only small pockets of raw materials, or large raw material supplies which are some distance from the market. In China where the transport infrastructure is weak, it is estimated that trucking cement a distance of more than 150–200kms adds 30–40 per cent to its cost.[30] This trade-off between scale, markets and deposits is not unique to DCs. A conventional large-scale RK plant producing 1mtpa over 60 years will require limestone deposits of over 50m tons. Thus the largest UK plant has a designed capacity of 3.5mtpa but only operates at 1.2mtpa. This is due to a combination of the spread-out nature of the domestic market and the virtual collapse of both domestic and export markets — factors inherently locational in nature.[31]

The use of VSKs is limited to only a few countries. Kenya operates two cement plants, one in the interior using semi-wet large-scale RK technology and the other at the coast which has two relatively large-sized vertical kilns.

This coastal plant has exported cement to the Gulf Region for some years. India has provided more of an incentive to mini-cement although it was not until the lat(1970s that any active steps were undertaken to either improve the technology's performance or increase the rate of diffusion. Between 1981 (when the first commercial plant was installed) and 1985, 19 had been commissioned and a further 57 were on order. Most of these were in the 39–99tpd category. By mid-1985 the mini-cement plants accounted for only 2.8 per cent of all India production (1.18mt out of 42.8mt), but if all new licences are taken up this will have risen to just over 10 per cent of total capacity by 1990.[32]

It is only in China that small-scale cement technology has flourished. The proportion of total cement provided by an increasing number of mini-cement plants has consistently risen over the years (Table 7.4), from 34 per cent in 1965 to around 75 per cent in 1983. This involved an increase in the number of these small plants from around 2,800 to over 4,800. What is especially interesting is that even after 1980 when China became much more receptive to imported technology, production by the large-scale plants virtually stagnated, whilst that of the small-scale sector has advanced both rapidly and consistently. In relation to the Indian experience it is worth noting not only the relatively large and growing share of the small-scale sector, but also the size of Chinese cement output. With only a third more population, Chinese cement production as a whole was over two and a half times that of India (Table 7.1). Yet the output in the Chinese large-scale sector was only about two-thirds of that produced by the large-scale sector in India and the superior Chinese cement performance arose entirely from production in dispersed and locally financed mini-cement plants. It also involved the use of small-scale technology which was less efficient than its Indian counterpart. (See Table 7.3 for relative energy-efficiencies.)

There are two major reasons why small-scale cement technology has

Table 7.4. Sectoral contribution of cement in China

	Total output (000 tons)	Large and medium sector (000 tons)	% of total	Mini-cement sector (000 tons)	% of total	No. of mini kilns
1965	15.0	9.9	66	5.1	34	200
1970	25.9	15.5	60	10.4	40	
1975	49.6	21.6	43	28.3	57	>2,800
1977	55.6	19.1	34	36.6	66	
1978	69.2	22.7	33	42.5	67	
1979	73.9	24.7	33	49.	67	
1980	79.9	25.6	32	54.3	68	
1981	82.9	25.1	30	57.1	70	
1982	95.2	25.9	27	69.3	73	
1983	108.3	27.2	25	81.1	75	>4,800

Source: Compiled from Sigurdsen (1979) and Li Mingyu et al. (1984).

thrived in China. The first reflects the overall policy commitment in the early post-revolutionary period to a technological policy of 'walking on two legs', that is encouraging both small- and large-scale production. This was in large part implemented through a decentralized rural industrialization programme. By throwing the onus of resource generation to the local-state level, central development budgets could be allocated to different uses. It is this mobilizing effect of the macro-economic environment in China which is stressed by Chinese cement planners

> About 50% of mini cement finds its usage in the rural construction and it is especially the case during recent years due to the new economic policy of agriculture practiced in our country. The capital construction of water conservancy works, the improvement on rural housings and the upsurge of industry in small towns stimulate a thriving development of mini cement industry. Moreover, due to the economical investment of mini cement plants, it is possible for the state, collectives and even individuals to raise funds for setting up such plants. (Li Mingyu *et al.*, 1984, pp. 4–5)

The second reason why small-scale cement was able to thrive in China relates to the official specifications of cement quality. Most countries in the world use the ordinary portland cement specifications as the minimum standard which can be sold. This is measured in terms of the 28-day strength of the final product (28 newtons/m^2), although it is common in many IACs for these standards to be exceeded. (It is around 44 newtons/m^2 in the UK.) Until the recent improvements in Indian small-scale cement technology in the early 1980s, ordinary portland cement could not be produced consistently. This meant that some output had to be wasted and a great deal of time and effort were required to sort out the cement of acceptable standard. This is probably the key factor explaining the slow diffusion of mini-cement technology in India.

By contrast the Chinese recognized a much more diverse set of requirements for cement. In earlier discussion it was pointed out that whereas in the IACs most cement was used for structures which required reinforced strength (such as bridges, high-rise buildings), this was not the case in DCs where the bulk of use was in simple houses and low-rise buildings. The Chinese recognized this diversity of use and instead of specifying a single grade of ordinary portland cement, they allowed for six grades of final product. Ordinary portland cement produced by the large-scale rotary plants was used for bridges and high-rise buildings, whilst simpler needs were met by the small-scale plants.

Differentiating between different categories of cementitious products offers considerable scope in many other DCs. In addition to different types of cement, other substitutes are possible. These are invariably of a lower grade than ordinary portland cement, but almost always associated with simpler and more appropriate process-technologies, which involve the use of cement substitutes based on lime, hydraulic-lime, gypsum and lime–pozzolana mixtures as well as the blending of cement.[33] Hydraulic lime or lime–pozzolana mixtures are normally strong and water resistant, but they set more slowly than cement and are of lower strength. (Thus if equivalent strength to cement is required, the replacement rate *vis-à-vis* cement will vary between 1.5 and 2.3.) Three basic raw materials are required for this set of products: limestone (not necessarily of high quality), burning fuel and a source of pozzolanic material, of which there are four major possibilities. These are volcanic products (pumice stone or ash), rice-husk ash, pulverized fly ash (a by-product of coal-fired power stations) and pulverized fired clay (including crushed bricks and tiles).

Whereas limestone is widely available throughout the world, suitable types of volcanic products appear to be confined to E Africa, SE Asia and Central America. Burnt clay is widely available, but except for marginal quantities of waste from brick and tile plants, it is an expensive type of input since it has to be not only quarried, but also fired. Coal ash is confined to the localities of suitable power stations and is, anyway, produced only in limited quantities. Finally rice-husk ash is widely available, but has other uses such as a fuel.

Blended cement is another possibility. This is widely practised in the global industry with various extenders being substituted for cement. Indeed in India this is now the dominant form of cement produced. There is a range of opportunities available, including not only coal-slag ash but also rice-husk ash and other types of pozzolanic materials. One of the virtues of this approach for developing countries is that it may not necessarily involve the production of cement itself as the extenders can be ground into the final product in a separate process. Another alternative is to use gypsum as an input. Its properties are different to those of lime (it sets rapidly, it is more porous, it has slightly lower strength and it is slightly water-soluble). This limits its use, largely to internal purposes where its fire-resistant qualities are especially valuable. A major advantage with gypsum-based materials is that their firing occurs at only around 170°C, around one-eighth that of cement. It is therefore a much more energy-efficient building material.

Most of these alternative cementitious materials can be manufactured on a small scale, generally less than 10tpd. Their technology, based upon lime-kilns which are generally similar to the VSKs of mini-cement, are simple and generally manufactured locally. They are more labour intensive and often produce a cheaper product.[34] Their potential is, however, limited in the following ways:

- suitable pozzolanic material is not available everywhere
- the quality of the final product is often inferior to that of portland cement, limiting its uses
- final quality (especially concerning its workability) results in resistance from users[35]

• national building standards often limit the extent to which these alternative materials can actually be used.

There are a number of lessons relevant for an AT-enabling state which emerge from this brief recounting of DC experience with appropriate cementitious materials: first, there are clear opportunities for these materials which are not being grasped, either in terms of their development or diffusion; second, it would appear that market-signals alone are not successful in promoting their further development; third, it would also appear that the nature of state intervention in most DCs is not adequate to the task. This latter conclusion throws the focus of investigation on the nature of state actions likely to promote the development and diffusion of appropriate products and materials such as these. This is the task of the concluding chapter.

CHAPTER 8
The AT-enabling state

For many decades the path of economic growth and development seemed to be unproblematic. A clear road was laid out, both for the industrially advanced and the developing worlds. This was based upon the use of an 'efficient' technology which maximized output by producing in ever larger factories, with cheap energy and unlimited material inputs, and which organized work in a hierarchical framework of highly divided tasks and skills. But as the post-war decades rolled on, it became ever clearer that this pattern of social and technological development was not only associated with undesirable social and environmental developments, but that its conception of 'efficiency' was flawed. The plant-level micro-efficiency which it espoused was often associated with meso- and macro-level inefficiency, since the growing scale of these ever larger plants (producing high volumes of poor quality standardized products) often made it difficult to capture these potential efficiencies. Nowhere was this more apparent than in the Third World where (as shown in Chapter 1) poverty is not only widely prevalent, but is of increasing severity. Growth rates have fallen and, seemingly everywhere, the environment is stretched to its carrying capacity.

This quest for micro-level 'efficiency', which, with its adverse economic, environmental and social consequences added up to a picture of macro-level inefficiency, involved a range of implementing institutions. The private sector, in its varying guises, was primarily responsible for the allocation of investment in the industrialized market economies, with public-sector investment generally limited to what were considered to be natural monopolies. In most of the Third World, too, the private sector played the primary role in resource allocation. However, as market conditions made it more difficult for private entrepreneurs to appropriate returns on new investment, partly because of the difficulty in running ever-larger factories efficiently, the state came to play an increasingly prominent role as a direct investor. In the socialist countries the state was the primary allocator of investment.

These private-sector investments took a number of forms, including TNCs, joint-ventures, publicly quoted companies, conglomerates and small family businesses. State investments also assumed diverse forms, although not as varied as those in the private sector. In all countries, socialist and capitalist, industrially advanced and developing, the state also played an important role in setting the ground rules in which investment occurred. It was generally within these boundaries that the market

199

provided the price signals which guided investment by individual institutional actors.

The appropriate division of responsibility between state- and market-allocation of resources is now a topic of intense debate. There is a strong, albeit ebbing, current of neo-liberal opinion arguing that the economic ills of many countries, including the DCs, are directly attributable to the over-weening role played by the state. This, it is believed, is as much evident in the choice and generation of technology as any other feature of economic performance. Rolling back the state has been pushed to the forefront of the policy agenda, with respect both to overall economic performance and the development and diffusion of AT. And yet, as can be seen from the case-study of Botswana in Chapter 6 and the evidence of resource allocation in all the other case-studies in earlier chapters, there is little evidence that private-sector participation in itself will lead to the wider diffusion of ATs.

The second part of the neo-liberal agenda is to get markets to operate more effectively. This has proved difficult to achieve. Markets are not merely a construct of state policy, but also a reflection of power relations. Their structure cannot easily be changed at the wave of a policy wand. Moreover, there is powerful evidence that even when markets function effectively, the resource allocation which results may not be necessarily socially desirable. Much pollution results from external diseconomies and is a natural consequence of profit maximization. 'Socially inappropriate' forms of work-organization which have degraded the quality of working life may not only be neutral with respect to market perfection, but 'progressive changes' may only diffuse slowly through their operation.[1] Thus, as the various case-studies contained in this book have shown, if resource allocation is left to the market alone, even a well-functioning market, it is unlikely that social welfare will be optimized. This is especially true in DCs, where not only do markets operate particularly imperfectly, but where there is also an absence of suitable institutional innovators to carry through socially efficient forms of investment.

But the evidence from countries confining investment to state-owned enterprises suggests that this route is also not optimal in the search for desirable forms of economic development. The absurdities of the large-scale mass production paradigm are probably more acutely represented in Eastern Europe than in any other part of the world economy. The world's single largest automobile factory is in the Soviet Union and attempts to assemble 750,000 cars a year, approximately three times the size of an optimal plant. And the most glaring example of inappropriate technology in this book involved the transfer of technology from socialist North Korea to socialist Tanzania. The inescapable conclusion is that a mix of state and market is required if ATs are to diffuse more widely.

Characteristics of the AT-enabling state

It is first necessary to consider the social basis of an AT-enabling state since certain political 'preconditions' are necessary if relevant policies are to be implemented.[2] White provides a taxonomy for analysing the state which has much wider application than the problems of socialist industrialization which he is considering.[3] He identifies three basic factors determining the effectiveness of state action:

- Its social nature. This concerns the extent to which the state represents the summation of individual interests (the perspective underlying the neoliberal paradigm), or those of particular groups, or whether it has a degree of 'relative autonomy' which enables it to operate with some independence from interest groups.[4]
- The state's politico-administrative capability. This involves its capacity to identify a policy direction, to administer these policies through bureaucratic procedures and a technical capability to analyse problems and formulate feasible solutions.
- The specific modes of involvement of the state. Here White distinguishes two types of policy: *'parametric'* measures in which 'the state's role is limited to providing a [basic] framework of institutions and resources conducive' to meeting its policy objectives — these may be regulatory, may define an institutional context in which its objectives are to be attained, and may include the provision of appropriate infrastructure; and *'pervasive'* measures in which 'state organizations become more directly involved in processes of industrial investment, production and circulation, eliminating or circumscribing the autonomy of economic actors ... In a capitalist context, the state may strive to establish a "social structure of accumulation" by nurturing the emergence of [a] financial and industrial bourgeoisie'.[5]

It is helpful to consider the characteristics of an AT-enabling state in the light of this taxonomy.

The social nature of the AT-enabling state

In the various case-studies of the development and diffusion of AT contained in earlier chapters, the social basis of the state played an important role in determining the nature of technological choice and development. In each case the state reflected the interests of different groups although in some cases their influence waxed and waned over time. For example, the Kenyan state has undergone a series of transitions, and these have had profound affects on the choice of technology.[6] In the early colonial period the state primarily responded to the needs of European settlers and this was a period in which the oligopolistic control of the bread industry (which has dominated the choice of inappropriate baking technology — Chapter 2) was defined. After the Second World War, and for the first two decades of Independence, it was the interests of foreign capital which predominated in the state, and this was reflected in part by the establishment of large-scale capital-intensive sugar mills (Chapter 5). As the post-colonial economy has progressed, a smaller-scale indigenous entrepreneurial class has emerged, and this is reflected in a number of schemes favouring the development and diffusion of AT: during the 1980s there has been a significant (but unmeasured) growth of smaller-scale bakeries in rural areas, reducing the dominance of the large-scale inappropriate tunnel bakeries; the success of the smaller-scale OPS sugar plant has begun to lead to a process of emulation, and a number of proposals are being actively pursued for new OPS plants; and, in the case of brick manufacture (Chapter 4), there also appears to be considerable dynamism in the private sector for small scale brick-pressing.

By contrast, neighbouring Tanzania did not have a large European settler community and for a long time its needs for manufactures were met not only from Europe, but also from large-scale plants in Kenya. There never was a powerful domestic entrepreneurial class which dominated state actions in the same way as in Kenya. Reacting against this, the post-colonial state acted with a considerable degree of 'relative autonomy', attempting to pursue a policy which it saw as favouring the interests of rural and poor groups. In this it was much influenced by the example of China where such policies led to the rapid development of rural industries utilizing ATs. (See Chapter 7 for the example of mini-cement technology in China.) Yet, despite this intent, and despite a considerable level of ambiguity in policies actually implemented, for the state itself is not homogeneous, the Tanzanian state seems in retrospect to have acted predominantly in its own interests. Investments were made in inappropriate technologies which had the effect of consolidating the power of the central state over the peripheral state and the state in general over private capital and labour.

What these various examples show is that the social basis of the state plays a key role in determining the pattern of technological choice and development. Thus for a policy environment to be developed which encourages the diffusion of ATs, the interest groups which benefit from these technologies have to be directly represented in the state. It is possible that this is beginning to occur in Kenya. There, after two decades of rapid agricultural growth, the lobby for small-scale and rural industry has been strengthened. In part this has been because of the change in political power from Central Province ethnic interests (centered around the capital city) to those emanating from the peripheral Western region. In part it is also because indigenous capital — often having at its disposal surplus generated in agriculture and rural trading — has found its expansion in the 'modern sector' blocked by the power of foreign investors. In China, at least until the late 1970s, rural interest groups exercised a powerful influence over state action, leading to rapid decentralized and small-scale industrialization.

Agricultural interests, too, influence the state to introduce policies favouring ATs. When agricultural development is given a clear policy emphasis, important linkages arise which foster the diffusion of AT. This is especially the case when such development occurs through small-scale farming rather than through large-scale enclaves, since this pattern is more likely to be associated with the local, and small-scale reinvestment of agricultural surpluses. The provision of infrastructure for agriculture, such as rural access roads, is also beneficial to the development and diffusion of AT.

The influence of rural interest groups in the state has accelerated the diffusion of ATs in both the Philippines and Taiwan.[7] In both cases increases in agricultural output led to more than proportionate increases in non-agricultural output and employment. This is especially true for Taiwan, where by contrast with other DCs such as Korea, small-scale AT has been especially prominent.[8] Ranis identifies a direct relationship between enterprise size and rural location (as proxies for appropriateness) and the influence of agricultural interests in the state:

> What is crucial here, and not yet fully understood, is the importance of agriculture and its relations to dispersed rural industry as a key to both successful domestic growth and the export-oriented performance which is so well known internationally. It is noteworthy, for example, to recall that, in 1951, only 34 percent of all the industrial establishments in Taiwan were located in the five largest cities, quite low by LDC standards; but even more spectacular is the fact that this proportion was unchanged in 1971, after two decades of rapid growth which culminated in Taiwan's reaching the end of her labor surplus condition. The proportion of the total number of persons in manufacturing employed in the larger cities actually declined, from 43 to 37 percent of the total, between 1956 and 1966, while the proportion for services also declined, from 41 to 34 percent. Employment in rural manufacturing, on the other hand, increased from 47 percent to 52 percent of the total and that in rural services from 49 to 56 percent of the total during this decade; the rest were located in small towns. (Ranis, 1989, pp. 4–5)

A final point concerning the social basis of the state relates to the policy prescription designed to 'get the prices right'. Particular price regimes do not emerge by accident. They materially affect social welfare and reflect the balance of power. For example, low real interest rates and high rates of inflation favour entrepreneurs investing in large-scale capital-intensive technologies. Similarly, the rural–urban terms of trade affect the levels of rural incomes and thus, as has been argued, the degree of rural linkages to small-scale technologies. Prices are responses to political pressures and consequently, however eloquently argued, the call to 'get the prices right' often misfires because the interest groups backing the new price regimes are not sufficiently powerful in the domestic polity, or within the state itself.

The politico-administrative capacity of the state

Almost all DC states are poor in the three key capabilities which define politico-administrative capacities: the ability to identify policy options, the administrative capability to implement them and the technical capacity to analyse the consequences of alternative policies. These capacities are particularly poorly developed in relation to the assessment of appropriate technological choices. There are three reasons why this is the case:

- As has been argued in earlier chapters (especially Chapter 2), many characteristics of appropriateness are inherently difficult to measure. This is especially the case in relation to the social and environmental dimensions of AT. Even in DCs it is not easy to measure the extent and impact of external diseconomies such as acid rain. These difficulties are compounded in DCs where basic knowledge of the environment is much poorer. Similarly, improvements in the 'quality of working life' or in social cohesion can only be imperfectly reflected through measurable indicators, for example, absenteeism and vandalism.

- The administrative machinery is not adequately trained to define the details of AT-enabling policy, nor to implement these efficiently. In most cases technology assessment has been reduced to the application of cost-benefit analysis. Most commonly this involves merely discounting financial costs and returns; in some cases it incorporates the use of shadow prices for key physical inputs and, even more seldom, for the weighting of 'social' inputs and outputs. But despite the rhetoric, these wider criteria in technology assessment have seldom affected real resource allocation.[9]

- Attitudes towards AT, particularly to small-scale and labour-intensive technologies, vary. Here interesting and important differences exist between Asia on the one hand, and Africa and Latin America on the other. In Asia, small-scale capital has played an historically important role in both industry and agriculture. The logic of small-scale production is clear and there is considerable receptivity towards AT in these state apparatuses. By contrast, in Latin America both agricultural and industrial development have occurred in the context of large-scale production, which is identified with modernity — the pervasive atmosphere is one in which small-scale production is treated with great scepticism. Similarly, and especially in Africa, AT often is at best regarded as a second-best alternative and at worst as a 'plot' by the IACs to keep DCs in a state of impoverishment. In both these continents there is a considerable degree of hostility towards AT, although it is interesting that as the old model of capital-intensive and large-scale production is proving increasingly unworkable, so the attitude towards AT is improving.

These factors explaining the weakness of the politico-administrative machinery in DCs are reflected in the performance criteria which influence decision-making. Wells (1973) characterizes the attitudinal problem as one of 'engineering man', a fixation with the most modern and technically efficient engineering solutions. James (1987) adapts this concept and refers to 'bureaucratic man', one in which the decision-criterion is reduced to output maximization. For various reasons, argues James, this leads to a preoccupation with new capital, and foreign exchange intensive technologies.[10] To these characterizations of attitudes, others could be added, reflecting a range of prejudicial anti-AT views: the preference for IAC over DC technologies; for urban- rather than rural-centered industrialization (as in Lipton's urban bias); the preference for machine-powered and machine-paced rather than human-powered and human-paced work organization; and so on.[11]

Another reflection of these attitudes to technology is that contained in the lending-criteria utilized by financing agencies. Since these are almost always based upon providing tangible security, they tend to focus on embodied rather than disembodied technology, and on capital- rather than labour-intensive plants. Since borrowers often have to provide security external to the enterprise itself (such as on land or cattle), these criteria tend to favour the better off rather than the poor. There are also a series of less obvious effects which have an impact on the pattern of industrial development. In Kenya, for example, the traditional pattern of land-holding was communal, and individualized tenure was introduced only in the 1950s. The process of land adjudication proceeded slowly and was initially confined to the richer Central Province in an explicit attempt to diminish support for the Mau Mau insurrection. The consequence, however, was that it reinforced the spatial unevenness of economic growth since only people with individual land-rights were able to borrow resources to diversify into small-scale trading and manufacturing. Thus it was only some decades later that small-scale manufacturing developed in other regions.

The development of a suitable politico-administrative apparatus thus requires three linked developments:

- Attention needs to be given to the methodology utilized to assess technologies. This cannot be confined to financial analysis and at the very least social cost-benefit analysis should be utilized. But this is only the starting point and a specific criteria approach, outlined in Chapter 2 (pp. 41–3), must necessarily be adopted.
- Specific training needs to be provided to administrative *cadres* in the state, to decision-makers in parastatals and to officers in lending agencies. In part this will acquaint them with the techniques of technology assessment, but it should also be designed to transform their attitudes towards AT. These are often a result of ignorance, rather than prejudice.[11]
- Lending criteria in financing agencies have to be adapted to take account of the intangibility of labour-intensive assets and the difficulty which poor people have in providing suitable security.

Modes of state involvement and the diffusion of AT

Two types of state involvement emerge from the analysis of state intervention in the industrialization process in DCs. Parametric actions set the general boundaries in which private entrepreneurs allocate resources and operate their businesses. Pervasive interventions are much more wide ranging and involve the state in the details of both choosing technology and in operating plants. Loosely speaking, the former type of involvement characterizes capitalist economies, and the latter is more commonly found in socialist states. (However, probably the most effective pervasive interventions have occurred in capitalist economies such as Japan and Korea.)

As analysis in earlier chapters has shown, there is not much evidence to suggest that socialist or capitalist economies are inherently good or bad at utilizing ATs. China's experience seems to have been positive, whilst that of Eastern Europe has been negative; Taiwan has seen an extensive role for small-scale technologies, Brazil has not. Even within the same country, as in the example of the Tanzanian state's involvement in brick production (pp. 91–4), the same (pervasive) state adopted contradictory policies towards the diffusion of AT.

This suggests that in itself the parametric/pervasive categorization of state involvement has little bearing on the diffusion of AT. More pertinent is the way in which state involvement is implemented. This turns the focus of discussion towards the heterogeneity of the state and the delivery systems utilized in affecting state policies. Institutional design is especially important here. Where policy towards technological diffusion is defined and executed within a single centralized division of the state and is based in the major cities, this will almost certainly lead to the support of inappropriate technologies. By contrast, when the institutional delivery mechanisms are diffused and rural based, they are more likely to underwrite the introduction of AT. Yet this is not an inevitable concomitant of a decentralized state, and attention will still need to be paid to the methodology of technology assessment, the attitudes of state officials, and the performance criteria under which they operate and which they use to guide the operations of their clients in the productive sector.

AT-enabling policies: an agenda for action

Stewart has observed of the AT movement that, until recently, most inputs have been aimed at the micro-level, assisting particular enterprises and developing individual technologies (see Chapter 1). Consequently the policy environment, which sets the parameters within which resource allocation occurs, has tended to be neglected. It is these sets of policies which are considered below. As mentioned earlier, the very relativity of appropriateness ensures that the specific policies which are adopted vary to reflect different operating conditions. Nevertheless it is possible to identify a few areas in which policies are most likely to have the desired effect.

Market efficiency and prices

It is helpful to begin by reviewing the main relevant conclusions which have been drawn about the price signals offered by markets in DCs. First, in all environments, IACs and DCs alike, markets function imperfectly. This is especially the case in respect to markets for technology and information. Since technology and information are what economists call 'public goods' (that is, they are not used up in their consumption), it is inherently difficult for entrepreneurs to appropriate the benefits of innovation, and their diffusion will always be socially sub-optimal.[13] The imperfect functioning of markets is also particularly apparent for 'non-economic goods', such as environmental quality and social factors. These are not only difficult to value, but especially in relation to the environment there is frequently a temporal and spatial disparity between the causes and the incidence of pollution.

A second relevant conclusion on markets is that they operate particularly inefficiently in DC environments. This reflects a range of causes, including poor physical infrastructure, highly imperfect flows of information and a low level of entrepreneurial development. Consequently, there are not many cases in which resource allocation has been overwhelmingly driven by market forces in DCs and even where this has occurred, as in Botswana, the consequences have not been especially beneficial to the development and diffusion of AT.

Of course, this does not mean that market-driven resource allocation is inherently inimical to AT, nor does it imply that the more efficient functioning of markets should be deliberately avoided, since there is evidence that the particular form of market imperfections found in many DCs is severely inhibiting of the development and diffusion of AT (see pp. 208–10). Thus there are many respects in which market and price reform are an important element in the policy package required.

The first relevant set of markets are those for factor inputs. Evidence provided by Haggblade et al.,[14] corroborated by many of the case-studies in earlier chapters, suggests that the diffusion of AT is not especially sensitive to the price of labour. This is not of course to suggest that they will diffuse at any set of wages, but merely that the elasticity of technology choice to wage costs is not high. Perhaps this is because the high levels of unemployment in most DCs force wages towards the minimum subsistence level and thus do not in practice lead to relatively large variations in labour costs between enterprises. By contrast, as Table 8.1 shows, there is evidence that small-scale enterprises face significant differences in their capital costs and many formal sector enterprises in fact experience negative real interest rates (due to capital charges being below the rate of inflation). Moreover, as was apparent in the diffusion of small-scale sugar technology (Chapter 5), the effective writing-off of capital costs in inflationary economies occasioned by depreciating on historic rather than replacement costs (particularly prevalent when these large-scale enterprises are state-owned) has meant that in many cases capital is virtually costless. This clearly benefits capital-intensive plants disproportionately. Hence, with respect to the reform of factor markets, it would appear that more efficient capital markets will benefit the diffusion of AT.

Table 8.1. **Real interest rates for formal and informal sector enterprises (per cent pa)**

	Informal sector	Formal sector
Ethiopia	66	8
Ghana	64	0
Ivory Coast	145	6
Nigeria	192	−2
Sudan	120	7
Sierra Leone	60	−3
India	15	−1
Indonesia	29	3
Malaysia	58	16
Pakistan	27	4
Korea	49	5
Sri Lanka	20	−1
Bolivia	96	5
Brazil	38	−7
Chile	52	−16
Colombia	40	16
Costa Rica	20	4
Honduras	37	6
Mexico	57	7

Source: Haggblade *et al.* (1986).

A second set of markets is that for capital, raw material and intermediate goods. The evidence here suggests that it is the trade regime which most adversely affects the diffusion of ATs. Haggblade *et al.* cite data from both Africa and Latin America which suggest that in so far as the trade regime has been designed to favour the import of capital goods, this has had a negative impact on labour-intensive enterprises. This is because many of the small-scale sector's capital goods are in fact intermediate and consumer goods, for example sewing machines, hand tools and outboard motors. Policies designed to promote industrialization tend to place lower tariff rates on capital than on intermediate and consumer goods. Consequently, they argue, there is an inherent bias in trade regimes against AT, and from this they proceed to argue the case for liberalizing trade.

This conclusion, that AT is harmed by trade interventions designed to promote import-substituting industrialization, requires further consideration. First, there is only a limited number of sectors in which capital goods are defined by the trade regime as consumer and intermediate goods. Even then, it is a relatively simple procedure to provide equivalent protection for the sewing machines and hand tools utilized by these small-scale enterprises. Second, as discussion in earlier chapters makes clear, AT cannot be reduced to this narrow range of absolutely small-scale, informal sector enterprises. Appropriateness is a relative concept, and there are many other sectors in which production through appropriate technologies does involve the importation of capital goods as defined in conventional trade categories. And, finally, as will be argued below, whilst the diffusion of AT may be furthered by the freeing of the trade regime, this will often not be the case for the development of AT, and there may thus well be a trade-off between the short- and medium-term diffusion of AT.

Intersectoral prices play an important role in the development and diffusion of AT since, as was shown above, there is extensive evidence that the diffusion in decentralized small-scale units is predicated upon the prior growth of the agricultural sector. When both the internal and international terms of trade are heavily weighted against agricultural production there is a consequent bias against AT. A particular component of this arises in relation to the international terms of trade since imports are disproportionately favoured compared to local inputs. In many DCs capital goods are not produced locally and thus an undervalued exchange rate may well be associated with large subsidies to capital-intensive projects. Haggblade et al. cite evidence that these subsidies may in some cases be as large as 25–40 per cent of capital costs.[15] This being the case, devaluation will improve the prospects for AT since it increases the costs of imported capital equipment. Other sets of markets are those for products and technology. Here there is much evidence of the need for policy reform, but this will be treated in greater detail on pp. 210–13.

Given that there are markets in which reform will be associated with a more sympathetic environment for AT, an important issue is what sort of reform is required. Two major alternatives are relevant. The first involves price reform in which factor, input and product prices are more closely aligned with opportunity cost. Many observers argue that 'price distortions' arise directly from state interventions. They conclude that prices can only be brought in line with opportunity costs when government intervention is removed and this is one of their major rationales for an assault on the *dirigiste* state in DCs.

A second type of policy reform is that designed to change the nature of government interventions in the market, rather than to remove them. The argument for this approach is that in the context of imbalances in power, freeing markets will in fact only further disfavour small-scale producers. An example of this can be found in the case of Zambia. After considerable pressure from the IMF, Zambia introduced a system of auctioning foreign exchange. However, virtually none of the auctioned currency went to small-scale and labour-intensive enterprises since they lacked the acumen and financial resources to bid at the auctions. Where financially rich trading intermediaries obtained the foreign currency to import inputs for these enterprises, the scarcity rents accrued to them and the small-scale enterprises found themselves in a no better situation. There clearly remains a need for state intervention in markets in order to ensure that resources are directed to enterprises using AT.

Policies to encourage the development of AT
In Chapter 1 the evolution of the AT movement was charted. An initial concern with political constraints gave way to the publicization of knowledge about AT; in turn this was superseded by attempts to develop new technologies. Subsequently the focus of attention turned to the diffusion of ATs. Most recently the debate has reverted to the political circumstances in which AT may flourish and the detailed policies which might be introduced to implement this political commitment.

It is helpful to distinguish between the development and the diffusion of AT. In part this is because some policies may have conflicting results, perhaps maximizing the short-term diffusion of existing technologies at the cost of long-term technological development and ultimately of wider patterns of diffusion. Earlier, the example was briefly cited of trade policy reform where a reduction in protection might undermine the development of appropriate technological capabilities. But, in part it is also because different sets of policies might be required to meet these two objectives. This discussion will concentrate on the problem of technological development.

It is possible to identify a number of different components of 'indigenous technological capability' (ITC). Each of these has relevance to the development of AT. The first element is the ability to search amongst technological alternatives. This includes those 'forgotten' technologies previously used in the IACs. This residue of technologies provides particular opportunities for DCs and it is significant that both of the technological developments which made small-scale OPS sugar technology viable were discarded IAC techniques.[16] The policy challenge here is to ensure that the wheel is not being reinvented. It is most likely that the institutionalization of a technology search will often be undertaken most efficiently by non-market institutions. A centralized search capability in the state, at the central or regional level, may be one policy response, but experience suggests that this activity is best undertaken at the sectoral level. There is a variety of search procedures available. One is patent data where holders are required to describe their inventions; once these patents have expired (usually 15–20 years after registration), they can be freely accessed and used without cost.[17]

The second major component of ITC involves an awareness of the implications of different mechanisms of transfer. Technology can be obtained via a number of mechanisms — through equity links, the purchase of licences, of capital goods, of blueprints and operating procedures, and through the transfer of human beings. The evidence from the most successful industrializers has been that the use of disembodied mechanisms of transfer, that is, the transfer of human knowledge and the purchase of know-how, provide the greatest returns in importing technology. But there is little systematic knowledge of the impact of these alternative mechanisms of transfer on the development of AT. One insight from the literature is that in so far as foreign investment and technology emanate from IACs rather than DCs, it is more likely to be relatively inappropriate. This is not so much because TNCs are inherently more prone to use inappropriate technologies when compared to locally-owned firms, but more because IAC-based TNCs manufacture products which involve the use of these inappropriate technologies (see pp. 34–5). For example, there is evidence that TNCs are more prone to meeting the input needs of their plants from affiliates abroad and they thus tend to have a higher import propensity.[18] The policy implications of this are fairly clear — a preference for disembodied mechanisms of transfer. In so far as embodied technologies are introduced, those obtained to satisfy local needs through foreign investment are more likely to be appropriate when the investors are from other DCs. In all of these cases the market will require 'direction' by the state since there is no necessary reason why technology importers will gravitate towards disembodied mechanisms of transfer, or why indigenous firms or small-scale enterprises in IACs will be involved in this process of transfer.

A third element of ITC relates to the ability to utilize technologies to their designed potential, and to adapt them to local conditions. This is an especially important component of an AT policy since it focuses directly on the relative nature of appropriateness. Technologies which might be optimal in a particular location may operate at different levels of productivity elsewhere, perhaps because of environmental factors, or because the skill composition of the workforce varies, or because the economic infrastructure is different. To operate effectively they may require changes in procedure and sometimes in the equipment itself. Many DCs are particularly poor at this problem of technological adaptation, and have tended to focus more centrally on the acquisition of new technologies. This has led to a great deal of wasted investment, and by focusing on the installation of new capacity rather than the adaptation and rehabilitation of existing equipment, has contributed to the inappropriateness of technology and worsened the economic problems of DCs. Specific policies can be introduced to encourage adaptation, perhaps by a change in the decision-criteria of parastatal enterprises (as argued by James — see Chapter 1). Whilst adaptation is most efficiently undertaken at the enterprise level, there may be a case for creating a specialized institution to deal with this.

It is probably only once capabilities exist to adapt technologies to local operating conditions that the two final elements of ITC can be developed effectively. The first of these is the ability to stretch machine designs beyond their design capacities. This is likely to be a much more labour-intensive route (per unit of output) to industrial growth than the acquisition of new technologies; it is also likely to be foreign-exchange saving. On the other hand it may well involve an increase in plant size and this may, in many circumstances, involve a diminution of appropriateness. Finally, ITC involves the ability to develop new technologies which may be more appropriate than those currently being utilized.

As policy and practice move away from search and identification towards development and research, so the scientific content in production is likely to increase.[19] This poses a major policy problem of endogenizing scientific activities within production. In many DCs, and also in some IACs, there has been a persistent tendency for the results of technological enquiry to be locked away within specialized research institutions, and this has been as true for AT as for other technologies. This failure to diffuse new ATs does not only apply at the highest level of knowledge. For example, in Kenya a demonstration centre of ATs was built near the capital city showing innovative ways of meeting basic needs. These included new stove designs and various water purifying techniques. The centre functioned mainly as a type of museum, largely frequented by admiring foreign visitors and involving few spin-offs into the domestic environment. Thus the problem of incorporating the 'Schumpeterian motor' into the development of new ATs has proved to be troublesome in many DCs and requires some form of effective policy response (issues considered further in Chapter 4).

Another important issue affecting institutional design in AT development is whose needs are represented in defining developmental goals. In Chapter 3 it was shown that the problems of developing more energy-efficient baking ovens were, technically speaking, relatively trivial, yet potential technological innovators concentrated instead on meeting the demands of the large-scale modern sector. In the same way that the AT enabling state itself requires a reorientation of perspectives, necessarily reflecting a change in its social base, so the same can be said for research and development institutions.

Finally, it is clear that particularly in relatively more science-based sectors, technological development takes time. Indian attempts to upgrade small-scale sugar processing took at least a decade of investment, as did the development of mini-cement technology. Similarly, IAC developments of the large-scale and capital-intensive variants of these technologies took many decades of sustained endeavour. Although the development of these appropriate technologies could have been speeded up, since the technologies involved are not complex, it is unlikely that even this more efficient process of technological development could have occurred without state support. In

India, as in many other countries, this support took two forms: financial subsidies to the research institutions and protection against imports for the final product.

The neo-liberal agenda argues that only one of these policy mechanisms, subsidies, is justifiable and that protection necessarily leads to 'directly unproductive economic behaviour', or 'rent seeking'. Yet there is considerable evidence that few of the successful rapid industrializers have managed to advance without an effective regime of protection. More importantly, the protection regime recommended by the neo-liberals — in Balassa's case, not more than 10–20 per cent effective protection for more than 5–8 years — is way out of line with this historical experience. Of course, this necessity of protection should not be taken to mean that protection in itself necessarily leads to technological development. Other policies are also required. In addition, to be effective, protection should not be of infinite duration. Here a political problem which arises is that the rents provided by protection often lead to political lobbies which make it difficult to remove tariffs once their function has been performed. This re-emphasizes the importance of the political basis of state power in any successful policy regime.

Policies affecting the composition of units

From the case-studies in earlier chapters, it was clear that a significant factor affecting the choice of technology was the identity of the entrepreneurs. This manifested itself in various ways. In India, small-scale rural entrepreneurs were responsible for the diffusion of appropriate sugar processing technologies, whereas the co-operative movement and the parastatals were oriented towards the large-scale technology. In Kenya, interest in small-scale sugar processing only intensified as an indigenous class of capital, finding itself blocked in the large-scale sector by foreign investors and parastatal corporations, searched for outlets to reinvest its profits. In food processing, the oligopolization of the industry derived from the colonial period, and represented the interests of institutional (mainly development banks) and private investors and the managerial class. Appropriate technologies were the domain of indigeous, small-scale rural capitalists. There is little evidence in any of the case-studies, or in fact from a wider reading of the AT literature, that foreign investors are associated with the development and diffusion of AT, especially if they come from the industrially advanced countries.

It could be read from these examples that state investment is necessarily associated with the use of inappropriate technologies. Yet, as the Tanzanian state's experience in the brick industry makes clear, the state is not homogeneous. While the 'central state' may have a tendency to use large-scale technologies, the 'local state' may be more often concerned with applying smaller-scale appropriate alternatives. China's experience with decentralized industrialization, represented in part by the cement and micro-hydro sectors (Chapter 7), illustrates this well. Finally, it is evident from

213

much of the AT movement's activities, that the NGO sector is an important conduit for innovation, for example in Botswana's brick industry. An especially significant component of this has been the role played by the international NGOs such as Appropriate Technology International (ATI) and the Intermediate Technology Development Group (ITDG). They were established expressly to promote the use of AT and are one of the most powerful 'units' accounting for its innovation.

Various conclusions can be drawn from this evidence:

- Technological choice seems to be so closely linked to institutional identity that unless policies can be introduced which directly affect the composition of units, it is unlikely that other policies designed to facilitate AT will have much impact. In this sense, it is probably one of the most important elements of the AT policy agenda.
- Common patterns emerge from various countries, and over time. TNCs (especially those from IACs) and parastatals representing the central state do not appear to be associated with the utilization of AT; nor do enterprises owned by what may be called the 'large-scale fraction of capital'.
- Despite common threads, there are important variations between countries, and undoubtedly also over time: parastatals might be responsible for introducing inappropriate technologies in some countries, but not in others; local large-scale capitalists in Asia seem less prone to pursuing the mania of mass production than those in Latin America; rural capitalists may begin by favouring the use of small-scale technologies, but over time their horizons may widen and they may become more prone to larger-scale technologies which allow them to more easily appropriate the surplus generated in production. Thus any policy designed to promote AT and fashioned on the composition of units will necessarily have to reflect local conditions.

One crucially important variable affecting the composition of units is that involving competition policy. Sectors in which large-scale technologies dominate are often associated with monopolistic or oligopolistic markets. There is a mutual interaction in this correlation between technological choice and market structure — large firms choose large-scale units because they diminish problems in control (as was clear from Kenya's bakery industry in Chapter 3) and large-scale technologies often require large-scale ownership (as has been the case until recently in power generation; see Chapter 6). Yet there is no inevitability behind this correlation since in many sectors there are often small-scale alternatives in both enterprise size and production technology. The policy task is thus to create a form of interacting dependency between small-scale firms and small-scale plants and one of the routes to this is an active policy on market structure. It can be seen from Chapter 3, for

214

example, that had the state been concerned to use pricing policy to undermine monopolistic tendencies in the market, rather than to maintain bread supplies in the short run, then a very different pattern of technological choice would have resulted.

Policies on product markets

There is a close identification between the choice of products and the choice of production technology. If products are tightly specified, then there is often only a very restricted choice of technology. For example, if a writing instrument is required then there is a great degree of choice, ranging from chalk (produced from local natural resources, often on a small scale and with labour-intensive technologies) to word processors (most often imported, and involving very large-scale and capital-intensive production). But if a Parker pen is required, then only a single technology is available, not only involving capital-intensive and large-scale production, but also almost certainly necessitating foreign investment. Similarly, there is a world of difference in solving transport problems through the use of bicycles and through the use of Mercedes Benz autos.

Thus the factors determining product choice are often crucial in the choice of technology. This was evident both from the case of cement in Chapter 7 (where India's insistence on the production of ordinary portland cement was one of the key factors ruling out small-scale production in the past) and bread in Chapter 3 (where the preference for Elliots' brand-name made it difficult for small-scale bakeries to compete). There is a variety of policy variables which potentially affect product choice. Langdon has shown how product choice affected technology choice and related this to the composition of units.[20] His research pointed to the key role played by TNCs in influencing consumer taste patterns in favour of internationally branded consumer products; this factor was also important in the breakfast foods industry in Kenya (Chapter 3) where the branded modern product was heavily promoted by comparison with the traditional staple. In all of these cases the production technologies required to manufacture branded products were inappropriate. Consequently an important element of policy designed to promote AT is that which affects the conscious attempts by producers to influence consumer tastes.

A second potentially relevant area of policy concerns income distribution. There is some evidence that highly unequal structures of income distribution are associated with patterns of demand which favour high-income (often branded) goods, and that these are produced by inappropriate technologies. Hence, as the ILO Employment Report on Kenya argued, a redistribution of income will change the composition of final demand, and this will feed through to the utilization of more appropriate technologies in production.[21] Whilst this is clearly the case in many, if not most, DCs, it is a policy conclusion which needs some care in implementation. A study of India in the early 1970s concluded that the overall employment effect of income redistribution would be neutral, since higher income consumers had a marginal propensity to consume labour-intensive services, whereas low-income families had a high marginal propensity to consumer products which involved relatively capital-intensive production.[22] Whilst there is obviously an important lesson to be learnt from this exercise in econometric modelling, there are nevertheless strong grounds for believing that, on balance, in most DCs income redistribution will have the effect of altering demand patterns in a way which will lead to the more widespread choice of ATs.

The state also has a role to play in setting product standards in a wide number of areas and invariably these have an important impact on technological choice. This is probably best evidenced in relation to building standards where regulations in post-colonial societies are often modelled on those of former colonial rulers. This not only affects the building materials used (for example, specifying ordinary portland cement rather than lime pozzalanas — see Chapter 7) but also the technology utilized in construction itself. Inappropriate standards leading to inappropriate production technologies are also widespread in the food processing industry.[23] Sometimes the impact is to be found in unexpected directions. For example, in Chapter 3 it was shown that the particular standard chosen to monitor bread weight, based on minimum rather than average loaf-weight, had the unintended side-effect of promoting capital-intensive moulding technology. This was because manual moulding was inherently more variable than machine moulding.

The state also makes a contribution to product choice through its own operations. This is both as a purchaser of inputs and also as a producer (in so far as production occurs through parastatals). Here the same mentality which has been characterized as 'engineering man' and 'bureaucratic man' (Chapter 1) is evidenced in product choices which favour modern products designed to international standards. This can often be an important stumbling-block to the wider diffusion of AT.

Regional policies and the local state
In general, policy formulation is considered in the context of central government action, designed to affect the whole economy. Yet from the various case-studies presented in earlier chapters it is clear that the state is not a homogeneous entity and that its component parts often act in very different ways when it comes to influencing technological choice. This is particularly true in the continent-sized economies of China and India, where many regional governments are very large by international standards. For example, the Uttar Pradesh government in Northern India which has assisted the development of small-scale sugar and cement technology, covers a population of over 100m people, almost twice as large as any sovereign government in Europe. Compare this with the total population of Botswana (just over 1.1m) and it is clear that 'the state' can take a number of forms.

216

Evidence that the local state has an important role to play is not confined to DCs. Italy's experience is particularly impressive since it relates directly to the composition of units. In a swathe of central Italy — which, significantly, has come to be known as the 'Third Italy' to distinguish it from the industrialized North and the less-industrialized South — local governments have acted to foster small-scale industrial development (see Chapter 6). This builds on local craft traditions and has helped traditional small firms cope with the centralizing consequences of growing indirect costs in design and marketing, as well as in heavy fixed costs in production. *Consorzia* have been established through these efforts by municipal governments which have fostered this inter-firm co-operation. It is significant that central government interventions in the same country have had the effect of consolidating firm size and in this respect have enhanced the inappropriateness of Italy's industrial development.

Since smallness is often in itself one of the criteria of appropriateness and since small-scale enterprises are often identified with the use of appropriate production technology, this link between local government intervention and the composition of units is suggestive of policies of decentralized industrialization, specifically designed to promote AT. Many DCs lend themselves to similar actions. Sometimes the most relevant level is below that of regional government, especially in very large countries. From the policy perspective, therefore, the frequent shortcomings of central government should not necessarily lead to a response of rolling back government intervention, but rather to one of pushing back this intervention to the local level.

The role of international agencies

The state played an important role in innovation in Japan's industrial development in the nineteenth century. The weakness of a local entrepreneurial class led it to invest directly in targetted areas, and then subsequently to pass these enterprises on to local capital. Only once these initial pioneering steps were taken did widespread diffusion occur. The history of AT in many DCs shows an analogous role played by the international AT movement. It was led to adopt a quasi-state role because of the failure of other potential actors — a weak class of small-scale capital, a state preoccupied with large-scale mass-production and import-substituting industrialization and IAC aid agencies involvement with large-scale projects. A clear example of this involvement by the international AT movement was provided by the experience of brick production in three African countries in Chapter 4. Government-to-government aid led to the introduction of particularly inappropriate technologies in Tanzania; state investment in Botswana was oriented towards large-scale technology; and local entrepreneurship was poorly developed in all three countries.

The role of the international aid agencies (as opposed to the role of the international NGOs addressing the problems of AT) is worth exploring since they have a potentially important role to play in the transfer of appropriate technology. Yet, particularly in the 1960s and 1970s, their aid was largely implemented at the project level, often associated with exports of capital goods from the donor country's own firms. This led to a series of technological disasters. The Aswan dam, with its devastation of the environment, its negative social impacts and the spread of bilharzia is a case in point. So, too, are the Amazonian mining projects (which are often part-funded by multilateral aid), and which are associated with the destruction of rain-forests. And in Sudan, the aid agencies have assisted in the design and in investment in a sugar production scheme designed to crush more than 20,000 tons of cane per day (tcd) even though maximum scale economies are exhausted at 10,000tcd and in the face of considerable evidence that DCs such as Sudan face recurrent problems in operating plants on a large scale.

These are not isolated examples — they reflect the general pattern of government-to-government aid as well as most aid from multilateral agencies. There is thus something about IAC government aid which leads to an association with inappropriate technology. A number of factors explain this link. First, the sociology of these aid institutions militates against the diffusion of AT. They are generally staffed by highly trained professionals who have not only absorbed the world-view of mass production, but also are accustomed to lifestyles which more than replicate those in their home countries. Most commonly, they live in ghettos insulated from the mass of the population and it is not uncommon for a person-year of technical assistance (especially that involving multilateral aid agencies) to cost more than $80,000. This structure of donor aid militates against the diffusion of AT.

A second reason why most donor-country aid is inimical to AT arises from the lobbying power of their own industrialists. Aid is often seen as a way in which donor-country industries can be assisted, although premised on the idea of mutual benefit. Where this occurs it is often because the technology offered by these assisted firms is inferior, otherwise they would not require assistance to compete. But, perhaps more significantly, IAC firms generally develop technologies suitable for IAC operating environments (which are the largest markets) and only see DC markets as a 'bonus'. Hence most of these technologies are likely to relate imperfectly to DC conditions.

Another reason why donor-country aid is often associated with the diffusion of inappropriate technologies is because the donor–recipient relationship is inherently a power-relation. It not only reflects and reinforces the dependence of the recipient (often leading to overt political pressures), but more relevantly also reflects power relations internal to the DC. Thus the existing internal power relations are likely to be reinforced by the distribution of aid. As is evident from the various case-studies contained in earlier chapters, the social basis of power in many DCs is inimical to the widespread diffusion of AT.

218

Donor aid agencies often also find it difficult to administer aid to small-scale enterprises. Their institutional costs are high and the tasks involved in disbursing small quantities (often only hundreds of dollars) of large aid budgets (generally in millions of dollars) to informal sector enterprises, often operating on a cyclical basis, are considerable. It is partly for this reason, and partly because of the recognition that government-to-government aid is inherently unlikely to diffuse ATs, that a variety of donor agencies have created specialized agencies to deal with AT. The largest and most prominent of these are ATI in the USA and ITDG in the UK. Donor agencies have also tried to make use of various NGOs, mostly voluntary agencies, both in their home countries and in recipient countries.

These voluntary agencies have played an important role in publicizing the virtues of AT and in developing and diffusing these technologies. In both sugar and cement their participation has complemented the efforts of Indian research groups, especially in so far as they have required foreign inputs or foreign travel. And in bricks, ATI has played a key role in developing kiln design, in promoting knowledge of small-scale brick presses, in funding their diffusion and in helping to create entrepreneurship. The activities of these international NGOs are not confined to foreign operations and many have also seen an identity between problems of technological choice in their own countries and those in other economies (see Chapter 1).

Yet, although these NGOs have come to play a crucial role in the development and diffusion of AT, they have not been free of problems. As was seen in Chapter 4, they often seem to find difficulty in getting down to the level of informal sector enterprises. In Botswana their aid was geared to the needs of domestic NGOs who used more appropriate technologies than those planned in the large-scale sector. But at the same time they neglected the slop-moulders operating at the lowest level of scale. A second problem confronting these international NGOs is that they find difficulty in responding to technologies which are relatively small by comparison with the large-scale sector, but are absolutely large by comparison with the informal sector. This is evident from the experience of both mini-sugar and mini-cement where the ATs involve investments of around $2m. The social basis of these NGOs, often funded in part by voluntary donations from the public, makes it hard to justify such large programmes. Yet they offer considerable social and economic potential and are often neglected by the existing pattern of resource allocation.

Related to this is the problem which these NGOs have in what might be called 'the operation of the Schumpeterian motor'. In Chapter 4 this process of endogenizing technical change in production was described. It is one in which capitalist enterprises (where competitive markets exist) are naturally led into developing new product and process technologies in the search for technological rents. Whilst this often leads to the introduction of inappropriate technologies, it does ensure a high rate of technological

219

progress. By contrast, the NGOs, which are insulated from market pressures, are more likely to develop ATs, but at the same time have a lesser incentive to incorporate these in profitable production — as seen by the experience of both mini-sugar and mini-cement technologies where technologically trivial developments took an unnecessarily long time. The NGO movement has not yet learnt to cope with this problem.

Finally, there is some evidence that ATs are best implemented in a packaged context. For example, the experience of small-scale sugar production in Kenya (Chapter 5) was one in which the full social impact of sugar processing could not be easily identified, since there were so many other interacting factors. To have most beneficial effect, the sugar-processing technology needs best to have been diffused simultaneously with other complementary technologies. These include economically appropriate and environmentally sound agricultural techniques and clean drinking water in new residences necessitated by changes in agricultural practices and new employment opportunities offered by the sugar plant. The inputs provided by the international NGO were confined to the process of sugar processing alone and, in this sense, were deficient.

The policy implications which follow from this experience of aid are that the international NGOs clearly have a productive role to play in the development and diffusion of AT. They are inherently more likely to meet the challenge than government-to-government aid. Yet attention needs still to be given to the programmatic nature of their activities, to their involvement in projects which are relatively small by international standards but large by the experience of the AT movement, and to the difficulties which they experience in endogenizing technical change and in maximizing the pace of diffusion.

Conscientization

A final issue on the policy agenda relates to the publicization of AT. Here the widespread diffusion of AT is hindered by related problems of prejudice and ignorance. In many countries there is a pervasive lack of knowledge of the achievements of AT. In Kenya, for example, senior decision-makers at the Kenya Sugar Authority have no faith in small-scale sugar processing. Their knowledge of the potential is confined to two failed investments in the mid 1970s and this has led them to give no credence to the prospects of the small-scale alternative. Yet a mini-sugar plant flourishes in the Western Province, in the midst of a cane region in which all of the large-scale mills are unprofitable and struggle to operate near their designed capacity (see Chapter 5). This ignorance is reflected in other sectors in Kenya and in many other countries.

The effect on policy is compounded by prejudice, especially in Africa and Latin America. At worst this views AT as a 'construct' of IAC interest groups trying to keep DCs underdeveloped. At best, it involves a belief that ATs have nothing to offer in the way of economic efficiency. This prejudice is not confined to DCs. Prominent observers in the IACs have argued that ATs are almost always inefficient. Moreover, since the efficient modern technologies are the property of TNCs, development in the Third World will be maximized through an increase in foreign investment.[24]

The various case-studies in this book, as well as a wealth of other empirical studies, expose the prevalence of both ignorance and prejudice. These attitudes are pervasive, indeed hegemonic. Consequently an important area for policy is to conscientize decision-makers to the potential offered by AT. When the endeavours of the large-scale sector are considered — Coca Cola spending $5m on making an advertising video for a product which can be considered highly inappropriate in many environments and which was withdrawn after a single showing! — it is clear that the existing efforts to publicize AT are much too modest.

Restructuring policies to favour AT: the room for manoeuvre

Whilst appropriateness is by its nature relative, it would thus appear that there are a number of areas of policy which are common to a variety of operating environments, especially those located in the Third World. Some of these can be implemented by a wide range of governments, since they do not represent any significant change in power relations. Yet, in general, most policy interventions which are likely to have a significant impact upon the development and diffusion of AT do directly impinge on underlying political power. Consequently, it is probably the social and political basis of the AT-enabling state rather than the intelligence of policy design which is the single most important factor determining the effectiveness of policy.

This change in power relations need not necessitate a change in the mode of production, that is from capitalism to socialism. Much more relevant is the type of socialism and the type of capitalism which is involved, since each of these can take different forms. In the case of socialism, for much of China's recent history the power relations were such that small-scale and decentralized industrialization, involving the widespread diffusion of AT, thrived. By contrast, in Eastern Europe socialism has been identified with the extremes of Fordism — pollution, large-scale production and social alienation. Similarly, in capitalist economies, variance is also to be found. The USA has pursued mass production, whilst parts of Italy have thrived on small-scale production. Taiwan has a long history of small-scale decentralized production, whilst the Republic of Korea has tended to favour large-scale production.

The differences between power relations in these countries should not be interpreted in a determinate way. They can, and do, change over time, as appears to be currently the case in Kenya. And there are circumstances in which a state (or part of a state) develops an attitude favourable to AT but finds itself confronted by a hostile pattern of power relations. Stewart suggests a taxonomy which distinguishes between 'zero-sum' (where one group's loss is another group's gain) and 'positive-sum' situations (where all groups gain).[25] Where policy changes are of the latter sort, they are relatively easy to implement. She suggests that this is most likely to be the case with 'policies to improve appropriate R&D and dissemination, to support agriculture, to improve rural infrastructure and to develop appropriate standards' and concludes that '[f]rom the perspective of identifying policies likely to be adopted, the aim should be to find non-confrontational policies'.[26]

In addition to zero-sum situations, another factor affecting the implementation of effective policies to develop and diffuse ATs is the external constraint on policy formulation. The external debt of many DCs has meant that structural adjustment loans (SALs) from the World Bank and the IMF have led to the imposition of a variety of detailed policies, not all of which are favourable to AT. Ranis and Stewart distinguish between SAL-related policies which are demand-restraining, those which are designed to switch resources (generally from industry to agriculture, and from local to foreign markets) and those which are focused on long-run supply.[27] They conclude that the demand-restraining policies have dominated SALs, and these have little relative impact on AT. The other two sets of policies have mixed consequences for AT. They believe that exchange-rate policies are favourable to AT since overvalued currencies undervalue capital. Yet in so far as these reforms are designed to encourage production for foreign rather than domestic needs, they are not unambiguously favourable to AT. But one of their major conclusions is that

> [m]any AT policies do not form part of the [SAL] package. These include, for example, policies towards science and technology, product policies, reforms in administration and in aid. An effective AT policy usually requires a more egalitarian distribution of income and assets, both to secure markets for appropriate products and to increase rural linkages. But this is not a concern of IMF/WB [World Bank] policy reform. (Ranis and Stewart, 1989, p. 45)

To these other areas of policy neglect might be added policies to change the composition of units, those fostering local development and policies designed to strengthen international and domestic ATs involved in development and diffusion.

To sum up, this book has been concerned to show that the quest for ATs has a number of different dimensions: social, economic and environmental. The evolving call for more appropriate technologies has arisen as a consequence of the degradation of a dominant form of industrial development, and affects all countries. This mass-production mode of accumulation is now in disarray as the world struggles to make the transition to a more efficient form of production. In this period of transition many new opportunities open up for the diffusion of AT, especially in regard to the scale of production. Here it would appear that the long-lived search for ever larger scales has led modern technology into a blind alley, and it is the economics of small rather than the economies of scale which now underlie best-practice production. Similarly, the destruction of the environment can no longer be ignored and ecological issues are currently high on the policy agenda in many countries. Finally, the old dehumanized organization of work is no longer optimal and new and socially more acceptable forms of work-organization are currently being implemented.

Despite the growing economic rationality of ATs, they will not develop and diffuse autonomously. There are too many vested interests in the old form of production, and markets are imperfect carriers of technological change, particularly of new ways of thinking. Consequently, there remains an important role for policy intervention, nowhere more so than in the Third World.

Notes

Chapter 1

1. Solow (1957) calculated that only 12.5 per cent of US economic growth between 1909 and 1945 could be attributed to increases in capital stock. The residue, he argued, was explained by technological progress. See also Abromovitz (1956).

2. The seminal contribution to this debate was made by Seers (1972).

3. Eckaus (1955) and (1987).

4. See Stewart (1978) for a summary of this literature.

5. Emmanuel (1982).

6. For a selection of different periodizations and explanations see the discussions in Freeman, Clark and Soete (1982), Hoffman and Kaplinsky (1988) and Piore and Sabel (1984).

7. More extensive discussion can be found in Hoffman and Kaplinsky (1988), Chapters 2 and 8.

8. See Freeman Clark and Soete (1982) for a compilation of these views.

9. Perez (1985) and (1988).

10. This has probably been most evident in relation to nuclear power in the US and the UK. The costs of decommissioning power stations at the end of their useful life has been so high that they are unable to produce energy at competitive rates.

11. UNIDO (1986).

12. All export figures calculated from various tables in GATT (1988), Vol II.

13. Inforpress, 30th April 1987.

14. All data from UNICEF (1989).

15. Three main elements have been common to these structural Adjustment Programmes — a reduction in budget deficits, currency realignment (that is, lowering) of exchange rates and a reduced role for the state. The implications for AT of this latter element are considered in Chapters 7 and 8.

16. Cornia (1988). The 'years' in this calculation refer to the number of years in which the individual countries experienced improved, significant or negative growth rates. It is worth noting that since only the countries accepting these conditions have been provided with additional external resources it would be expected that their economic performance would be better. In these circumstances it is surprising that the relative 'success' of these countries was not even more marked.

17. Ellis W N, McRobie G and Darrow K (1979).

18. See Rosenbrock (1985) and Cooley (1984).

19. For a discussion of the effectiveness of Volvo's attempts at job redesign, see Aguren et al. (1976) and (1984).

20. Nader (1972), Carson (1963).

21. The accuracy of these predictions is not relevant here since our concern is to document the rise of the environmental critique of technology. However a penetrating commentary is to be found in the collection of papers edited by Cole et al. (1973) in which Freeman characterizes the Club of Rome's report as 'Malthus with a Computer'.

22. One of the most widely-used managerial paradigms being pursued is that of 'flexible specialization' — see Piore and Sabel (1984).

23. See Eckaus (1955).

24. This phenomenon is not restricted to AT. Evans and Tigre (Forthcoming) show this also to have been the case in the development of the computer industries in Brazil and Korea.

25. See Juma (1989).

26. Numerous examples of these blended technologies are to be found in Bhalla (1984) and Bhalla and James (1988).

27. See Pickett et al. (1974).

28. Wells (1973).

29. James (1988).

30. Nelson and Winter (1977).

31. An example of this is urban transport where instead of favouring public transport facilities which have positive economic externalities, the price system favours technologies for private transport. This increases the production of pollutants.

Chapter 2

1. These are set out by Reddy (1979).

2. Lancaster (1966) has been particularly influential in developing this conception of product technology. These ideas have been extended to incorporate the problems of appropriateness, especially in DC environments by Helleiner (1975), Stewart (1978) and James and Stewart (1981).

3. See especially Langdon (1981) as well as the discussion on breakfast cereals in Chapter 3 below.

4. For example in South Africa, 'as a source of light, candles are 173 times more expensive per unit of energy (mJ) than electricity. Even wood, a major source of fuel used by more than half (57 per cent) the households living in non-electrified areas near Cape Town, costs nearly three times as much' (Wilson and Ramphele, 1989, p. 47).

5. This is of course a hotly debated issue. On the one hand some commentators point to Lenin's naivety in believing that capitalist technologies could be utilized in post-revolutionary Russia without any effect on socialist relations in the workplace (Muchie, 1986). On the other, a recent comparative study of the use of computerized machine tools observes that whereas these were associated with a skill-polarized labour force and exclusive managerial control in the UK, in West Germany the same equipment was associated with craft labour and worker control over machine reprogramming (Sorge et al., 1983).

6. These issues are treated further in Chapter 7.

7. This is because the greater the rate of discount, the less future costs and benefits are represented in net present value terms. This illustrates the possibility of conflicts between AT objectives since while a high rate of discount might be desirable to induce the choice of labour intensive technologies, it will simultaneously tend to undervalue the cost of long-term environmental damage. Methodologies to reconcile these conflicts are considered below, pp. 41–3.

8. This specific criteria approach is most closely associated with the work of Frances Stewart (1987a).

9. See Stewart (1975) and the Special Issue of *World Development*, Vol. 6, Feb. 1978.

Chapter 3

1. A brief discussion of similar patterns in other sectors in Kenya can be found in Kaplinsky (1982b) and for other sectors in other countries see James and Stewart (1981).

2. For most of the post-war period, bread was not even considered in the basket of goods in the African cost of living index.

3. This is not atypical. The UK Monopolies and Mergers Commission observed that 'Econometric studies suggest that the demand for bread is inversely related to the level of national prosperity and average disposable incomes' (1959, para 59).

4. The name 'peel-oven' derives from the spatula used to load baking trays into these ovens.

5. The major variant involves the separation of individual bags which are then opened by brief bursts of air. Sometimes the timing of this goes awry, and the empty bags are blown all around the bakery!

6. It is this which explains the freshness and lack of storability of French and other European breads. Unlike the British and US products which are made from high-protein 'hard' flours, continental breads are made from 'soft' flours.

7. These calculations of relative profitability in the Kenyan bakery industry were based upon detailed investigations of relative prices and factor productivities for the 60 most active bakeries. The particularities of their operations and a discussion of the difficulties in estimating profitability can be found in Kaplinsky (1981), Chapter 6.

8. The formula used for this annual capital charge is

$$\frac{AC}{1 - \dfrac{1}{(1 + r)^n}} \cdot r$$

where AC is the acquisition cost, r the rate of discount and n the estimated economic life of the machinery.

9. In order to test these assertions, 15 loaves were bought from each bakery and then weighed.

10. Unlike many other DCs, capital markets in Kenya are not so imperfect that rural borrowers pay higher rates of interest than urban borrowers.

11. This is not unique to the bread industry in Kenya. For example the most energy-intensive form of food in Europe is North Sea fish. This is largely because of the energy sunk in the construction of all metal boats.

12. Oil-based hydrocarbons generate less carbon dioxide per unit of energy than does wood; natural gas generates even less, but is unavailable in Kenya.

13. The data in Table 3.9 refer only to the share of production by the 58 largest active bakeries, all of whom were interviewed. It is possible to measure with some precision those bakeries (approximately 17) outside this sample by reference to flour deliveries from the mills. These excluded bakeries (most of them in rural areas utilizing brick ovens) accounted for a tiny 3.8 per cent of total flour consumption. If they are assumed to all use brick ovens and to be located in the rural areas, then the share of rural bakeries rises to 29.2 per cent, of brick-oven bakeries to 5.9 per cent and those of tunnel-oven bakeries and Elliots fall to 67.7 and 60.5 per cent respectively.

14. See Stewart (1987a and 1987b).

15. This discussion is informed by Huxley (1935 and 1957), McGregor Ross (1927) and by company files held at the Registry of Companies in Nairobi.

16. The exclusion of Africans and Asians from commercial farming has been widely documented. See, for example, McGregor Ross (1927).

17. Here the management had 'window-dressed' the Board with three well-known moderate politicians, C W Rubia, C Malemba and J Murumbi. They featured on the Boards of many similar white-owned enterprises and were consequently both disinclined and too busy to involve themselves in either detailed or strategic management.

18. These hard wheats have a high protein content and are necessary for bread production since without them the bread will not rise adequately. Globally these hard wheats are grown in countries with severe weather conditions such as North America and the Soviet Union.

19. One urban bakery said that it merely sprinkled caraway seeds over its regular bread and then sold it as Ksh 1.85, rather than Ksh 1.40 per loaf. But most bakeries did produce bread of a different nature, including raisin-bread, bread with added fats and cakes and scones.

20. See Langdon (1981) and Kaplinsky (1979).

21. A disaffected local academic observed of Kenya that the national motto might well be 'Be Kenyan — Buy Foreign'!

22. The small-scale hammer-mills which mechanize maize grinding only produce 100 per cent extraction flour.

23. Based upon an eight-hour operation for only 200 days a year (a conservative estimate).

24. Not only does *ugali* have to be cooked, but the 100 per cent extraction hammer-mill flour takes longer to cook than does the sifted maize flour.

25. See Langdon (1981).

Chapter 4

1. See Chapter 7 for references.

2. The discussion in this chapter is focused on bricks made from clay rather than alternative materials such as cement or soil. Thus unless specified to be made from any of these other materials, 'bricks' always refers to claybricks.

3. Schumpeter (1961).

4. The choice of AT in cement manufacture is discussed in Chapter 7.

5. It would appear that bricks are probably a cheaper form of construction material in Kenya as well, although the evidence gathered to support this contention is not as robust as for Botswana and Tanzania.

6. The calculations for these two countries are based upon the output price of bricks produced by small-scale brick factories in the local regions. They are not comparable between the two countries since it is not clear what exchange rate to use, especially in the case of Tanzanian prices. There, in 1986 when the fieldwork was undertaken, the difference between the official and unofficial exchange rates was 7:1. In addition in Botswana bricks are compared with equivalent-sized cement bricks, whereas in Tanzania the bricks are compared with much larger-sized cement blocks.

7. Although some authors, such as Keddie and Cleghorn (1980), distinguish a greater number. In their case it is 6, namely clay winning, clay transport, clay mixing, brick forming, drying and firing.

8. However, in one British brick factory, very large-scale clamp-firing is combined with mechanized pressing to produce a final product which is characterized by its non-uniformity of appearance. In a culture of uniformity these bricks earn a premium price and sell for as much as three times the price of the homogeneous-looking automated-kiln variety.

9. Indeed this is the methodology used in Keddie and Cleghorn (1980).

10. Based upon operating experience it is assumed that the smaller-scale pressing plant would operate at 45 per cent in the first year and thereafter at 90 per cent of rated capacity, whereas the medium-scale pressing plant would build up from 33 per cent capacity in the first year to 60 per cent in the second and thereafter at 80 per cent of rated capacity. These are fairly conservative assumptions and contrast with the estimates for the large-scale plant of 60 per cent capacity after 18 months, rising to 80 per cent in the second year and to 100 per cent thereafter. This latter assumption is particularly unjustified given the fact that the total brick market in Botswana will only allow for the utilization of 50 per cent of production capacity and export prospects are limited.

11. However, the market size of 25m bricks is based upon the selling price of P325 per 1,000 for imported bricks. If locally produced bricks were available at a lower price then the market for bricks would increase, thereby diminishing the degree of excess capacity.

12. For significant parts of the year much of Tanzania's transport system is idle due to a lack of imported fuel oil. This is especially the case in the interior where the brick factories are located.

13. The process of invention is not being considered since the various types of brick manufacturing technologies are well known and have been in existence for some time.

14. White (1984) distinguishes between a parametric role for the state in which it sets the broad parameters under which investment occurs, and a pervasive role when the state becomes more actively involved in facilitating investment. It is in this latter, pervasive sense, that this point is made. See Chapter 8 for further discussion.

15. The role which Botswana played as a conduit for this capital flight is discussed in Chapter 7.

16. This was ultimately provided by its parastatal affiliate which exports cement and is therefore able to use some of these earnings to cover its own equipment needs.

17. Unfortunately no details are available for the Bulgarian-supplied large-scale plant in Dar es Salaam.

18. See Rebublic of Kenya (1986).

19. Of course these are often conflicting objectives.

20. This is especially apparent for mixing, where poorly functioning equipment has led to an increase in wastage, from about 10 per cent to 25 per cent of total production.

21. These jinko-liners are inserted inside the charcoal-burning cooking stoves which are widely used throughout Eastern Africa and in many other parts of the world. When well made they can save up to 20 per cent of energy costs and have a payback period of less than five months.

22. These building standards are based on British regulations, but do not apply outside of urban areas — see Allen (1984).

23. The neglect of technologies which have obvious potential for DCs is one of the major recurring themes in all the case-studies of this book.

24. The role which another international NGO played in sending entrepreneur B to Thailand to learn about jiko-lining technology is also an important background to this story of technological invention and development, since it funded the acquisition of the necessary technological skills.

25. See Lal (1983) and Little (1982).

26. See Wade and White (1984).

27. Leys (1975) is especially illuminating in illustrating how access to the state provided the rents required to fund productive investments. See, also, Swainson (1980).

28. See James (1987).

29. It has not only been ATI of the US which has been involved in the brick industries of these countries. The Intermediate Development Technology Group has also played an important and complementary role.

Chapter 5

1. See the introductory and concluding chapters in Stewart (ed., 1987).
2. Only the choice of cane-processing technologies is considered in this chapter. The alternative technology producing cane from beet is largely confined to temperate climates.
3. The reason for this particular cycle is that sugar cane has a long gestation period. The high prices spur farmers to plant an additional cane which matures after 2–3 years and hence leads to an excess supply. Since the cane can be recropped at least twice, it takes an additional period before it is uprooted and supplies become scarce.
4. For various estimates of the recurrent costs of production, see Lone (1989).
5. The acronym OPS stands for open pan sulphitation. 'Sulphitation' refers to the process used to clarify the crushed juice.
6. An interesting point emerges from this detailed costing analysis by Tribe (1989). Small-scale VP plants running at the same rate of under-utilization as large plants suffer a disproportionately large penalty on unit costs. This is because of the scale economies inherent in the process, since fixed costs are a higher proportion of unit costs for small plants.
7. See Baron (1975) and Forsyth (1977).
8. The reason why inhibition could be utilized by VP and not by OPS plants was because of the VP technology's ability to boil juice under semi-vacuum conditions. This made it much more feasible to drive off the extra water contained in the juice.
9. The share of the VP mills had increased steadily from just over 20 per cent in 1951–2. But whether this was at the expense of jaggery or OPS production is unclear since the published data on the utilization of cane make no clear distinction between these two end-uses. The estimation of 10 per cent given over to OPS is derived from Garg (1979).
10. This particular form of 'market distortion' led to a concentration of centrifuge size which bore no relation to economic or social needs; it mererly reflected the specificities of the fiscal legislation.
11. For a detailed discussion of these costings, both for India and Kenya, see Kaplinsky (1983a).
12. It is interesting that if the social welfare economic approach (involving the estimation of shadow prices and the determination of the greatest net present value) is utilized in the measurement of AT (see Chapter 2), then the OPS technology would almost certainly be considered optimal. This is because the greater land-utilizing characteristics of the OPS technology have already been taken into account through the greater cost of cane. Unless crop market prices are relatively skewing of social opportunity costs of cane compared to other crops, the financial analysis suggests that this would result in a higher aggregate net present value if OPS technology accounted for total sugar production.
13. An insightful analysis of the role played by KNTC levies in the process of class formation in Kenya can be found in Leys (1975).
14. Mumias's loss in 1980–81 was K£77,000. Subsequently, as the 1980s progressed, changes in the price structure and improvements in productivity allowed Mumias (but none of the VP mills) to move into the black.
15. This is derived from the experience of establishing a new VP plant on an adjacent site in 1982, and is towards the lower range of costing estimates — see earlier discussion (p. 116).

16. In fact so large is the Mumias plant on which this analysis is based (7,000 tcd) that only 2.6 of these sized plants would be required.

17. Makanda (1989). These conclusions are corroborated by the detailed research of Odada et al. (1986).

18. This latter fact is confirmed by Makanda (1989).

19. Odada et al. (1986).

20. Lemmings (1989).

21. Ibid.

22. Ibid.

23. For a discussion of the character and degree of inequality and of its changing nature see Kaplinsky (1979) and Godfrey (1986).

24. In 1962 a number of Kabras area smallholders attempted to plant coffee but were stopped from doing so by agricultural officers (Makanda, 1989).

25. I am grateful to Ian McChesney for details on these costs of rehabilitation.

26. Mlaki (1989).

27. The fact that many prominent Western and Nyanza politicians (including President Moi) became large landowners in the sugar belt is not unimportant.

28. The neo-liberal critique of the state does not see things in this way — it argues that the state has become a 'predator', fuelled by the rent-seeking behaviour of its officials. See Chapters 7 and 8.

29. For the case of tin-can manufacturing technology, see Bell et al. (1973). For a more general analysis of Taiwan and the Philippines see Ranis and Stewart (1989).

30. Baron (1975), Forsyth (1977).

31. See Bell (1982).

32. In the case of Booker McConnell, the 1976 nationalization of the sugar industry in Guyana was especially significant in inducing a change in corporate direction.

33. Schumpeter argued that firms attempt to escape competitive pressures by introducing new product and process technologies. Thus technological change is endogenized within the process of capitalist accumulation. See Chapter 4.

Chapter 6

1. Wood (1978).

2. See Piore and Sabel (1984), Kaplinsky (1988), Hoffman and Kaplinsky (1988) and their bibliographies for more detailed discussion.

3. The failure of some countries, such as the UK, to use 'scrubbing technologies' to clean up emissions from carbon-based power stations is a major issue of technological inappropriateness.

4. All figures from 'Laying a bet against OPEC', *Financial Times*, 4 December 1989.

5. I am indebted to George McRobie for this information.

6. Peters (1987).

7. Peters and Waterman (1982).

8. Leen (1984).

9. Pratten (1971) p. 3.

10. Cited in Pratten (1971) pp. 3–4.

11. Silberston (1972).

12. See Stewart (1978) and Pratten (1971).

13. Stewart (1978).

14. To this could be added a general tendency for large enterprises to pay higher wages. This is a widely observed phenomenon in the Third World (see, for example Little, Mazumdar and Page, 1987), but also occurs in the IACs (see Wood 1978, pp. 168–70).

15. But sometimes labour can also become a fixed cost, for example when legislation forbids redundancy without compensation or when labour scarcities make entrepreneurs reluctant to let labour go. Energy is a variable cost, but it does not rise in a constant proportion to output, especially when stopping and restarting production requires the refiring of furnaces.

16. Aylen (1988) calculates the following scaling factors in sub-processes of the steel industry: 0.66 for the sinter plant, 0.60 for the blast furnace, 0.66 for oxygen steelmaking and 0.30 for hot strip rolling. The exceptional value for strip rolling arises because it is the only sub-process which does not occur within containers.

17. See Chandler (1977) for an extensively documented study of this process.

18. Although it is common to refer to this process as one of deskilling, what in effect was happening was the increasing polarization of skills. For many workers, the skill content was diminished, whilst at the same time a smaller number of more highly skilled workers were required. Thus whilst in some notional sense the 'average' skill-content of work improved this was not the case for the bulk of line-workers.

19. An example of an industry which produces on a large scale despite the absence of technological imperative to do so is the shoe industry in the UK. By comparison in Italy and Brazil firms tend to be of a smaller scale and (whether this is related to size or not) much more flexibly attuned to changes in market conditions.

20. By 1976 there were something like 11,000 TNCs with some 82,600 affiliates. Of these the largest 371 accounted for around two-thirds of total sales. In 1980 the 350 largest TNCs had total sales equivalent to 28 per cent of the GDP of all non-communist economies, employing 25 million people which was equivalent to approximately one-quarter of total manufacturing employment in these economies. They also accounted for one-third of total industrial output. (Hoffman and Kaplinsky, 1988).

21. For example, one of the largest chemical TNCs, Monsanto, reduced its dependence on bulk chemicals from 26 to 3 per cent in five years (Peters, 1987).

22. Ibid., p. 32.

23. See Scriberras (1979) for a discussion of the TV industry and Altshuler et al. (1984) for the auto industry.

24. Kaplinsky (1984) discusses the systemic characteristics of the new micro-electronics-based automation technologies.

25. I am indebted to John Surrey for helpful advice on this section.

26. M Wilkinson, 'The boom in small scale power', Financial Times, 1 July 1988.

27. But see earlier discussion where product and plant descaling tendencies in these sectors were highlighted.

28. Ayres and Miller (1983).

29. Hoffman and Rush (1988).

30. Business Week, 26 August 1985.

31. Hoffman and Kaplinsky (1988).

32. See Kaplinsky (1984), Chapter 7.

33. See Buttell et al. (1985) for a stimulating review of the potential impact of the biorevolution in agriculture.

34. See Rada (1982) for a discussion of this in relation to the semiconductor industry.

35. See Piore and Sabel (1984), who first mapped out the significance of this form of inter-firm cooperation.

36. Institute of Development Studies (1988).

37. Institute of Development Studies (1988).

38. See Kamata (1982) which details the nature of work-conditions in Japan as well as to Ron Dore's insightful introduction in which he draws links between this system and pre-Meiji feudal Japan.

Chapter 7

1. See Colclough (1990) for a review of the literature and an extended discussion of the issues.

2. This section of analysis is informed by the comprehensive survey paper of Haggblade, Liedholm and Mead (1986). Although their survey relates to the problems of small-scale enterprises, in many DCs these are often synonymous with enterprises using AT. This is not always the case but in the absence of any literature review which focuses on factor price distortions in relation to the broader characteristics of AT, their survey serves as a good proxy.

3. It is interesting that these calculations do not take into account cases where equity investments in large-scale plants are effectively written off or where capital recoupment procedures are inadequate. Both of these phenomena were very significant in the study of sugar processing in Chapter 5 and benefited the inappropriate large-scale VP mills. They are also found in many other cases of large-scale enterprises in DCs.

4. This information can only be taken as indicative of more general trends. For example, Hendersen (1988) shows that Hong Kong's reputation as being free of labour market distortions is wrong, and that the state has consistently subsidized wages. Many authors (see, for example, Wade and White (eds), 1988, and Leudde Neurath, 1986) have shown that the characterization of South Korea, Taiwan and Singapore as having followed neo-liberal prescriptions is heavily flawed.

5. A more extended analysis of Botswana's industrial policy can be found in Kaplinsky (1989b).

6. The share of the service sector, almost entirely made up of traditional labour-intensive services and those provided by the state, remained static during this period of two decades.

7. Harvey, Lewis and Sharpley (1990).

8. Kaplinsky (1989b).

9. Colclough and Olsen (1983).

10. Large-scale enterprises (initially with an investment cost of P750,000) were eligible for the AFA scheme (see the next section) if they were new projects. In the case of CFA grants (see below) they would not only have to show the 6 per cent economic rate of return, but a full 20-year discounted cash-flow analysis should be conducted to ensure the project's long run viability. In other words, much more discretion was built into assistance for these large-scale projects.

11. For enterprises outside peri-urban areas, the rates were marginally higher.

12. Not more than 40 per cent of total fixed investment in urban areas, on a sliding scale to a maximum of 70 per cent in the far west of the country.

13. The percentages were regionally determined, ranging from 80 per cent for the capital city to 120 per cent for the far west.

14. Defined in official statistics as comprising firms employing more than 10 people.

15. The original scheme was designed to run on an Apple IIe, but as computer power increased and prices fell, the central ministry converted to IBM-compatible format. This meant that data-bases between various ministries were wholly incompatible. Coupled with the absence of effective training, the implementing staff were unable to 'mine' these data bases, either to generate an overview on the extent of loan commitments and disbursements or to analyse the trends of applications.

16. One recent and especially troubling source of competition emanates from Zimbabwe, where two *dirigiste* policy initiatives have led to low export prices and growing exports to Botswana and elsewhere. The first is an export subsidy and the second, and perhaps even more important innovation, is to allow Zimbabwean firms

to keep a percentage of their export revenues to import intermediate inputs and capital goods. Many of these products are exported at dumping prices, and this precludes production by Botswana enterprises operating on the market without subsidies.

17. Some years ago Vaitsos made the same point succinctly: 'In the formulation of the demand for information, as in all other markets, a prospective buyer needs information about the properties of the item he intends to purchase so as to be able to make appropriate decisions. Yet, in the case of technology, what is needed is information about information which could effectively be one and the same thing. Thus the prospective buyer is confronted with a structural weakness intrinsic to his position as purchaser with resulting imperfections in the corresponding market operations'. (1974, p. 87)

18. Although in Italy it is the district state which is important. However in many cases the resources commanded by these district-level authorities are larger than those available to the central government in Botswana.

19. These have been pitched at the upgrading of informal sector enterprises, such as tailoring, furniture manufacture and elementary metal-working, and have not ventured into sectorally-shared facilities or more technologically complex industries and services. Even in the traditional sectors, the sorts of inputs provided are at the basic level and offer none of the help required to penetrate foreign markets, for example design intelligence or common marketing in garments.

20. Open-door policies can block the development of indigenous technological capability (see Chapter 1).

21. Even the Thatcher government in the UK recognized this and maintained (and in fact strengthened) a scheme it had inherited from the previous socialist administration which was designed to promote a productive services sector.

22. See Harvey, Lewis and Sharpley (1990) for corroboration of this judgement.

23. The first patent granted to Aspdin in 1824, named portland cement because of its similarity to the portland stone on the South cliffs of England where he lived, was in fact a roman-type hydraulic lime. The first true portland cement, involving firing at sufficiently high temperatures, was not produced until 1845.

24. This is one of the major factors lying behind the expansion of the cement industry in China (Li Mingyu *et al.* 1984).

25. By this is meant the proportionate increase in cement consumption in relation to the growth in per capita incomes. Thus a 1 per cent increase in per capita incomes associated with a more than 1 per cent increase in cement consumption is seen as a high income elasticity, whereas a cement consumption growth rate lower than the increase in per capita incomes is seen as income-inelastic.

26. See p. 196.

27. This widely quoted view, which is based upon the development of mini-cement technology (Garg and Bruce, 1980) and which relates to the principle of heat transfer, is not universally accepted. A senior R&D engineer interviewed thought that the engineering logic was flawed, and was certainly much more complex than that specified by Garg and Bruce.

28. It is widely acknowledged that the dry-process is more fuel-efficient, but in some cases raw materials do not make this possible, and in other cases heavy investments in wet-process machinery are not fully depreciated. Even in 1986 around 25 per cent of UK production occurred in wet-process plants, which is substantially higher than the 1958 figure for Japan (18.8 per cent). There is a virtual absence of wet-process kilns in Germany and Japan today.

29. The economic analysis of this section rests heavily on the work of Economic Development Associates (1985).

30. Li Taoping (n.d.).

31. The domestic market for cement in the UK fell from 20mtpa to 12mtpa in slightly more than one decade.

32. Economic Development Associates (1985) p. 113.

33. A comprehensive survey of alternatives to cement can be found in Spence (1979 and 1986).

34. Spence calculates these as ranging between 25–50 per cent. On the other hand, Allen and Jones (1986) show that Botswana's blended cement is 30–40 per cent more expensive than imported portland cement. This is partly due to production inefficiencies and partly to the absence of suitable local extenders.

35. This can sometimes be advantageous. For example in Botswana the longer setting time of the blended cement was an important attribute in the very hot climate. Nevertheless because of the higher price and generally lower quality of the blended product, there was great consumer resistance to its use (Allen, 1984).

Chapter 8

1. This is now the case with a new form of work-organization which not only improves the quality of working conditions, but also improves firm competitiveness. Despite their attractiveness and their profitability, these innovations are diffusing only slowly. Another example concerns the slow spread of quality consciousness in the IACs. The gurus of this movement, Deming and Juran, began preaching the importance of quality in the 1930s. Their ideas were only taken up by the Japanese in the 1950s and by their fellow-Americans in the 1980s.

2. The social basis of the AT enabling state in the IACs will not be considered here. But it is one of considerable importance, as well as being of academic interest. In Chapter 1 it was argued that whilst the three major currents of the AT movement (the social, the economic and the environmental) reflect a common response to the degradation of the mass-production paradigm, this does not mean that they share a common platform in constructing a society in which more appropriate technologies predominate. This political challenge, reflected in part by a simultaneous growth of ecological parties and a 'greening' of the established political order, remains to be confronted in the IACS.

3. White (1984).

4. There is a variety of sets of analyses here. The classical Marxist view is that the state acts as an instrument of the capitalist class. More recent Marxian perspectives (for example Poulantzas, 1975) distinguish different sub-sets ('fractions') of capital. Lipton (1977), in his seminal analysis of India, offers an alternative, non-class based perspective of the common interests of different classes within the urban areas, leading he believes to a phenomenon of 'urban bias'.

5. All quotes from White (1984), p. 100.

6. There is an extensive literature on the changing basis of the Kenyan state. See, *inter alia*, Leys (1975), Langdon (1981), Kaplinsky (1980) and Swainson (1980).

7. See Ranis and Stewart (1990) and Ranis (1990).

8. For a comparison of scale between Korea and Taiwan, see Mody (1989). For a description of the evolution of small-scale technologies in the tin-canning industry in Taiwan, see Bell *et al.*, (1974).

9. This is apparent not only for DC states but also in the World Bank's lending programmes where despite a long commitment to considering social and environmental criteria in project evaluations, this has seldom been evidenced in the projects funded.

10. See Chapter 1 for an elaboration of these views.

11. Not the least of these are attitudes to gender. Even within the AT movement, biases are prominent — 'engineering man', bureaucratic man', etc.

12. A case in point here is the surprise registered by official visitors to the small-scale OPS sugar factory in Kenya. Instead of the ramshackle heath-robinsonish informal sector plant of their expectations they are confronted with a modern, but labour-intensive and small-scale sugar factory. Many visitors have their attitudes towards AT transformed in a single visit.

13. Arrow (1962).

14. Haggblade *et al.* (1986).

15. Op cit, p. 29.

16. The shell furnace which enabled the burning of wet bagasse was extensively utilized in the nineteenth century in Europe. The design for the screw expeller was based upon the verbal recollections of one of the last survivors of Quebec's small-scale molasses crushers — no formal designs had ever been published.

17. Both the ideas of sectorally based technology-search capabilities and the systematic use of expired patents are on the policy agenda in Cyprus. See Institute of Development Studies (1987 and 1988).

18. See Langdon (1981) and Kaplinsky (1979) on the link between product choice, transnational ownership and technology choice.

19. Of course there are clear sectoral variations. For example, the ability to search for appropriate biotechnologies may require a much higher skill content than the development of new brick-pressing technologies. Nevertheless the principle certainly applies within most sectors and is probably also generally applicable across sectors.

20. Langdon (1981).

21. See ILO (1972).

22. Berry (1977).

23. Baron (1980).

24. Emanuel (1982) and Eckaus (1987). See Chapter 2 for further discussion.

25. Stewart (1987b).

26. Ibid., p. 297.

27. Ranis and Stewart (1989).

Bibliography

Abromovitz M (1956), 'Resources and output trends in the United States since 1879', *American Economic Review*, Vol. 46, pp. 52–3.

Adams, W and Brock C (1986), *The Bigness Complex: Industry, Labor and Government in the American Economy*, New York: Pantheon Books.

Aguren S, Hansson R, and Karlsson K G (1976), *The Volvo Kalmar Plant: The Impact of New Design on Work Organization*, Stockholm: The Rationalization Council.

Aguren S, Bredbacka C, Hansson R, Ihregren K and Karlsson K G (1984), *The Volvo Kalmar Revisited: Ten years of Experience*, Stockholm: Efficiency and Participation Development Council.

Allen W J (1984), 'Alternative cements in Kenya and Tanzania', *Report Prepared for Intermediate Technology Development Group*, Rugby.

Arrow K J (1962), 'Economic welfare and the allocation of resources for invention' in *The Rate and Direction of Inventive Activity: Economic and Social Factors*, National Bureau of Economic Research, Princeton University Press.

Aylen J (1988), 'Privatisation of the British Steel Corporation', *Fiscal Studies*, Vol. 9 no. 3, pp. 1–25.

Ayres R and Miller S (1983), *Robotics: Applications and Social Implications*, Cambridge, Mass: Ballinger Publishing Co.

Baron C G (1975), 'Sugar processing techniques in India' in Bhalla A S (ed.), *Technology and Employment in Industry*, Geneva: International Labour Organization.

Baron C G (ed.) (1980), *Technology, Employment and Basic Needs in Food Processing in Developing Countries*, Oxford: Pergamon Press.

Bear M, Almond F and Taubmann H (1985), *Mini Cement Technology: Appraisal Report of the ATDA Mini-Cement Project*, Washington/Rugby: ATI/ITDG.

Bell R M, Cooper C and Kaplinsky R (1974), 'An international comparison of the choice of manufacturing techniques in the production of cans in Kenya, Tanzania and Thailand', *Report Prepared for the ILO*, Geneva.

Bell R M (1982), *Technical Change in Infant Industries: A Review of the Evidence*, Brighton: Science Policy Research Unit, University of Sussex, mimeo.

Berry R (1977), *Inequality, Demand Structure and Employment: The Case of India*, DPhil Dissertation, University of Sussex, Brighton.

Bhalla A S (1979a) 'Technologies appropriate for basic needs strategy' in Bhalla A S (ed.) (1979).

Bhalla A S (ed.) (1979b), *Towards Global Action for Appropriate Technology*, Geneva: International Labour Organization.

Bhalla A S (ed.) (1984), *Blending of New and Traditional Technologies: Case Studies*, Dublin: Tycooly.

Bhalla A S and James D (eds) (1988), *New Technologies and Development: Experiences in 'Technology Blending'*, London: Kynne Reinner.

Birla Institute of Scientific Research (1981), *Cement Industry (An Inter-Sectoral Appraisal)*, New Delhi.

Brooks C, Jones M, Kaplinsky R and McChesney I (eds) (1989), *Cane Sugar: The Small-Scale Processing Option*, London: Intermediate Technology Publications.

Brusco S (1982), 'The Emilian model: productive decentralisation and social integration', *Cambridge Journal of Economics*, Vol. 6 no. 2.

Buttel F H, Kenney M and Kloppenburg J (1985), 'From green revolution to biorevolution: some observations on the changing technological bases of economic transformation in the Third World', *Economic Development and Cultural Change*, pp. 31–55.

Carson R (1963), *The Silent Spring*, London: Hamish Hamilton.

Cembureau (1982), *World Cement Market in Figures, 1913–81*, Paris.

Cembureau (1985), *World Statistical Review*, Paris.

Cement (1986), Vol. XIX no. 2.

Cement Manufacturers' Association (1978), *Workshop on Towards Self-Sufficiency in Cement*, New Delhi.

Cement Research Institute (1981), *All India Seminar on Cement Manufacture (3 vols)*, New Delhi.

Chandler A D (1977), *The Visible Hand: The Managerial Revolution in American Business*, Cambridge, Mass: Harvard University Press.

Chilton C H (ed.) (1960), *Cost Engineering in the Process Industry*, NY: McGraw Hill.

Colclough C (1990) 'Structuralism versus neo-liberalism: an introduction', in Colclough and Manor (eds) (1990).

Colclough C and Manor J (eds) (1990), *States or Markets? Neo-Liberalism and the Development Policy Debate*, Oxford: Oxford University Press.

Colclough C and McCarthy S (1980), *The Political Economy of Botswana: A Study of Growth and Distribution*, Oxford: Oxford University Press.

Colclough C and Olsen P (1983), *Review of Incomes Policy in Botswana: 1972–83*, Gaborone: Ministry of Finance and Development Planning.

Cole H S D, Freeman C, Jahoda M and Pavitt K L R (eds) (1973), *Thinking About the Future: A Critique of the Limits to Growth*, London: Sussex University Press and Chatto & Windus.

Cooley M (1984), *Technology, Unions and Human Needs*, Geneva: International Metalworks Federation.

Cornia A C (1988), 'Adjustment policies 1980–1985: effects on child welfare' in Cornia *et al.* (1988).

Cornia A C, Jolly A R and Stewart F (eds) (1988), *Adjustment with a Human Face, Volumes I and II*, Oxford: Clarendon Press.

Dickson D (1974), *Alternative Technology and the Politics of Technical Change*, London: Fontana.

Dunn P D (1989), *Appropriate Technology: Technology with a Human Face*, NY: Schocken Books.

237

Eckaus R S (1955), 'The factor proportions problem in underdeveloped areas', *American Economic Review*, Sept.

Eckaus R S (1987), 'Appropriate technology: the movement has only a few clothes on', *Issues in Science and Technology*, Winter, pp 62–71.

Economic Development Associates (1985), *A Technology for the Intermediate Entrepreneur: The Place of Mini-Cement in the Indian Economy*, Lucknow.

Ellis W N, McRobie G and Darrow K (1979), 'Appropriate technology developments in the United States and their relevance to the Third World', *OECD Development Papers*, Paris: OECD.

Emmanuel A (1982), *Appropriate Technology and Underdevelopment*, Chichester: J Wiley.

Evans P B and Tigre P B (forthcoming), 'Going beyond the clones in Brazil and Korea: a comparative analysis of NIC strategies in the information industries', *World Development*.

Feichtinger F, and Koltermann M (1983), 'Ex post and ex ante development of world cement demand — its mathematical quantification', *Zement-Kalk-Gips no. 9*, pp. 409–14.

Feichtinger F, le Corre C Y, Lammer A and Koltermann (1985), 'Cement production growth trends in countries with different degree of industrialization — trend projection up to the year 2000', *Zement-Kalk-Gips no. 9*, pp. 245–9.

Floor W M (1979), 'Activities of the UN system on appropriate technology' in Bhalla A S (ed.), *Towards Global Action for Appropriate Technology*, Geneva: ILO.

Forsyth D (1977) 'Appropriate technology in sugar manufacturing', *World Development*, Vol 5 no. 3, pp. 189–202.

Fransman M (1986), *Technology and Economic Development*, Brighton: Wheatsheaf.

Freeman C, Clark J, and Soete L (1982), *Unemployment and Technical Innovation: A Study of Long Waves and Economic Development*, London: Frances Pinter.

Garg M K (1979), *Project Report and Feasibility Study of Appropriate Technology and Mini-Sugar (OPS Khandsari)*, Lucknow: Appropriate Technology Development Association.

Garg M K and Bruce R (1980), *Mini Cement Project Proposal and Feasibility Report*, Lucknow: ATDA.

GATT, *International Trade 87–88*, Vols I and II, Geneva: GATT.

Godfrey M (1986), 'Kenya to 1990: Prospects for Growth', *EIU Special Report no. 1052*, London.

Gopa Consultants (1983), *Republic of Botswana Building Materials Sector Study*.

Greeley M (ed.) (1987), *Energy and Poverty*, IDS Bulletin, Vol. 18 no. 1.

Hagelberg G (1989), 'The structure of world production and consumption' in Brooks *et al.* (eds) (1989).

Haggblade S, Liedholm C and Mead D C (1986), 'The effect of policy and policy reforms on non-agricultural enterprises and employment in Developing Countries: A Review of Past Experience', Dept of Agricultural Economics, Michigan State University, *MSU Working Paper no. 27*, Michigan.

238

Harvey C, Lewis S and Sharpley J (1990), 'Botswana' in Riddel R (ed.), *Industrialisation in Sub Saharan Africa*, London: James Currey.

Helleiner G K (1975), 'The role of multinational corporations in the less developed countries' trade in technology', *World Development*, Vol. 3.

Hendersen J (1989) 'High technology production in Hong Kong and the making of a regional core' in *Proceedings of International Symposium on Technology Policy in the Americas*, Stanford, 1–3 December 1988.

Hoffman K and Rush H (1988), *Microelectronics and Clothing: Impact of Technical Change on a Global Industry*, Geneva: ILO.

Hughes H, Bautista R, Lim D, Morawetz D and Thuomi F (1976), 'Capital utilization in manufacturing in developing countries', *World Bank Staff Working Paper* no. 242, Washington: World Bank.

Huxley, E (1935), *White Man's Country: Lord Delamere and the Making of Kenya*, 2 vols, London: Macmillan.

Huxley E (1957), *No Easy Way: A History of the Kenya Farmers Association and Unga Ltd*, printed in Kenya by East African Standard Ltd, Nairobi.

Institute of Development Studies (1984), 'Developmental states in East Asia', *IDS Bulletin*, Vol. 15 no. 2.

Institute of Development Studies (1987), *Cyprus Industrial Strategy*, Report for UNIDO/UNDP, Brighton, mimeo.

Institute of Development Studies (1988), *Cyprus Technology Strategy*, Report for UNIDO/UNFSTD, Brighton, mimeo.

International Labour Office, *Employment, Incomes and Equality: A Strategy for Increasing Productive Employment in Kenya*, Geneva: ILO.

Isaksen J, Kaplinsky R and Odel M (1984), *Report on Evaluation of Financial Assistance Policy*, prepared for Government of Botswana, Bergen: Christa Mickelsen Institute.

James J (1987), 'The choice of technology in public enterprise: a comparative study of manufacturing industry in Kenya and Tanzania' in Stewart (ed.), *Macro-Policies for Appropriate Technology in Developing Countries*, Boulder: Westview.

James J and Stewart F (1981), 'New products: a discussion of the welfare effects of the introduction of new products in developing countries', *Oxford Economic Papers*, Vol 33 no. 1, pp. 81–107.

James J and Watanabe S (eds) (1985), *Technology, Institutions and Government Policies*, Geneva: ILO.

Japan Productivity Centre (1958), *The Cement Industry in Japan*, Tokyo: Cement Industry Productivity Study Team.

Jequier N (1976) (ed.), *Appropriate Technology: Problems and Promises*, Paris: OECD Development Centre.

Jequier N (1979), 'Appropriate Technology: some criteria' in Bhalla A S (ed.), (1979).

Jequier N and Blanc G (1983), *The World of Appropriate Technology: A Quantitative Analysis*, Paris: OECD.

Jolly A R and Cornia A C (eds) (1984), *The Impact of World Recession on Children: A Study Prepared for UNICEF*, Oxford: Pergamon Press.

Juma C (1989), *The Gene Hunters: Biotechnology and the Scramble for Seeds*, London: Zed Books.

Kamata H (1982), *Japan in a Passing Lane*, Harmondsworth: Penguin.

Kaplinsky R (1979). 'Export orientated growth: a large international firm in a small developing country', *World Development*, Vol. 7 nos 8/9, pp. 825–34.

Kaplinsky R (1980), 'Capitalist accummulation in the periphery: the Kenyan case re-examined', *Review of African Political Economy*, No. 15.

Kaplinsky R (1981), *Appropriate Technology in a Developing Country: The Bakery Industry in Kenya*, DPhil Dissertation, Brighton: University of Sussex.

Kaplinsky R (1982a), *Computer Aided Design: Electronics, Comparative Advantage and Development*, London: Frances Pinter.

Kaplinksy R (1982b), *Fractions of Capital and Accumulation in Kenya*, Brighton: Institute of Development Studies, mimeo.

Kaplinsky R (1983a), *Sugar Processing: The Development of a Third World Technology*, London: Intermediate Technology Publications.

Kaplinsky R (1983b), 'Firm size and technical change revisited', *Journal of Industrial Economics*, Vol. XXXII no. 1, pp. 39–60.

Kaplinsky R (1984), *Automation: The Technology and Society*, 2nd ed, Harlow: Longmans.

Kaplinsky R (1990), 'Industrialisation in Botswana: how getting the prices right helped the wrong people' in Colclough and Manor (eds) (1990).

Keddie J and Cleghorn W (1980), *Brick Manufacture in Developing Countries*, David Lingstone Institute Series on Choice of Technique in Developing Countries, Edinburgh: Scottish Academic Press.

Lal D (1983), *The Poverty of 'Developmental Economics'*, London: Hobart Paperback 16, Institute of Economic Affairs.

Lancaster K (1966), 'Change and innovation in the technology of consumption', *American Economic Review*, Vol. 56, May.

Langdon S (1975), 'Multinational corporations, taste transfer and under-development: a case study from Kenya', *Review of African Political Economy*, no. 2.

Langdon S (1981), *Multinational Corporations in the Political Economy of Kenya*, London: Macmillan.

Leach G, 'Energy and the urban poor' in Greeley M (ed.), *Energy and Poverty*, IDS Bulletin, Vol. 18 no. 1.

Leen O-Young (1984), *Smaller is Better: Japan's Mastery of the Miniature*, New York: Kodansha International.

Lemmings L (1989), 'The Kabras experience: an exploratory socio-economic impact analysis of the West Kenya sugar factory' in Brooks et al. (eds) (1989).

Leudde-Neirath R (1986), *Import Controls and Export Oriented Development: A Reassessment of the South Korean Case*, London: Frances Pinter.

Leys C (1975), *Underdevelopment in Kenya: The Political Economy of Neo-Colonialism*, London: Heinemann.

Li Mingyu, Yuan Guangpu and Ding Weidong (1984). *Cement Industry in China*, UNIDO Asia-Pacific Region Mini-Cement Workshop.

Li Taoping (nd), *Cement Industry in China*, China Cement Development Centre, Tianjin Cement Design Institute, paper presented to 20th International Cement Seminar.

Lipton M (1975), *Why Poor People Stay Poor: A Study of Urban Bias in World Development*, London: Temple Smith.

Little I M D (1982), *Economic Development: Theory, Policy, and International Relations*, New York: Basic Books.

Little I M D, Mazumdar D and Page J (1987), *Small Manufacturing Enterprises*, Oxford: Oxford University Press/World Bank.

Lone H (1989), 'The sugar industry in developing countries: import substitution, government policy and scale of production' in Brooks *et al.* (1989).

MacGregor Ross W (1927), *Kenya from Within*, London: Allen & Unwin (reprinted 1968).

Makanda D (1989), 'Sugar policy in Kenya: a farmer's dilemma' in Brooks *et al.* (eds) (1989).

Mallorie E (1989), 'Economic viability of small-scale sugar production in Kenya' in Brooks *et al.* (eds) (1989).

McRobie G (1981). *Small is Possible*, London: Jonathan Cape.

Meadows D H, Meadows D L, Randers J and Behrens W W (1972), *The Limits to Growth: A Report for the Club of Rome's Project on the Predicament of Mankind*, London: Earth Island Ltd.

Miles D (1974), 'History of cement manufacture before 1824', prepared for Seminar on Cementitious Materials, London: ITDG

Mlaki W A (1989), 'The future of small-scale sugar processing in Tanzania' in Brooks *et al.* (eds) (1989).

Mody A (1989), 'Strategies for developing information industries', *European Journal of Developmental Research*, Vol. 1 no. 1.

Monopolies and Mergers Commission (1977), *Flour and Bread: A Report on the Supply in the UK of Wheat Flour and of Bread Made from Wheat Flour*, London: HMSO.

Morawetz D (1974), 'Employment implications of industrialisation in developing countries: a survey', *Economic Journal*, Vol. 84.

Muchie M (1986), *Capitalist Technology and Socialist Development*, DPhil dissertation, Brighton: University of Sussex.

Nader R (1972), *Unsafe at any Speed*, NY: Grossman.

Nelson R and Winter S (1977), 'In search of a useful theory of innovation', *Research Policy*, Vol. 6 no. 1. pp. 36–76.

Nyongesa D P and Mbuthia J I (1989), 'Policy and performance of the sugar industry in Kenya' in Brooks *et al.* (eds) (1989).

Odada J E (ed.) (1986), *Incentives for Increased Agricultural Production: A Case Study of Kenya's Sugar Industry*, Nairobi: Friederich Ebert Foundation.

Pack H (1988), *Productivity, Technology and Industrial Development: A Case Study of Textiles*, NY: Oxford University Press/World Bank.

Pack H and Westphal L (1986), 'Industrial structure and technical change: theory versus reality', *Journal of Developing Economies*, Vol. 22 no. 1, June 1986, pp. 87–128.

Pearson R (1977), 'Technology, innovation and transfer of technology in the cement industry', *UNECLA Working Paper no. 9*, Buenos Aires.

Pearson R (1982), *Technology Transfer and Technological Dependence: A Case Study of the Argentine Cement Industry 1875–1975*. DPhil Dissertation, Brighton: Universtity of Sussex.

Perez C (1985), 'Microelectronics, long waves and structural change: new perspectives for developing countries', *World Development*, Vol. 14 no. 3, pp. 441–63.

Perez C (1988), 'The institutional implications of the present wave of technical change for developing countries', paper prepared for World Bank Seminar on Technology and Long-Term Economic Growth Prospects, November.

Peters T J (1987), *Thriving on Chaos: Handbook for a Managerial Revolution*, New York: Harper & Row.

Peters T J and Waterman R H (1982), *In Search of Excellence*, New York: Harper.

Phan-Thuy N, Betancourt R R, Winston G C and Kabaj M (1981), *Industrial Capacity and Employment Promotion: Case Studies of Sri Lanka, Nigeria, Morocco and Over-all Survey of Other Developing Countries*, Gower: Farnborough

Pickett J, Forsyth D, and McBain N (1974), 'The choice of technology, economic efficiency and employment in developing countries', *World Development*, Vol. 2, March.

Piore, M J and Sabel, C F (1984), *The Second Industrial Divide: Possibilities for Prosperity*, NY: Basic Books.

Poulantzas N (1975), *Classes in Contemporary Capitalism*, London: New Left Books.

Pratten C E (1971), *Economies of Scale in Manufacturing Industry*, Cambridge: Cambridge University Press.

Rada J (1980), *The Impact of Microelectronics*, Geneva: ILO.

Ranis G (1990). 'Rural linkages and choice of technology' in Stewart *et al.* (ed.) (1990).

Reddy A (1979) 'Nations and Regions Technology Groups and Institutions: an Assessment' in Bhalla (ed.) (1979b).

Republic of Kenya, *Sessional Paper no. 1 of 1986 on Economic Management for Renewed Growth*, Nairobi: Government Printer.

Robinson A (ed.) (1979), *Appropriate Technologies for Third World*, Proceedings of a Conference held by the International Economic Association at Teheran, Iran, London: International Economic Association/ MacMclelland.

Rosenbrock H (1985), *Engineers and the Work that People Do*, Manchester, mimeo.

Schumacher F (1973), *Small is Beautiful*, London: Blond & Briggs.

Schumpeter J (1961), *The Theory of Economic Development*, Oxford: Oxford University Press.

Sciberras E (1979), 'Technology transfer to developing countries — implications for member countries' in *Television and Related Products Sector Final Report*, Paris: OECD.

Seers D (1972), 'What are we trying to measure?', *Journal of Development Studies*, Vol. 8 no 3.

Sheriff A (1988), 'The competitive product position of automobile manufacturers: performance and strategies', International Motor Vehicle Program, Cambridge Mass: Massachusetts Institute of Technology, mimeo.

242

Sigurdson (1977), *Small Scale Cement Plants*, London: Intermediate Technology Publications.

Silberston A (1972), 'Economies of scale in theory and practice', *Economic Journal*, March, pp. 369–91.

Silva D (1980), 'Location and plant size in the Mexican cement industry', *International Institute of Management Discussion Paper 80–77*, Berlin.

Singer C, Holmyard E J, Hall A R and Williams T (eds) (1958), *A History of Technology, Vol V: The Late Nineteenth Century c1850 to c1900*, Oxford: Clarendon Press.

Singer H W (1977), *Technologies for Basic Needs*, Geneva: ILO.

Sinha S (1990), *Mini-cement: A review of Iranian Experience*, London: Intermediate Technology Publications.

Smith C, Kaplinsky R, Menz J and Selabe B (1988), *Evaluation of the Financial Assistance Policy: FAP and its Role in Botswana Business Development*, Government Printer, Gaborone.

Solow R (1957), 'Technical change and the aggregate production function', *Review of Economics and Statistics*, Vol. 39, pp. 312–20.

Sorge A *et al.* (1983). *Micro-electronics and Manpower in Manufacturing: Applications of Computer Numerical Control in Great Britain and West Germany*, Gower: Aldershot.

Spence R J S (1986), *Cement Making in Developing Countries: The Development of Indigenous Cementitious Materials*, Nairobi: United Nations Centre for Human Settlements.

Spence R J S (1980), *Small-scale Production of Cementitious Materials*, London: Intermediate Technology Publications.

Stewart, F (1975), 'A note on social cost benefit analysis and class conflict in LDCS', *World Development*, vol. 3, No. 1, pp. 31–9.

Stewart F (1978). *Technology and Underdevelopment*, 2nd ed., London: Macmillan.

Stewart F (1979), 'International mechanisms for Appropriate Technology' in Bhalla A S (ed.) (1979).

Stewart F (ed.) (1987a), *Macro-Policies for Appropriate Technology in Developing Countries*, Boulder: Westview.

Stewart F (ed.) (1987b), 'Macro-policies for Appropriate Technology: An introductory classification' in Stewart (1987a).

Stewart F (ed.) (1987c), 'Overview and conclusions' in Stewart (1987a).

Stewart F and James J (eds) (1982), *The Economies of New Technologies in Developing Countries*, London: Frances Printer.

Stewart F, Thomas H and de Wilde T (eds) (1990), *The Other Policy*, London: Intermediate Technology Publications.

Stewart F and Ranis G (1990), 'Macro-policies for Appropriate Technology: a synthesis of findings' in Stewart *et al.* (ed.) (1990).

Swainson N. (1980), *The Development of Corporate Capitalism in Kenya, 1918–1977*, London: Heinemann Educational Books.

Taubmann H J (1986), *Technical Report on ATDA Mini Cement Plant Technology*, Rheinfelden: Buro fur Systemtechnik.

Thomas G (1985), 'Indian cement industry: the encouraging outlook', World Cement Vol. 16. no. 7, pp. 269–76

Tribe M (1989), 'Scale considerations in sugar production planning' in Brooks *et al.* (eds) (1989).

UNCTAD (1988), *Trade and Development Report, 1988*, NY: United Nations.

UNICEF (1989), *The State of the World's Children 1989*, Oxford: Oxford University Press.

UNIDO (1986), *International Comparative Advantage in Manufacturing: Changing Profiles of Resources and Trade*, Vienna: United Nations Industrial Development Organisation.

United States Central Intelligence Agency (1977), *China's Cement Industry: A Research Paper*, ER 77–10704, Washington: National Foreign Assessment Center.

USAID (1976), *Proposal for a Program on Appropriate Technology*, Washington: US Government Printing Office.

Vaitsos C V (1974), *Intercountry Income Distribution and Transnational Enterprises*, Oxford: Clarendon Press.

Wells L T (1973), 'Economic man and engineering man: a choice of technology in a low wage country', *Public Policy*, Vol. 21, no. 3, pp. 319–342.

Westphal L (1978), 'Research on Approprate Technology', *Industry and Development*, no. 2, pp. 28–46.

White G (1984), 'Developmental states and socialist industrialisation in the Third World' in Kaplinsky R (ed), *Third World Industrialisation: Open Economies in a Closing World*, London: Frank Cass.

Willoughby K W (1990), *Technology Choice: A Critique of the Appropriate Technology Movement*, Boulder: Westview.

Wilson F and Ramphele M (1989), *Uprooting Poverty: The South African Challenge*, NY: W W Norton and Co.

Wood A (1978), *A Theory of Pay*, Cambridge: Cambridge University Press.

Woodward J (1965), *Industrial Organization: Theory and practice*. London: Oxford University Press.